How to Start A CLOTHING EMPIRE

THE APPAREL BUSINESS

© 2006-2013 Bruno Marino

All Rights Reserved. No part of this book can reproduced by any means, digital, mechanical, photocopying or otherwise without the express written permission of the author.

ISBN 978-1-300-16027-4

DISCLAIMER FOR CONTACT INFORMATION

The contact information (such as suppliers, websites, trade shows etc.) contained in this book should be fully investigated prior to using an/or contacting. The author and publisher make no claims or warrants on any of the business' or business products or services mentioned, and has no direct or indirect affiliation with the contact information. All contents of this book should be used for informational purposes only.

ACKNOWLEDGMENTS

OK, here is the page where I thank everyone for making it all possible. I am sure most readers skip this page as they feel it has nothing to do with the contents of the book.

However, to understand a person's success story is as important as recognizing all of the elements which have participated in making a business grow and flourish.

My brother is without a doubt the number one person I wish to thank. From the very beginning, he has been there through thick and thin. Sure, we've had the typical sibling disagreements over the years, but whenever called upon, he was there without question. I can honestly say I don't think I would have been able to reach the heights I have without his generous support.

Next on the list are my parents. It's true what they say, we are all by-products of our family. My parents both came to North America in search of a better life. To call them working class is a definite understatement. I recall most of the hardships they endured in order for my brother and I to enjoy a better life. I want to thank them for instilling the necessary ingredients that made me start, grow, and have the confidence to operate a successful business.

I would also like to thank each and every employee I had over the years, good and bad. It was all part of the learning experience. I especially want to thank my managerial staff Nicolas (formerly Nicky J), Tania, Antonett, Natalie, and Sara. You have all given me enough stories to reminisce for the rest of my life.

Finally, I would like to thank my customers. Because at the end of the day, you are the reason the business was able to blossom into an empire. Thank you.

CONTENTS

Chapter 1 - My Story 1
Chapter 2 – Getting Started 8
    Your First Day 8
    Most common Start-up Costs 9
    Business Set Up 10
    The importance of the Telephone 12
    Alarm System and Monitoring 13
    Banking 14
    Electricity and Gas 16
    First and Last Month's Rent 16
    Stationary and Office Supplies 17
    Additional Security 18
    Hiring Staff 18
    Advertising 19
    Leasehold Improvements 21
    Chattels and Fixtures 22
    Miscellaneous 23
Chapter 3 – What Type of Store do I Set Up? 25
    The Boutique 26
    The Outlet/Warehouse Store 29
    The Shopping Mall 31
    Strip Plaza 33
Chapter 4 – Where Do I Set Up Shop? 34
    How do I find the right location? 34
Chapter 5 – What do I sell? 41
    Does your supplier have an in-stock program? 41

    What happens if I receive my order late?............... 42

    What is the turn around time for re-orders?.......... 43

    I made changes, am I still obligated?...................... 43

    Can I get a credit on my order? 44

    What if the items don't sell?..................................... 46

Chapter 6 – Where Do I Find Merchandise?............. 48

    Trade Shows... 48

    Internet

    Trade Consulate... 57

Chapter 7 – Signing the Lease 59

    Real Estate versus Clothing.................................... 61

Chapter 8 – Hiring Employees....................................... 63

    Hiring Beauty or Brains.. 63

    Employee Training... 66

    Set Guidelines and follow them 66

    Sample Employee Manual...................................... 67

Chapter 9 – Creative Advertising 89

    Customer Profile.. 89

    Magazine Print Ads... 90

    Television.. 92

    Radio.. 93

    Newspaper Ads 94

    The Internet 95

    Door-to-Door Flyers.. 95

    Club and Value Packs 96

    Yellow Pages and other Directories 97

    Business Cards 97

    In store advertising.. 98

Celebrity Endorsements 103
Chapter 10 – Creative In-Store Selling 105
    Send out Regular Advertisements 106
    Hire more Staff 106
    Have Staff wear merchandise 106
    Mannequin Displays 107
    The Power of Price Tags 107
    Being Courteous 107
    Product Knowledge 108
    Rotating Stock 108
    Door Crashers 108
    Inventory Control 109
    Return Policy 109
    Birthday Promotions 109
    Point of Sale items 110
    Appearances 110
    Variety versus Quantity 110
    The Power of a smile 111
Chapter 11 – The Internet & Ebay 112
Chapter 12 – Expanding Your Business 122
    Setting up Multiple Locations 122
Chapter 13 – Other Useful Information 128
    From Concept to Garment 128
    Theft: What works and what doesn't 129
    Surveillance Cameras 129
    Security Tags 130
    Wire and Lock Systems 132
    Posting Signage 132

Staff Awareness 133
Computers: Friend or Foe? 135
Preparing for the Big Sale 138
My Theory on Discounting 140
Useful Buying Tips 140

Chapter 14 – Becoming an Importer 142

Getting Started 143
How to find merchandise to Import? 148
Company Image 149
Freight Forwarder 150
Air versus Sea Shipping 152
The importance of Trucking 153
Quota Restrictions 154
Country of Origin 154
Licensing 155
Importing a well known Brand 155
Importing your own Label 157
Importing Private Label 158
Exclusivity Agreements 159
How much do I buy? 160
Buying Direct from Importer 161
Customs Broker 161
FOB: Freight on Board 162
Foreign Currency 162
Methods of Payment 163
Grey Market Importing 166
Counterfeit Merchandise 168
What to do next? 168

Chapter 15 – The World According to Wholesale ... 170

Sales Rep/Agency 171
Scouting for a Great Rep 171
You're Hired 173
Offer Incentives 174
Go national in a week 174
The Next Steps 175
Sample Purchase Order Form 1 177
Sample Purchase Order Form 2 178
Sample Credit Application Form 178
Sample Reference Letter 180
Credit through a Factor Company 181
How not to bury yourself 182
Government Documents 182
Shipping and Supplies 184
Sample Packing Slip Forms 187
Substitutions 188
Managing Returns 189
End of Season 189

Chapter 16 – Creative Financing 191
Sample Business Plan 191
Use your own Suppliers 198
Friends and Family 199
Home Equity Mortgage 200
Consignment 201
Personal Credit Cards 203
At the End of the Day 203

Glossary of Terms 205

Appendix 208
Secret Designer Clothing OFF PRICE list 208

Sample Birthday Ad	211
Sample Club Card	212
Sample Lease Agreement	213
Sample Partnership Agreement	220
Sample Job Application	222
Fashion Schools	224
Industry Organizations	228
Surface Treatment	237
Yarn Suppliers	240
Textile Label Manufacturers	245
Fabric Suppliers	247
Promotion	265
Image and Branding	266
Model Agencies	268
Public Relations	272
Popular Industry Links	275
Order more Books	285

Chapter One

MY STORY

It was a real rush to drive my new *Mercedes* past the crowd of shoppers who gathered outside my new store, eagerly waiting for its doors to open. I felt like I was on top of the world.

This was my third location in less than four years and business was booming. Everything I touched seemed to turn to gold. That day broke an all-time record, with sales exceeding $80,000.

Things didn't start out this way.

I'd like to take you back to the very beginning. The following events are real. They are the circumstances which lead to the rise of my clothing empire.

My story begins at the ripe "old" age of twenty. I was extremely ambitious and equally fearless. Okay, let's face it. I was young, naïve, and ignorant in the ways of the world.

This naivety was to be a blessing. Dumb luck, and a lot of common sense, turned my suit and a rolling rack full of clothes into four thriving retail clothing stores as well and two warehouses providing wholesale service.

I was one of only two children, so it was fitting that my brother chose me to be his best man for his wedding. Instead of going the traditional route of rent-a-tux, my brother opted for more classic dark navy suits for me and the rest of the wedding party.

As luck would have it, our next-door neighbor's boyfriend was a wholesaler of private label suits, which meant that he provided the suits to companies which put their own label on the inside pocket. He gave us what seemed to be a great deal, at $170 a suit. The cost to rent a tuxedo was over $100, so in effect I got a great new suit for an additional $70.

The night of the wedding went off without a hitch. We received rave reviews. Compliments on our off-the-rack no-name suits came from almost everyone in attendance.

A light went off in my mind. I began thinking that I could sell suits like this and make a nifty profit. So I Did.

The initial reaction was more than positive. Orders began flowing in, so I convinced my brother to do a cash advance of $2,000 on his credit card to cover my orders. Now I felt like a real businessman, but after making my buy I realized I had no place to display my goods. I did what any aspiring entrepreneur would do, I set up shop in my parents' basement.

Business boomed. Customers routinely came in and out, using my bathroom as a fitting room. I had everyone on the take. That's street lingo for profit sharing. Whoever referred new clients got a cut of a sale.

But something didn't feel right. When my dad began offering customers a glass of his homemade wine, I knew that it was time to move on. I thought it would be a good idea that instead of customers coming to my dingy basement, I would go to their home or business, providing door-to-door service.

I became known as the hatchback boutique.

I gained momentum, but after hitting the road for several months my sales began to dip. I had tapped all my resources. After all, how many no-name suit buyers were out there?

I began thinking some more. What if I provided clothing other than suits to the same customers who had already bought from me? Surely they couldn't refuse other great deals.

I was right.

While driving past a clothing store up the street from where I lived, I noticed a BLOW OUT SALE sign in the window. I decided to check it out. The veteran salesman/owner convinced me to buy a bunch of dress shirts (the ones he couldn't sell).

That proved to be the turning point.

Now that I was moving shirts, my customers began making requests for pants, jackets, ties, underwear—you name it.

I began to scour the earth, going into every store, buying up whatever I thought was saleable. As my clientele grew, so did my contacts for merchandise. I was getting calls from everyone from uptown to downtown.

Once again, it was time to move on. A chance encounter with a competitor lead me to a small store located in a quiet suburban area, about half an hour from where I lived. It was appealing for two reasons. One was that the store was set up for clothing, completely renovated with fixtures. The second was that the rent was only about $600 a month.

I was as nervous as I was excited. The thought of having my own fully furnished clothing store was a dream come true. I knew it was the next logical step in order for me to grow. My meeting with the landlord went well. It helped that we both spoke Italian. I didn't even sign an offer to lease, if you can believe that. With a handshake and first and last month's rent, I sealed the deal.

I was ecstatic!

Unfortunately, my family didn't share my newfound joy. My father, who had always been a hard-working man, didn't believe in taking risks. He was convinced I'd made a mistake, but wished me well.

As I began to prepare for the big move I realized that my rolling rack wasn't enough to fill my new store with merchandise.

I was desperate, but short on funds. I began calling everyone I knew to see whether they would help me out.

Only one person stepped up to bat. He was an up-and-coming designer who only made shirts and pants, but what did I care? I was willing to take anything I could get my hands on. I convinced him to give me whatever stock he had on hand on a consignment basis. That way I didn't have to use any money and he had the chance to sell whatever was sitting in his warehouse.

That was the idea, but I somehow stretched the truth. I let him think that he would be getting a whole new world of exposure, and the hundreds of my soon-to-be customers would relate to his product as a household name synonymous with *Armani* and *Calvin Klein*.

The big day finally arrived. I began moving in with everything from the clothes to my stereo, to *Windex*, to my old beat up rolling rack, which I thought would come in handy in the back stockroom. The store was set up within two weeks. My feelings were like nothing I'd experienced of imagined.

I invited everyone for my grand opening. That was true feeling of accomplishment.

What lay ahead was another story.

Sales for the first week were promising. I made a point of visiting every business in the area, hoping they would stop by. Some did. Most did not.

More surprising was the fact that my original customers were not showing up, despite numerous phone calls. They still expected me to make house calls, and that, combined with the fact that the store was in a remote suburban area, half hour out of the city, didn't help.

I was only twenty, so nothing was going to hinder my success.

I closed shop from Monday to Wednesday. That gave me much-needed time to do buying and promotion, and created an illusion that my store was not a store but a special place to find good prices. My sign on the door read: OPEN TO THE PUBLIC THURSDAY, FRIDAY, AND SATURDAY ONLY.

I wanted to create the image that I was a large importer/wholesaler, and that it was a privilege to even come through my doors.

In truth, the store was a store, nothing more, nothing less. What did I care? It was working for the time being, and I needed all the help I could get.

The store saw a dramatic increase in sales during the following weeks. More traffic generated more sales, as word spread, business became steady.

I was excited! Christmas was just around the corner, and that could only be a good thing.

I was wrong?

As I slept one winter evening, the phone rang with disturbing news. It was the alarm monitoring company. There had been a break in.

With dire thoughts racing through my mind, I got out of bed and dressed. It was still dark, cold, and to top it off my car was buried in snow. I drove to the store, which looked like a crime scene. The police officer asked me a thousand and one questions for his report. His closing words were very comforting: "Don't expect this stuff to pop up anytime soon."

Thanks.

But I couldn't get my mind off the fact that I had an empty store. I called a glass replacement company to replace the front door, which had been smashed in. I spent the rest of the day cleaning a big mess. Dazed and confused is the best way to describe how I felt.

The most nerve-racking feeling was to call my insurance company with the bad news. I made an appointment with the adjuster three days after the incident.

I restored everything as best I could, putting out whatever was left in the stockroom. The next day I was back in business. Less than a week later my phone rang again. It was deja vue all over again. The store had been broken into once again.

Was I dreaming?

The police officer on duty said that this was very common.

Not to me!

The burglars had finished what they started. I had to repeat everything from a week ago.

My appointment with the insurance adjuster had been rescheduled to that very day. I couldn't believe what happened. The adjuster must have seen the devastation in my face. That, or he had become numb to these matters. I could imagine that he'd heard it all.

Thank God for insurance!

I was completely covered, including the cost of replacing the glass in the front door.

To make a long story slightly shorter, they broke in ten times within a six-month period. I had no choice but to move out. The landlord completely understood and gave me little resistance. I began looking for something closer to home.

In keeping with the wholesaler/importer theme, I moved into a second floor office. This time I was in the city, with easy access to all major highways. My hours remained the same. My merchandise changed to a more casual format. That was what my clients were demanding.

My customer base kept increasing, and soon I had people at my door waiting for me to open. I knew I was onto something. Business continued to grow. The more sales I rang up, the more merchandise I could buy. I kept reinvesting everything I made back into my company. I grew at a staggering rate.

My first Boxing Day (Canada's version of Black Friday) was unbelievable. There was a line of people down my staircase that stretched to the end of the block. A television news station used my store to illustrate the frenzy of Boxing Day shopping. That was great publicity; the kind of marketing money can't buy!

I soon had more inventory than I had room for. The deals just kept coming my way. I continued to buy up everything in sight. To me, having inventory was better than having money in the bank.

It was time to expand once again. My second location was a breeze to set up, as was my third. If you can believe it, my workload was less than when I started. I'd learned to manage my time wisely. Having the right employees didn't hurt either.

My fourth location was an accident. Overstock had become an increasing problem. While driving by a busy downtown street, I noticed a large vacant store front. The Holiday season was fast approaching and what better time for shopping? I convinced the landlord to let me test the spot for a one-month trial. The rent was outrageous but, trusting my instincts, I went for it.

The results were beyond my wildest expectations. The gross sales exceeded any previous location. To my surprise, items that had been sitting in boxes forever were the first to sell. I cleaned out most of my unwanted inventory.

I wasn't prepared to stay, nor was it my intention to do so. I packed up and began looking for a smaller location in the area, which I would use strictly as clearance center. Approximately a year later, my fourth location was born.

I'm sure that most of this story seems simple, if not vague. I can assure you it was not. In the following chapters I will reveal, step-by-step, the results of my thirteen-year career in the clothing business.

My writing style is designed to make sense, which is the basis of my entire business: **Common Sense**.

Forget what they taught you in school for the time being. This is a real life story with real life experiences, and nothing will come as close to retailing reality.

You'll learn everything from setting up your first store to managing multiple locations, and even how to tackle the wholesale game.

This book is ideal for the beginner as well as the small business owner wanting to improve. I promise you that after reading my book you will walk away with a better understanding of what works and what does not.

You may already be in business, so I'm hoping that you can grasp some powerful techniques that have worked wonders for my business.

The moment when we feel we know it all is when our days are numbered.

Information is the most valuable commodity.

In the rapidly changing pace of business, there is always room for improvement. My hope is that this book will provide that for you. I hope you will enjoy reading the next pages as much as I enjoyed writing them for you.

Chapter Two

GETTING STARTED

YOUR FIRST DAY

So you've decided to get into the "smutta" business. This is a Jewish term which implies that you're in the clothing business. I include the term because I'm sure you'll hear it from time to time, and I wouldn't want you to make the assumption that it is derogatory as I did.

The biggest mistake made by up-and-coming businesses is poor planning. Gone are the days when everything was in demand. We're not looking at those old timers who set up shop thirty years ago with dumb luck riding over their shoulder. In today's world it's either kill or be killed. "There are no substitutes," I remember my college professor telling me, "you must decide early on if you're a shark or a dove." That may sound strong, but unfortunately that's what the business world is. Everyone is chasing the same dollar.

Back to planning. Invest in a binder or folder to store all your documents. Papers will accumulate rather quickly, so it's a good idea to develop organizational skills from the beginning. Most obvious is where you stand financially. Are you borrowing the start-up capital or are you using your life savings? Either way, you must budget accordingly. The last thing you want is to be 80% complete and run out of funds.

Let's look at an itemized breakdown of the most common start up expenses. The budget will vary drastically pending on what type of store you decide to open. Along with the approximate costs, here is an overview of general expenses.

MOST COMMON START UP COSTS

BUSINESS REGISTRATION	$100-$500
PHONE + INSTALLATION	$150
ALARM SYSTEM	$300-$1000
INSURANCE	(pending content value)
BANKING	$100
ELECTRIC	$500
GAS	$500
FIRST/LAST MONTHS RENT	(pending location)
STATIONARY	$500
ADDITIONAL SECURITY	$400-$1500
PERMITS	N/A
EMPLOYEE HIRING	(agency and adversting)
ADVERTISING	N/A
LEASE HOLD IMPROVEMENTS	N/A
CHATTELS AND FIXTURES	N/A
SIGNAGE	N/A
PROFESSIONAL FEES	$500
MISCELLANOUS	$1000

This <u>price does not include</u> the N/A (not available) items, that is, the costs which can vary widely, and the most important line item of all... CLOTHING.

Let's examine these costs more closely. To make matters easier we'll use a mens and ladies casual wear store.

There are three basics areas to cover when starting out.

BUSINESS SETUP. This includes company registration, banking, phone, utilities, etc.

FINDING A LOCATION. This is not as easy as it sounds, and it's crucial to your success. The right location can make your business or the wrong location can break you. You are not driving all around town looking for the first empty spot! There are many factors to consider.

WHERE TO BUY MERCHANDISE. Seeking out the right contacts is the difference between a highly profitable company and one that is not so profitable. I will discuss in great detail how to deal with your supplier.

BUSINESS SETUP

COMPANY REGISTRATION. When you set up any business, you must register the company in the city where you live.

Although the laws differ from city to city or state to state, the principles usually remain the same. Check with your local government registration office for details.

Let's decide what your business will be called. It's important to choose your name wisely, as it will stay with you for years to come. It will be how most people identify what type of business you do. It's always wise to include what you do in the name itself. For example, if the name is Laura's Fine Fragrances, shoppers know immediately that this business is involved in cosmetics or perfumes.

Sometimes the name has nothing to do with what you sell but rather how you sell. *Best Buy* is an example of this. We all know who they are by their massive ad campaigns. Their name puts emphasis on their prices. What about *BMW*, the automaker? We all know the car, but how many of us can say what the letters stand for?

Let's assume that you don't have millions of dollars to promote your business. Let's try to come up with a name that will ring out every time people hear it.

Once you decide on a name, it's time to visit your registration office. You will usually have three choices: Sole propriership,

Corporation, or Partnership. I would like to point out that the information provided is relevant to Toronto, Canada, where I live, so be sure to check with your local offices for more accurate details, and what each choice means under the laws where you live.

When going into business by yourself, the cheapest way to set it up is **sole propriership**. This costs under $100 and will allow you to conduct business as usual. However, there are limitations. You may register a name and find out months down the line that someone else has been using your name for years. How did this happen? Maybe you didn't do a proper name search (the search looks to see if anyone else is currently using your name).

Don't forget that the basic registration is very limited in what it covers. The reason most businesses opt for a corporation is that there is what is called limited liability. Simply put, you are not personally liable for anything over and above the business.

CORPORATION is perhaps the most popular form of registration. When you see company names with INC., LTD., or CORP. after their name, they've been incorporated.

There are two types to choose from, a numbered company, a name corporation or both.

The numbered company is suited for real estate purchases or circumstances that do not require a name, so let's presume that the name registration is the way to go. This method can cost usually around $300 to $500.

Let's assume that you'll call your company **ABC Clothing, Inc.** You now must do whats called a *Naun* search report. This is a nationwide search, making sure nobody else is using the same name. Next, you register your new company. You'll need to fill out forms called **articles.** You'll also need to answer some basic questions, such as your personal info, the nature of the business, and list all share holders, if any. This method can cost slightly more, usually in the neighbourhood of around $1,000, especially when you're using an accountant or lawyer.

PARTNERSHIP is identical to both propriership or corporation except for, you guessed it, partners. Sounds confusing? You can easily avoid all this by hiring a lawyer or accountant to do the filing for you, but at a premium of about $1,000 or more.

THE TELEPHONE

The reasons for installing a telephone are obvious. Customers will call for hours, directions, and make general inquiries about your products. But did you also know that your telephone is often connected to your alarm system? It sends a signal to a monitoring station, which lets them know if there is an intruder.

The most common mistake new store owners make is to fill their store with merchandise, only to learn that they're not insured unless the alarm has been connected.

When you call to set up a new business line you may be told there is a two to three week wait for installation service. There isn't much you can do about it.

Sure, there are different companies to choose from, but make sure they're reliable. It would be wise to know someone who's already using the service and ask about their experience.

Telephone lines are also used for credit/debit card transactions. All your transactions are electronically deposited to your bank account by telephone.

Fax machines are also connected to the phone line. Although most communication is done via email, when running a business it is always wise to maintain all lines of communication.

The Phone Company may issue a temporary phone number when your order is placed. DO NOT rush to put this number on your business cards or other stationary! This temporary number is just that: temporary, and may change.

You can see that something as simple as a phone number should not be overlooked.

Also, with the ever-growing use of the Internet, it would be wise to use your telephone as a creative tool to support your business.

Most Internet connections are via phone lines. The Internet is a powerful marketing tool, which I'll talk about in more detail later in this book.

ALARM AND MONITORING

With clothing being the second most popular item of choice for theft (the first is electronics), an alarm system with monitoring is mandatory.

Prices were expensive when I started out, but today I'm finding that more and more companies will install alarm systems for free. Be aware that most of these deals require that you sign a three to five year monitoring contract, at a premium. It's wise to shop around and save. I've found monitoring companies which charge as low as $10 a month.

Most insurance companies will require a **certificate** from the alarm monitoring company to verify that you are indeed using their service.

You may opt to buy your own system. The cost will vary. Alarm systems can cost as little as $150 and as high as several thousand. Can you imagine the cost of a jewelry store's system or, for that matter, a bank's?

Remember these words, which I will repeat from time to time. COMMON SENSE!

When one of the tech guys visits your store to set up the system, have him do his job properly. After all, you're paying him with your hard-earned money.

They usually come by and install your system exactly where the last company had it. Maybe that's fine.

However, make certain that you address the following concerns. Did they install a proper siren, not some rinki-dink siren that a mouse won't hear in the middle of the night? Do not place it in arm's reach, example right by the door, so that your thief can walk in and rip it off the wall in two seconds flat? Install it in a hard-to-find, out-of-reach area.

Can they install an exterior siren? You want the alarm noise to be heard on the outside as well as the inside, this may be violating a by law not to mention disturbing your nieghbours so look into this prior to installation.

Have the entry delay time set for no more than thirty seconds. This will allow for a very short time to get to your keypad to disarm the system. Some stores have a two to three minute delay, allowing your employees to walk in, turn on the lights, and find a resting place for their latte. A thief, could break in and have that much time to do some serious damage.

The shorter the entry times the better. Any police officer will tell you that thieves are often in and out within seconds.

Another option is a detailed **entry report**. This may be useful when there are key holders and managers minding your business. What this service will do is provide a printout of each and every person accessing the system, with date, time, and employee code. That comes in handy to make sure you keep everyone honest. The last thing you want is to have your drunken manager bringing his date by in the middle of the night and making a mess (believe me it's happened).

There are more expensive measures you can take.

BANKING

It pains me to admit it, but to function as a business you must use the banking system and all the wonderful fees that go with it. For the purpose of setting up a business or current account, you must first call to make an appointment with the person in charge of setting up new accounts. You will need to provide them with your business registration papers and fill out and sign a bunch of papers. You can scrutinize them all you want. However, if you want to do business with that particular bank, you'd best be signing. Their rules and regulations are written in stone.

A nice security feature the bank will have you sign is the **signature card.** This is the best way to identify when there is any discrepancy. Try to sign the same way each and every time. Your signature will be your first line of defense against any would-be forgers.

The bank will make efforts to sell you certain packages, which allow you more perks than the average client, such as lower service fees, additional insurance and a list of freebies. Don't bother with these packages at this time. Try to stay as basic as possible. Change the package as your needs change.

At this time you should deposit your start-up funds into your newly formed account. Remember that everything you purchase for your business will be tax deductible, so it's important to keep track of every purchase and expense.

Each check written will be sent back to you either as a hardcopy or photocopied version, along with a statement, on a monthly basis.

Next, order your **business checks**. They will be numbered in sequence. This makes it simple and easy to retrieve any payment information. I recommend starting at a high number, this will give the impression that you have been in business longer than you have.

Next, set up a **credit card terminal**. The must-haves are *Visa*, *MasterCard*, and *Debit card*. You can set up other cards, such as *American Express*, but I strongly doubt you'll lose a sale with the main three. Besides, Amex and others usually charge a higher service fee than the rest. Your bank will provide the necessary info on who to call and how to get started.

Once you call, you the representative in your area will make an appointment to see you. After filling out and signing the documents, you're in business.

They will assign you a percentage fee on all transactions. This fee is based on your sales. It usually runs between 2 to 3%. Debit cards are pennies per transaction, with no percentage. There is little you can do when you're a new account, but it doesn't hurt to ask for the lowest possible fee.

There have been circumstances where Merchant Services have not approved a new applicant. They may request funds for a security deposit. This is extremely rare, and I highly doubt it will happen to you. If it does, appeal it at all costs. You don't want your funds tied up in a security deposit

ELECTRICITY/GAS

I have combined these two items. The setups are essentially the same.

To get the electrical service set up, simply call your local electric company and ask for a new account.

You may be required to provide a security deposit of about $500. This will be refunded at the end of your term or it may be credited as you go along provided the account is in good standing. The reason for this deposit is so you don't run up a large bill and decide to skip town.

The gas company, on the other hand, keeps the account in the landlord's name. More than likely the bill will get forwarded to you with a copy of the original. In fact, demand to see the copy to avoid over billing.

FIRST AND LAST MONTHS RENT

When a lease or rental agreement is signed, you will be required to pay the landlord the first and last month's rent in one lump sum. Some places call the last payment a security deposit. This is to insure that the landlord is somewhat compensated in the event that you do a midnight run (break your agreement) or cause damage to the property.

If the store is considered to be a hot location in a desirable area, the landlord may request first, last, and a security deposit. This will always be up for negotiation. However, time is of the essence. If you have been searching long and hard for the right spot, don't let a couple of bucks spoil the chances of locking a great spot.

The same is true when deciding between two properties. Don't let the better location escape on the account of a couple of dollars. A $200 dollar difference adds up to just over $6 a day. The better location is sure to fetch that much more in business.

STATIONARY

This includes business cards, receipts, accounting journals, paper, pens, markers, etc. General office supplies.

Although it might appear to be a non-issue, stationary products can quickly eat up the budget, Especially when business cards and invoices are concerned. If your budget allows for it, great, the sky's the limit.

However, if you're working with limited funds I propose you start off with blank carbonless copy receipt books. They're available for a couple of dollars at your local *Business Depot*. Print an address label including the business number and stick it on the top of each receipt.

Next is your business card. Printers often offer packages with cards and all your stationary needs at one low price. The difference between 500 cards and 2000 is often under $20-$30.

There are also many easy-to-use computer programs which allow you to create a very impressive look at the touch of a mouse.

Don't be fooled into thinking that your business card represents what type of store you are. Although this may be true for exclusive boutiques, it literally has no effect on the average store. Believe me when I tell you that a fancy business card simply serves to satisfy your own ego. Chances are you won't lose a sale if you have a not so impressive business card.

Buy stationary as you go along. Visit places like *WalMart*. You'll be more than impressed by their selection, as well as their prices.

ADDITIONAL SECURITY

A simple adjustment or upgrade can save you a lot of aggravation. There may be a cheap average back door lock, or a flimsy window. It's worth the extra couple of bucks to make sure you keep thieves out.

The most common security precaution is metal bars over the windows and doors, though I personally hate what this does to the look of any store. To go this route, you will need to hire an experienced welder, as it will most likely be a custom-fit job.

The most expensive, and I believe the best-looking, system is roll cages. There are many different types, from electronic versions that move up and down to manual systems that roll across into a hidden compartment. These systems are extremely expensive, so you may want to hold off until the business is up and running. Some insurance companies will insist that you take extra measures to insure a safe and secure store.

HIRING STAFF

If the business is new, it is assumed you (the owner) will manage day-to-day operations as well. Although your goal is to save as much money as you can, it would be wise to hire a part-time employee. This will not only free your time from doing daily chores, but also free your mind to concentrate on more important issues. You're the boss, so start acting as one.

A common mistake made by small business owners is that they want to take on everything themselves (otherwise known as micro manage). That's an invitation to burn-out, aside from being an inefficient way to run a retail business.

Know how everything works, but don't get absorbed in it. You might think that hiring staff is as simple as posting a sign in the window. Though you can do that, I wouldn't advise it. People from all walks of life, who couldn't possibly do your job, will apply wasting valuable time.

Instead, place an ad in the classified section of your local newspaper or job sites such as Monster.com. Craigslist and Kijiji may also produce results. This will get the attention of people who are seriously looking for work. It will also give you the opportunity to properly screen those who respond. If possible use the newspaper's message box service or an anonymous email address. This will save you time by avoiding direct communication with candidates.

I strongly recommend pleasant and outgoing types. Think about it. Who'd buy from a person who is frowning or half asleep?

Make certain of the following: Don't hire your niece or your girlfriend/boyfriend! That's a disaster waiting to happen. There is always the exception to the rule, but best to stick to the rules. Remember its business. I find that the hardest-working employees are those who have bills to pay (rent, car payments etc.). They need the money. They're motivated to do a good job.

It may become expensive if the ad keeps running without finding the person you need. If you haven't found anyone within a month, try another classified or website. There is also the option of using a job placement service.

It's important to note that most part-timers aren't going to make a career out of this job. Most are trying to make a couple of extra bucks so they can stay in school and party on the weekends. Don't be disappointed or surprised when they call in sick frequently. Expect it. Have a back-up. And, if you find a part-timer who really does the job and isn't always looking for time off, that may be the person you want to hire full-time, when you're ready.

Employees are a constant weeding process. As the old saying goes, "you're only as strong as your weakest link." I have included my employee manual in this book, which is sure to give you a few pointers.

ADVERTISING

Getting the word out is what will bring people into your store.

Initially, many people who set up a new business use up most of their funds before they budget for advertising.

I can't stress how important it is to effectively advertise your location. Why do you think giant corporations like *Nike* and *Coca Cola* spend millions of dollars annually to market (advertise) their products? We all know what they sell, but they continue to pour obscene amounts of money into promos and celebrity endorsements.

They spend so much on advertising **because it works!**

Consumers can be persuaded to buy almost anything. Think of those tacky infomercials that sell a new diet plan every couple of months. You and I know it's bull, but they're on the air continuously. They play with human emotions and it does the trick.

I'll get into effectively promoting your store in a later section, but for now let's discuss an easy and cost-effective startup plan.

First things first: Put a sign in the window trumpeting the message,

Coming Soon!
New Designer Outlet Shop!....Grand Opening (DATE)

That will let all the passers-by know what's new on the block. Believe it or not, it will create a buzz, so put up that sign the day you sign your lease. You can change the opening date accordingly.

Second, introduce yourself to your neighbors. Give them a business card, and maybe even offer them a discount. The last thing you want is a bad relationship with your neighbors! It's not good for business!

Third, place a small ad in the community paper. They're usually free, and are read by most locals. Try to see whether they can offer you a special rate for being a new business in the area.

Churches, community centers, and arenas have bulletin boards for posting events such as **Grand Openings.**

Hire a kid to go door-to-door or car-to-car with a flyer. This is a tried and true way to bring people through the door.

Go to your local dry cleaners, restaurants, or parking lots and ask whether they'll hand out your flyer with their ticket stubs.

I've given you some examples of inexpensive ways to put your store on the map. If the funds are available, I strongly recommend you make use of some of the techniques found in the advertising section of this book.

Get creative.

There are no limits on how to promote. Remember, the more people that come through the door, the more likely you are to sell. It's all a numbers game.

LEASEHOLD IMPROVEMENTS

When you decide between one location or another, the deciding factor may well be the interior. I'm always amazed at what general contractors charge for what seems to be child's play. You may have found an excellent spot, but if it needs some repair work you may want to reconsider. Repairs or renovation will surely affect the startup budget.

Before signing the lease, have a qualified contractor come by to make an overall inspection. Simply tell him or her that you want to know what it will cost for a paint job or to knock down a wall, or whatever is needed.

Most contractors give free estimates. That's one of the ways they generate business. Have them come by when you set up a second visit with the realtor or the landlord.

The last thing you want to do is to sign a binding contract, only to find out that it will cost thousands of dollars for additional renovations.

Another option is to have the landlord absorb some of the costs. Keep in mind if it's a hot spot, the chances are slim to none. Shop around when hiring contractors; their prices can vary dramatically. Make sure that whatever price you agree on is in writing.

A written estimate should include what they're doing, to the letter, and the cost, line by line, with an itemized breakdown of the materials they are using.

Be sure that a completion deadline date is written in. Often, jobs are accepted and put on the back burner because your contractor is juggling five jobs at once. Ask whether they're the ones actually doing the work. Most contractors specialize in certain areas. As a result, they sub-contract some of the work to others, usually at a premium to you.

Check the local yellow pages or do a google search. If there's a contractor referral service in your area, it can be a valuable resource. I find that using your neighbor's friend does more harm than good. Furthermore, you feel obligated. If you're unhappy for any reason, feel free to fire away. It's difficult to judge someone's work before it has been completed.

My last piece of advice is to not always hire the contractor who offers the cheapest price. As the old saying goes, "you get what you pay for."

CHATTELS AND FIXTURES

Again, sky's the limit.

I've known of super-exclusive boutiques spending millions of dollars. Before you walk into a fixture shop, search online. You'll be surprised at the deals available in the slightly used department. Clothing stores, like any other business, open and close all the time. Why spend thousands when you can spend hundreds?

It's important to have a certain image in mind. Don't buy scratched and beat up equipment if it will degrade the attractiveness of what you're selling. Ask clothing suppliers whether they can point you in the right direction. They know who is shutting down or downsizing. They may even have fixtures themselves that they're willing to part with.

Chattels are the items which become permanent, like lights, a drop ceiling, and new bathrooms. Once chattels are installed, they automatically become property of the landlord, so unless you're 100% sure that this is the location for you, limit what is spent.

It's difficult to know how to allocate funds without a location in mind. When I started, it cost me no more than a couple of cleaning products to move in.

MISCELLANEOUS

Starting out is never easy, nor is knowing exactly what's needed to set up shop. With all the years under my belt, it's still impossible to avoid the expenses lumped under "miscellaneous."

Another table, an additional mirror or mannequin, more hangers, or perhaps a simple extension cord are just a few examples. However small on the surface, these unavoidable costs can grow into a financial dilemma. Each new business will encounter its own set of unforeseen costs.

Don't panic if you're short a couple of bucks. Simply open your doors and raise the capitol as you go along. The last thing you want is to delay the grand opening because there isn't a sound system.

Who cares?

Open the store!

Don't wait for the weekend or that sunny day. The faster you're in business, the faster you'll know what else you forgot to buy. Believe me, there's always something!

As you can see there are significant costs involved in setting up shop. This section should have given you an overview on the most common fees associated with starting up.

My figure was just under $5,000, not including the N/A items, for which you'll have to fill in the blanks for your specific store and situation, and of course the clothing itself. Proper planning will not only assure longevity but will also avoid financial disaster

Chapter Three

WHAT TYPE OF STORE DO I SET UP?

The choices depend on a number of factors. The obvious factor is how much start-up capital you have. Another key factor is what type of environment you're trying to create.

The business which will hopefully become your livelihood should represent your lifestyle. Do you want to drive up in a Mercedes and turn the key to a posh boutique, or would you prefer to drive a truck to a gigantic warehouse?

This is not to say that one is better than the other. The most important factor is to define your goals. Remember that money may be the one and only concern, but for others it may be having a business that they can be proud of, one that fits their lifestyle.

Each of us must be honest and ask ourselves what we want from our business. The answer will vary between one person and the next, of course. We're all different, hence the wide variety of businesses out there.

Let's look at the most common types of stores. Decide which route will work best for you. It may be possible to combine elements of each, thus creating the best of both worlds. Some of this information will be further explored in Chapter Four, "Where Do I Set Up Shop?"

The Boutique

Perhaps the most expensive of the clothing stores, a boutique according to Webster is defined as a small shop selling articles of fashion. The true meaning of most business terms have been distorted over the years. I define a boutique as a small location selling very expensive designer labels in a very desirable area. Boutiques are usually owner-operated.

A boutique will clearly require substantial startup costs. A key ingrediant will be to set up in a desirable area, surrounded by other high-end establishments.

The goal here is to be in an area which has the right traffic flow. By right, I mean people with money. New York has Park Avenue, Beverly Hills has Rodeo Drive, and Toronto has the Golden Mile on Bloor St.

Every city has its own super-expensive areas. They're not difficult to find. Simply look for the flagship stores of your favorite designers. Try to locate in their vicinity. The price of rent will seem astronomical, but it's all relevant to the customer you are catering to and the product you will be selling. High end customers look for expensive areas and the shops in them

Next is the location itself. This can be where the bulk of the finances will be needed. Leasehold improvements should reflect the area the store is located.

The last thing we want is to have a great location and have Uncle Guido do the paint job. This is the time to call upon a professional. Hire a designer, give him a budget, and have him work on some sketches for your approval. Terms such as Italian Marble and Stainless Steel staircases will sound exciting—until you're hit with the price tag.

Interior designers consider themselves to be artists, not accountants, so it's your job as the proprietor to oversee and approve all decisions. Don't feel embarrassed to cut certain costs if they will put you over the top financially.

Next, if you can afford it, hire a project manager. His or her job is to coordinate all the contractors to assure that they complete their tasks in a timely fashion. He or she will, presumably, make your life headache-free. The goal is to have the renovations completed by a certain deadline. When you're paying thousands of dollars for rent, and potentially will earn thousands of dollars of revenues, you want to assure that you set up shop in a timely manner.

The added expense to this type of operation is more of a psychology one, playing off the emotions and expectations of a specific buyer. If I'm rich and have money to burn, I become accustomed to shopping in a plush environment. There are no sale racks and door-crasher tables.

Now we have the clothing.

This is what will make or break your business.

It's your job to investigate and possibly import a very exclusive and desirable label, one that will stand on its own next to the big boys. Remember, price is not an issue. Do your homework, and try to find out as much information on potential clientele—their age, sex, income, and lifestyle; everything which will affect their spending habits. This is called **demographic research**.

Due to the expenses involved, it's wise to sell a product which allows for a larger than normal mark-up. I recommend at least cost times three. The traffic flow will most definitely be slower than for the average-priced or shopping mall location, so make every sale count.

We've all heard the old saying, "perception is reality." We're trying to project the right image. A dress will have a greater chance of selling for a higher dollar amount if the presentation is correct. We can't expect to fetch the same dollar value should the same dress be hanging on a rack in a giant warehouse.

The most overlooked factor is the service. Be certain to hire an adult who will conduct him or herself in a professional manner. The last thing a rich, pretentious shopper wants is to have some smart aleck kid working part-time between classes serving them. The goal is to have that customer return with a smile and blank a lot of plastic.

I don't advise a novice or beginner to start off with such an undertaking unless they have several years of experience under their belts. What you need to keep in mind is that you're attempting to create a boutique that sells lifestyle as well as fashionable clothing.

Should you opt for a boutique, I recommend starting off in an area that's less expensive and more manageable. Once a clientele is built and you've perfected the art of catering to the needs of your customers, then and only then should you consider moving up to where the money flows like a river.

This formula will also work on a much smaller scale. The principals will remain the same wherever you decide to set up shop.

Follow the 80/20 rule!

Many years ago an Italian economist named Vilfredo Perato made an observation that later became known as the Perato Principal. Some examples are that we use 20% of our wardrobe 80% of the time, we use 20% of our phone numbers 80% of the time and you guessed it, 20% of our clients account for 80% of our sales. Although this may not be an exact science it is definitely note worthy and should be applied in terms of customers and customer service.

The Outlet/Warehouse Store

This type of setup has become very popular over the years, and with good reason. **People want to save money.**

Unlike a boutique, the outlet store is usually situated in a remote area oustide the city amidst industrial-type businesses. It is usually a destination point for those eager consumers. A location's main attraction should be price and size.

Don't be afraid to move into a rough space which may be larger than anticipated. Over time, and before you know it, the space will fill up with racks and shelves. The reason is that your buying is done in bulk and the sales floor becomes the stock room as well.

The largest part of your expenses will go toward your inventory, and perhaps to advertising. All that's required for a warehouse store is a clean and organized space. Tables, rolling racks, shelving, signage, and a fresh coat of paint are the basics to get started.

I've had great success using this very basic concept. I've literally used open cardboard boxes as display cases, with items still wrapped in their original packaging. Customers seemed to love the idea of rummaging through boxes in search of that special piece. I've also attended warehouse sales that didn't permit items to be tried on, yet the sales were more than successful.

The clothing you'll buy for a warehouse location must be purchased at a considerable discount in order for the business to flourish. Factory overruns, bankruptcies, samples, balances, and even factory seconds will provide the price needed to draw customers. Simply approach manufacturers and suppliers and ask whether they have clearance merchandise for sale. I recommend buying COD. This will entice them to sell.

Choose the items wisely. You want to be sure you can sell what you buy. The last thing you want is to purchase 500 lime green skirts because they were a brand name and you could buy them at an unbelievable price, and then discover that the reason for the unbelievable price is that nobody wants to wear them at any price.

Try to stick to staple items that will stand the test of time. It's worth spending slightly more to buy the right product rather than to save and buy items which don't sell. I'd buy a thousand white classic shirts over a few polka dot ones any day.

THE KEY TO A WAREHOUSE STORE IS TURNOVER!

Always try to have fresh and new items in order to keep customers coming back.

The structure of a warehouse will serve better if it's designed to let customers help themselves. Have large, easy-to-read, signage providing price and descriptions. Due to the nature of the store, customers will tend to make a mess. That's why it's essential to hire as many people as needed to keep each section organized and presentable. Have the staff familiarize themselves with the general layout so they can direct shoppers where to look. Keeping the store tidy takes priority over customer service. There are not enough hours in the day to be dealing with a finicky shopper, especially in a warehouse enviroment.

Once again, it would be wise to build slowly before taking a giant leap. Always buy what the market is asking for. This will change as you get a feel for whom the clientele will be.

The Shopping Mall

The shopping mall provides the greatest traffic flow of customers without the need to do any advertising. Although this comes at a premium, it should not be overlooked. A mall location offers the greatest chance for expanding your business into a large chain.

A shopping mall location will require considerable start-up capital and a proper business plan. Above all else, you need experience in the retail field. You may have worked retail in the past, but this will not prepare you for the fast-paced environment of a shopping mall.

A shopping mall is usually located in a rural or suburban area, where there are abundant residents and newly-developed subdivisions.

When investigating which mall to set up shop in, it's wise to know what other stores are tenants. The fact that there may be other clothing stores is actually a good thing. Competition is always healthy. In every mall, there will always be your anchor stores, usually a major department store or two, which sell clothing, of course. The Gap, Banana Republic, Roots, and Foot Locker all sell clothing geared towards a youth market, yet have managed to coexist and flourish together.

You benefit when these anchor or name-brand store advertise, because they bring people who are shopping for clothing into the mall. Those customers will look at what the big stores have, and then browse the rest of the mall in search of bargains or something different.

The leasehold improvements in a mall will be as expensive, often more expensive, than those of a boutique. In order for the shopping mall to keep a certain level of appearance, in keeping with the image it wants to present, it will require that all prospects provide a detailed plan of their designs and concepts for approval. Cutting corners will prove to be more than impossible. Sadly, this is why most mall businesses are multinational chains with deep pockets.

Whenever possible, try to obtain exclusivity on any brand you decide to carry. This will arm you with the competitive edge needed to succeed. If you're the only person in the mall selling a hot label that everybody wants, think of what this will do to sales.

I find that selling low to medium priced goods is the way to go, because it appeals to the masses, who in all likelihood will be the customer your store attracts.

Having the proper staff will reflect on your sales. Establish and maintain a proper training program. Bring in a professional, if need be.

The average price to set up shop in a mall, from start to finish, can run you over $250,000. Don't jeopardize that kind of investment with a poor staff. Have a proper pay structure with commission rates and bonuses. Pay management a premium salary to insure optimal performance.

Most successful mall stores are brands that sell directly to the public. Keystone mark ups will not be enough. I recommend having your own label mixed in that allows you mark ups as high as 10 times the cost. YES this is possible.

STRIP PLAZA

The strip plaza will be very similar to a shopping mall in the setup process and costs, but possibly with fewer restrictions and shorter operating hours. By all accounts it may be less expensive, but rest assured the overall structure will remain the same.

Chapter Four

WHERE DO I SET UP SHOP?

Location, location, location! That's a phrase you've heard over and over, and with good reason. The location you choose can make or break your business.

In this section, We'll look at the various types of places to set up shop such as the street store, the strip plaza, the warehouse, and the shopping mall. The choice will be entirely up to you.

How do you find the right location?

There are many ways this can be accomplished. You can visit your local realtor and give him a budget to work with. He or she has access to the MLS (multiple listing service), where all available properties are posted. The best part is this is totally free.

The landlord of the property you sign a deal with will pay the agent's commission. A word to the wise, however—don't have the real estate agent pressure you into signing a deal unless you feel comfortable and are sure that this is the right location for you.

Remember that they're making a commission, which is based on the type of deal you sign. They usually get the first and last month's rent, or a percentage of the entire lease amount.

Another way to find a location is to simply take a drive around the city. A good idea would be to know where you want to set up shop. This will narrow the choices significantly.

There will be either a realtor's sign or a private sign letting you know the property is vacant or soon will be. Take down the number and call to get as much info as possible. You want to know such things as how large the store is, the price per square foot, whether this includes all taxes, how long of a lease they're looking for, are there any restrictions on usage, does it have parking, and is the basement finished? And so on—everything you need to know about a property before even bothering to look at it, and certainly need to know before you sign a lease.

Make your own checklist to address your own concerns.

I don't advise using your agent if you find a suitable property on your own, as it may leave you with less negotiating power. On the other hand, Realtors are able to give you detailed information on the property through their system, like how long the property has been vacant and whether there have been any legal problems with the premises.

The street store is perhaps the most economical way to set up. This location is usually found on main streets throughout the city. They are usually in buildings which may or may not have apartments or offices on the second level.

I'm sure you know the city where you live. Therefore, you should know what type of location you're looking for, and what you're looking at when you find one that appears doable.

What type of people live and work in the area? Is there walk-by traffic? What kind of other stores are near by?

Don't get turned off if there are other clothing stores in the area. That will actually bring more business for everyone. The only drawback is that it may prevent you from carrying certain labels if they are already on the block.

I don't recommend hiring a high priced designer when you're starting out. Their cost will eat a large chunk of your capital. There are better places to spend (invest) your money. Clean walls, nice fixtures, and clothing is all you need.

Ask the landlord when you can take possession. Be sure that you have ample time to make arrangements. If the location is a fixer-upper, ask the landlord whether he or she is willing to subsidize the cost of the project. You can point out that you should be able to expect a clean space and shouldn't have to do the renovations yourself, starting from scratch, or cleaning up the mess left by some previous tenant. You usually won't get direct help from the landlord, but there's a good chance that you can negotiate and get a couple of month's free rent.

There are many advantages to a street-level location. You can set your own hours and pay a reasonable rental rate. I feel this is by far the best way to go when you're starting out. It will enable you to grow, while a mall or warehouse may turn into a larger than expected project, which will hinder and delay your success.

The strip plaza is very similar to a street store. The only difference is that the complex may be governed by a management company instead of by individual owners. The costs of setting up in a strip plaza are slightly higher, and more restrictions may apply. There are usually higher taxes and maintenance fees, but they're justified. The restrictions and/or management company policies may prevent you from using certain signage, and even regulate when you can hold a sale. Be sure the regulations won't stop you from doing something you need to do to make your business prosper.

For example, if you want to set up a store dealing in close-out, budget-priced merchandise, you don't want limits on when you can advertise a special sale, since you're marketing the "Blow-Out Sale!" aspect of the clothing business.

The strip plaza concept is similar to that of a shopping mall, except that the stores are situated outside rather than all the stores being within one huge building.

There are usually a wide variety of stores to increase the flow of shoppers. This may not be a good thing. If you're the only clothing store in the plaza, it may do more harm than good. The last thing you need is a seventy-five-year-old walking through after visiting the nearby senior community center.

A great idea would be to find a plaza specializing in fashion, though they will be hard to find. You're more likely to find a general plaza which has several clothing stores in its mix of businesses.

As suburban areas expand, so does the strip plaza concept. If you want to get away from hectic city traffic, this may be a nice alternative.

The warehouse is another term for big store.

This concept originated when a factory or wholesaler opened its doors to the public, often for only a few days for a "Special Sale." The idea expanded to become factory warehouse stores, which are more common today.

The term has become way overused and is often untruthful, unfortunately. Have you ever seen signs reading messages like BIG WAREHOUSE SALE, or, BUY DIRECT FROM IMPORTER?

This is a gimmick, which I find has become outdated. The consumer is much too intelligent to fall for this type of sales pitch. The setup is just like a street store, except that it's usually located in a remote industrial area.

The rent may be substantially less, but there's much more space to fill, and much more advertising must be done to draw enough customers to make the store turn over a profit.

When you're starting out, avoid going this route. It may have some initial momentum, but if you're not offering something extremely special on a constant basis it will be difficult to sustain a steady flow of traffic.

Shopping is all about convenience. Unless you live in a remote small town, there will be little that's exclusive. The warehouse will be a destination point for shoppers.

Ask yourself, "Why is anyone going to drive out here to buy this top or that skirt in this garage-like warehouse?"

If, on the other hand, years have passed, your stores have succeeded, and you've built up an excess of inventory and require a warehouse for normal and legitimate reasons, you may find that it's a good idea to promote an occasional sale at your warehouse. That is the definition of a true WAREHOUSE SALE.

If your customers come to expect that you'll have a GREAT WAREHOUSE BLOW-OUT SALE at certain times of the year, for example in January, which is typically a slow month, after the Christmas rush, they may flock to your sales.

The shopping mall is last on my list, for many good reasons. If you're a beginner with little or no experience, you may wind up closing your doors faster than you opened them.

The mall is a place where you can find everything under one roof. It's become a place where the young socialize and the old walk around and waste time (just kidding).

Because clothing is an impulse item, it's to your benefit to have herds of people walking through your door. Sadly, malls have become giant corporations, catering to the needs of chains and franchises. There is little or no room left for a small to medium-size company.

The screening process for a new mall business is difficult at best. There are a number of variables that will determine whether your business is a qualified candidate.

Most of us are under the impression that there's a waiting list for a mall which is in demand. This is not entirely true. A mall must have the right blend of businesses to stay afloat. If you're just another shoe store and there are already five shoe stores in the mall, your chances are diminished. They're looking for new and exciting ventures that will draw more crowds to support their other stores.

If your store has a new and exciting concept, your chances of becoming a tenant improve greatly.

But not so fast.

The mall management will do a background check on you, the owner. They want to make sure there are no bad credit reports, lawsuits, or anything else negative about your personal and business history. Anything negative will affect your chances.

Next, you'll need to show them the type of business experience you have in your chosen field. If you've been in construction work for the past ten years and decide to get into clothing, that will not qualify you as an experienced person!

The mall may require a minimum of five year's experience, and may want to see what type of operation you're running at present.

Next, they'll check you out financially. They need to know how stable you and your business are. The last thing they want is a deadbeat on their hands; someone who experiences a couple of bad months and is forced to close the doors.

Next, they'll want to know your intentions. Some high-end malls may accept certain designs but will only allow you to use short list of accredited contractors. A mall is all about image, so they can't afford to have you let your uncle Joe's neighbor to do the hardwood flooring. They have a list of reputable contractors who you must use for any work done on your space in their building. Their policies and approved contractors even include the signage of your store front.

Of course, some malls are far stricter than others. It's said that having a business in a mall is a make or break situation. There is no in between. You're either going to do well or close your doors.

The disadvantage to a mall location is there are too many restrictions placed on you, and you must be open during their hours of business, which may be twelve-hour days, seven days a week. This may not seem like much, but if you stop to add up the wages for all those hours it will make more sense. You have to draw enough business to pay your staff and make a profit, whatever the required hours of operation may be.

The other disadvantage is the competition factor. Ever wonder how giants like the Gap are able to afford massive ad campaigns and have armies of staff, not to mention a merchandising department? The reason is that they're involved in every aspect of the process from design to manufacturer to retailer. Their markup is astronomical.

As a small merchant in a mall, you will certainly have to go up against such companies, so prepare yourself. Do your homework. The best solution is to visit your competitors to see what similar items are selling for. If your black t-shirt is $19.99 and the chain or department store has a similar black t-shirt at $9.99, you may have a problem.

The best question to ask yourself is what makes your store different; what makes it stand out against your competition.

What are you offering your customers that the chains and department stores are not, and perhaps cannot?

Making the correct choice depends entirely on your current situation. Do not attempt to bite off more than you can chew. After all, the old saying that Rome was not built in a day remains true, and remains good advice.

Chapter Five

WHAT DO I SELL?

Clothing is a vast industry, consisting of everything from swimwear to maternity wear. The choices are endless.

I recommend that you sell what you enjoy wearing.

If you're in your late 20's and consider yourself trendy, why would you consider selling work wear?

I feel that your working environment should be a pleasurable experience. It should reflect your personality and lifestyle. You may be a new parent and find that infant clothing is your passion.

There's no greater feeling than waking up every morning, looking forward to work.

When I started out with formal wear, I was in my early 20's. It wasn't me. I was forced to deal with men twice my age. Later, I ventured into casual wear, which seemed like a better fit. I began interacting with my customers on a personal level. Some even invited me to their weddings. The odd date from the occasional customer didn't hurt, either.

Visit the trade shows. See what's out there. I'm sure you'll find your niche.

Once you've decided on what to sell, it's time to interact with your supplier(s). This is perhaps the single most important relationship you will form during the course of the business. The following is a brief list questions that should be addressed prior to buying.

Does your supplier have an in-stock program?

This is when a supplier will stock inventory of the line over and above the orders received. It seems obvious, but it's not always the case. Once upon a time, when business was booming, wholesalers stocked large amounts of everything they carried, so you didn't have to place large orders. Stock was always readily available.

You could have easily dropped in when you needed an item or two and be accommodated. When hard times hit, the suppliers became wiser, ordering only what had been purchased by retailers, thus limiting the amount on hand.

The larger agencies, which carry the big brands, may order a percentage more than their purchase orders (usually 10 to 20%), but don't rely on that. Those items are usually reserved for premium customers, those like you're trying to become.

This is not always the case, however. Sometimes orders are cancelled, rejected, or shipped incorrectly from the manufacturer. If you're at the right place at the right time, you may be able to capitalize and take advantage, and you'll usually save a buck or two.

Smaller agencies, those just starting out or those that carry less well-known brands, tend to take more risks. So always ask! Never hesitate to ask your suppliers for what you need!

If you know there will be merchandise available when you need it, you can reduce your original order and buy as items sell. Play it safe, and buy accordingly.

What happens if I receive my order late?

For economic reasons, most clothing is made overseas. Therefore, there may be delays in getting your order on time. This may be due to transportation problems, poor communication, manufacturer back orders, or any number of reasons. You don't care about these problems. All you care about is how this affects your business.

The best way to handle this situation is to prepare in advance. When you're filling out the purchase order, write in a cancellation date. This is the best way to protect yourself. By including a specific date by which the merchandise must be delivered, you have the right to reject any merchandise you ordered if it doesn't arrive on time. This is standard practice for major department stores. You can't be sitting around with an empty store, waiting for stock to arrive. That will damage your sales.

If merchandise is late, that's a great time to negotiate a discount. Most suppliers keep track of the situation and will advise you of any changes in arrival dates. Then it becomes a judgement call. Ask yourself:

How important are the goods you ordered?

Do you have customers waiting for them?

Will this affect the relationship with your supplier?

Can you find goods fast enough to replace this order?

In business, problems will always arise. It's important to deal with them in the best interest of your business. Don't let your ego get in the way of the right judgment call.

What is the turn around time for reorders?

If an item sells out quickly and is in demand, the supplier will usually restock it. If the brand is domestic, they'll often have a central distribution center where repeat items may already be in stock. Foreign brands may be more difficult.

Some suppliers are involved in the actual manufacturing process. They'll be able to tell you exactly how long it will take to remake and deliver popular items.

I made changes and no longer want the merchandise I chose last season. Am I still obligated?

Legally, no. Don't let anyone tell you otherwise. Business is constantly evolving, so how can anyone possibly know where he or she will be six months from now? If you ordered black jeans, and six months later everyone is asking for blue, why would you accept your black jean order?

I find that being straightforward is always the best approach. In business, if you plan on being around for the long haul, you want everyone to respect you. Call, write, or visit your supplier to tell them the bad news. If they're a busy company, they may not even care.

If you get some slack, deal with it as best you can in a professional manner. Put it into your head that whatever is said and done, you are not accepting the merchandise. End of story. Hopefully this will not ruin your relationship with the supplier.

Can I get my order on credit?

You've heard the old expression that credit is what makes the world go round. It can also make your world go upside down.

Gone are the days where a handshake was all it took to seal the deal. These days they want your soul. To put it simply, credit means I'll pay you later.

You'll hear terms like NET30 and NET60. This means that the balance is due in either 30 or 60 days, upon receipt of merchandise. PDC (post-dated check) is another common transaction you'll hear about, but these terms only apply when there's an established relationship between you and your supplier.

You will most commonly hear the term COD (cash on delivery) when starting out with no credit. This does not mean you must carry an actual suitcase full of money. It's an old term that means you're going to pay upon receiving your goods. A check is fine. Suppliers may want it certified to make sure it doesn't bounce because you don't have sufficient funds in the bank. The banking term is NSF, an acronym for non-sufficient funds.

Let's assume that your purchase is $5,000. There are two common ways to apply for credit. One is that you'll go through an application process with a **factor** company. This is a company that works somewhat like a bank. They've set up an agreement with your supplier that they'll make sure all the accounts are paid, less a small percentage to them. They're a finance company that deals exclusively with the apparel industry.

Sounds easy enough right? However, they are more difficult to get approved from than a real bank. They'll require a great deal of information from you to process the deal, starting with your personal information. They will obtain this info (with permission) from a credit bureau, just like a bank. If there are any missed payments, late payments, or NSF checks, it will show and reflect accordingly.

Next is your business information. They'll request banking information, other suppliers as references, etc. It's difficult to provide a history when you're starting out, because you have no business history. A good idea would be to call your suppliers and let them know that you have used their company as a reference. This can increase the chances of getting approved.

Now it's time to cross your fingers.

Here's a common scenario. Your personal information checks out okay, but there's not enough on your business profile, so the finance company contacts your supplier and lets them know that they're approving you for only $1,500 out of the original $5000.

All is not lost. At this point, it's up to your supplier to take the risk on the balance of your order. In the event that you default on payment, your supplier will only receive $1,500 from the factor company. The rest is an out-of-pocket loss for the supplier.

The second way is for the supplier to absorb the entire deal. This is most common in smaller businesses. To not lose the sale, the supplier will still make you fill out an application and fax it around to others in an attempt to learn your spending habits. They may go so far as to subscribe to a credit bureau, just like the factor company, to get as much info as possible. Remember, your credit bureau file is sensitive information. Any unauthorized use is strictly illegal. Usually you will be required to sign a waiver allowing your supplier to view your file. Don't let any of this discourage you; it's all part of the process.

The biggest advantage to credit is that you're not tying up your own funds. Before striking a deal with your supplier, see where you stand financially. If funds are low when you start out, knocking on enough doors will surely find someone to give in to your needs.

Be aware that this may cause more harm than good. When I started out, I refused to use credit. Why? Sure, it's been said that you should use other people's money (OPM) instead of your own. Although this may ring true, people often get carried away with spending, especially when it's not coming directly out of their pockets, but eventually it does. It's very easy to overbuy. Debt accumulates at an alarming rate.

Discipline is the key.

I'll discuss some creative finance strategies in a later section.

What if the items I pick don't sell?

Don't panic. This has happened to us all. If you buy a batch of merchandise that nobody's even glancing at, chances are you have a loser on your hands.

This is the time to weigh your options. Consider yourself lucky if you can go back to where you bought the goods and exchange what you couldn't sell for something new and exciting. This is not common practice, but it's a possibility for those suppliers who stand by their product or wish to take care of their customers. Certain brands are now offering exchange programs whereby allowing unsold items to be exchanged for credit on a new order.

Let your claws show. If there's nothing that excites you, try to get a credit for a future order. Demand it!

If that doesn't work, you must take drastic measures to sell it off by any means necessary. Mark the items down to cost or take a loss. The key is to not get stuck with merchandise.

What I find amusing with certain labels is that there are restrictions about when their products may go on sale. Their reasoning is this protects the integrity of the line. No major label wants to have everyone selling at different prices. However, if you get stuck and your supplier isn't willing to agree with exchange or credit, it will leave you with not much choice.

I cannot stress how important it is to have a good rapport with whomever you do business with. It will always prevail in difficult times. There are always many different solutions to every problem. Hopefully, through experience you'll learn to conquer them all.

These are some of the most common concerns I have encountered when dealing with suppliers. You may encounter your own as you go along. The most important thing is not to be bashful.

ASK! ASK! ASK!

You have nothing to lose, only to gain.

Don't stop here; ask for whatever pertains to your individual situation.

Chapter Six

WHERE DO I FIND MERCHANDISE?

I'm not exactly sure why, but suppliers are a closely guarded secret. When I started out, nobody would give me any information. I was sent on wild goose chases all over the city.

You will no doubt deal with different suppliers as the years pass. A great head start is to visit various trade shows. Here is a small list to get you started. Check listings as shows are subject to change or cancel without notice.

Alberta Gift Show
www.albertagiftshow.com
180 Duncan Mill Road, Suite 400,
Toronto, ON, M3B 1Z6
T 416-385-1880 | F 416-385-1851
Description: Western Canada's largest wholesale gift show (includes apparel, fashion accessories, and jewelry)

Apparel Salesmen's Markets
1625 rue Chabanel Ouest,
Montreal, QC, H4N 2S7
T 514-849-9497

Can-Am Western Apparel Trade Show
T 403-936-5620 | T 403-995-1003 | F 403-936-5367
Description: Western & English style apparel, horse equipment & tack, boots, hats, gifts, workwear, open to the trade only.

Canada's Bridal Show
www.canadasbridalshow.com
136 Winges Road, 2nd Floor, Unit 10,
Woodbridge, ON, L4L 6C4
T 905-264-7000 | F 905-264-7300
Description: Consumer bridal show

Clothing Show, The
www.theclothingshow.com
T 416-516-9859
Description: Consumer show featuring the hottest in and off-season new designs and vintage treasures, one-of-a-kind, handmade clothing and accessories, antique to contemporary design jewelry, also vintage bedding and textiles, new screen printed home accessories, vintage records, shoes and more.

Mode Accessories
www.mode-accessories.com
220 Duncan Mill Rd., Suite 611,
Toronto, ON, M3B 3J5
T 416-510-0114 | F 416-510-0165
Description: Canada's only wholesale trade show devoted to women's fashion accessories, casual apparel and fashion items.

Montreal Gift Show
www.montrealgiftshow.com
180 Duncan Mill Road, Suite 400,
Toronto, ON, M3B 1Z6
T 416-385-1880 | F 416-385-1851
Description: Over 350 exhibitors with more than 50 of these companies exhibiting exclusively at the Montreal Gift Show, international, national and regional giftware lines, plus new products designed especially for the Quebec market, Canada's only bilingual wholesale gift show.

National Womens Show, The
www.nationalwomenshow.com
60 Renfrew Drive, Suite 105,
Markham, ON, L3R 0E1
T 905-477-2677 | F 905-477-7872
Description: Consumer show exhibiting products targeted to women.

One of a Kind Show and Sale
www.oneofakindshow.com
10 Alcorn Ave., Suite 100,

Toronto, ON, M4V 3A9
T 416-960-3680 | F 416-923-5624
Description: Consumer show featuring the finest, freshest creative offerings from more than 450 North American artisans, artists and designers from the West to the East Coast.

Ontario Fashion Exhibitors Market
www.ontariofashionexhibitors.ca
160 Tycos Drive, Suite 2219, Box 218,
Toronto, ON, M6B 1W8
T 416-596-2401 | F 416-596-1808
Description: One of the largest fashion trade shows within Canada. To participate as an exhibitor, individuals need to join OFE and the Canadian Association of Wholesale Sales Representatives (CAWS)

Toronto Shoe Show
www.torontoshoeshow.com
49-6A The Donway West PO Box 701,
North York, ON, M3C 2E8
T 416-444-0005 | F 416-391-2928
Description: Trade show for shoes, sponsored by the Ontario Shoe Travellers Association.

Trends the Apparel Show
www.trendsapparel.com
P.O. Box 66037, Heritage Postal Outlet,
Edmonton, AB, T6J 6T4
T 780-455-1881 | F 780-455-3969
Description: Alberta Mens Wear Association Tradeshow, the first event of its kind in Canada that involves the participation of agents representing mens, ladies, children, sports, street, work & western wear

Vancouver Gift Show
www.vancouvergiftshow.com
180 Duncan Mill Road, Suite 400,
Toronto, ON, M3B 1Z6
T 416-385-1880 | F 416-385-1851
Description: Gift trade show for wholesale reps.

Western Apparel Markets
www.passporttofashion.com
28 - 910 Mainland Street,
Vancouver, BC, V6B 1A9
T 604-682-5719 | F 604-682-5719
Description: WAM members provide markets that bring retailers and sales representatives together to launch and complete seasonal buying of ladies wear fashion merchandise

Western Canada Children's Wear Markets
www.caws.ca
1951 Glen Drive, Suite 264,
Vancouver, BC, V6A 4J6
T 604-682-5110 | F 604-689-3170
Description: Affiliate show of the Canadian Association of Wholesale Sales Representatives

US FASHION TRADE SHOWS

Accessories the Show
www.accessoriestheshow.com
185 Madison Avenue, 5th Floor,
New York, NY, 10016
T 212-686-4412 | F 212-686-6821
Description: The marketplace for hot, new directions in edited accessories

AmericasMart Atlanta
www.americasmart.com
240 Peachtree Street, Suite 2200,
Atlanta, GA, 30303
T 404-220-3000 | F 404-220-3030
Description: Wholesale facility open to the trade only

ASD/AMD Trade Show - Las Vegas
www.merchandisegroup.com
2950 31st Street, Suite 100,
Santa Monica, CA, 90405-3037
T 310-396-6006 | F 310-399-2662
Description: 7,500 booths, 3,300 companies and thousands of

products, the nation's number one variety and general merchandise show

California Gift Show
www.californiagiftshow.com
888 S. Figueroa Street, Suite 600,
Los Angeles, CA, 90017
T 213-362-5640 | F 213-362-5660
Description: Prestigious gift industry event, the California Gift Show features 11 product divisions in over 3,000 booths

Chicago Apparel Market - Women & Children
www.merchandisemart.com/womensandchildrensshow
T 312-527-7600 - general questions | T 312-527-7750 - fashion office
Description: Women's and children's apparel and accessory resource.

Chicago Fabric and Trim Show
www.aibi.com/html/events.html
350 North Orleans Street, Suite 1234,
Chicago, IL, 60654
T 312-836-1041 | F 312-923-9076
Description: produced by the Chicago Apparel Industry Board, for the trade only

Dallas Fabric Show
www.dallasmarketcenter.com
2100 Stemmons Freeway,
Dallas, TX, 75207
T 214-655-6100 | F 214-655-6238
Description: features over 160 mills and coverters of decorative fabrics, laces, trims, leather, and related supplies. Held twice a year, this temporary show caters to the diverse needs of manufacturers who buy by the bolt

Designers & Agents
www.designersandagents.com
80 West 40th Street,
New York, NY, 10018

T 212-302-9575 | F 212-302-9576
Description: Independent, international alternative marketplace for over 400 collections and thousands of retailers who define the cutting edge in fashion and lifestyle

Direction - International Textile Design Show
www.directionshow.com
PO Box 115,
Maplewood, NJ, 07040
T 973-761-5598 | F 973-761-5188
Description: Major international textile design event, exhibitors showcase original textile designs and lifestyle concepts for a variety of markets including apparel, home and novelty.

Fabric@MAGIC
www.magiconline.com
6320 Canoga Avenue 12th floor,
Woodland Hills, CA, 91367
T 818-593-5000 | F 818-593-5020
Description: fabric, trim

Fashion Avenue Market Expo (FAME)
www.fameshows.com
227 Chelmsford Street, Suite S,
Chelmsford, MA, 01824
T 978-256-4604 | F 978-256-5748
Description: Mix of price points and merchandise attracts thousands of retailers each season, over 20,000 retailers have shopped and raved about clean, sophisticated and easy-to-shop format. Exhibitor's features, the set up, breakdown and overall operation is smooth and hassle free.

Fashion Centre Dallas
Women's & Children's Apparel & Accessories
www.dallasmarketcenter.com
2100 Stemmons Freeway,
Dallas, TX, 75207
T 214-655-6100 | F 214-655-6238
Description: Comprehensive variety of apparel and accessories lines. Permanent showroom and temporary exhibitors. From

moderate to designer, categories include: children's, women's (apparel and accessories including footwear) men's (appareal, furnishings and footwear)

Fashion Coterie
3 East 54th Street,
New York, NY, 10022
T 212-759-8055 | F 212-758-3403
enkshows@enkshows.com
Description: Known for its handpicked designers comprised of both established names and the young avant garde of fashion

Fashion Industry Gallery
www.fashionindustrygallery.com
1807 Ross Avenue,
Dallas, TX, 75201
T 214-748-4FIG
Description: a new boutique wholesale fashion venue showcasing the best in Women's Contemporary Bridge and Sportswear, Accessories and Better Men's within a modern, high-design environment in downtown Dallas

Florida Fashion Focus Show
www.floridafashionfocus.com
777 N.W. 72 Avenue Suite 3D19,
Miami, FL, 33126
T 305-718-4320 | F 305-718-4323
Description: Premiere women's apparel & accessories show, organized five times a year, a wholesale market, open to the Trade only

Footwear News
www.footwearnews.com
750 Third Ave 10th Fl,
New York, New York, 10017
T 212-630-4880 | F 212-630-4485

International Fashion Fabric Exhibition
www.fabricshow.com
1 Park Avenue, 2nd Floor,

New York, NY, 10016-5802
Description: The largest textile, trim and leather show in North America

Los Angeles Fashion Week
www.californiamarketcenter.com
110 East 9th Street, Suite. A727,
Los Angeles, CA, 90079
T 213-630-3600 | F 213-630-3708
Description: The Califorrnia Market Center hosts several market shows each year, in addition to the markets many showrooms are open for business year-round, the Mart is a wholesale facility open to the trade only

Los Angeles International Textile Show
www.californiamarketcenter.com/markets/latextile.php
110 East 9th Street, Suite. A727,
Los Angeles, CA, 90079
T 213-630-3600 | F 213-630-3708
Description: hundreds of fashion & home-interior fabrics & trimmings exhibitors from the U.S., France, Italy, and around the world. Plus design studios, trend forecasters, technology services, and essential seminars

MAGIC Marketplace - WWDMAGIC
www.magiconline.com
6320 Canoga Avenue 12th floor,
Woodland Hills, CA, 91367
T 818-593-5000 | F 818-593-5020
Description: Collaboration with Women's Wear Daily, the show is 200,000 square feet of high fashion, new resources and exciting discoveries, also includes state-of-the-art, highly-edited runway shows

Material World & Technology Solutions
www.material-world.com
1395 South Marietta Parkway Building 400, Suite 210,
Marietta, GA, 30067
T 678-285-3976 | F 678-285-7469
Description: An event of the American Apparel & Footwear

Association, the premier global trade event for the sewn products industries, trend-driven event focuses on the specialized needs of the textile, trim and related product sectors of the Americas

Moda Manhattan
www.modamanhattan.com
185 Madison Avenue 5th Floor,
New York, NY, 10016
T 212-686-4412 | F 212-686-6821
Description: provides a concise mix of carefully-juried RTW

New York Accessories Market Week
www.accessoriescouncil.org
390 Fifth Avenue, Suite 710,
New York, NY, 10018
T 212-947-1135 | F 212-947-9258
Description: A weeklong market showcasing the spring collection.

Nouveau Collective Trade Show
www.nouveaucollectivetradeshows.com
241 Lafayette Avenue,
Cortlant Manor, NY, 10567
T 914-736-0030 | F 914-736-0333

Pool
www.pooltradeshow.com
3924 W. Sunset Blvd #5,
Los Angeles, CA, 90029
T 323-666-5587 | F 323-666-4009
Description: Minimal rail trade show designed for the directional boutique market. New and established designers. Features men's, women's, denim, tees, accessories and shoes. Guest DJ's spin daily, accompanied by art installations and a full bar.

Print Source
www.printsourcenewyork.com
200 Varick Street, Suite 507,

New York, NY, 10014
T 212 352 1005 | F 212 807 0024
Description: Trade show for designers sourcing prints, embroideries, knit swatches, silhouettes, yarn dyes, trend forecasting services and vintage swatches and clothing

Swim Show
www.swimshow.com
777 NW 72nd Avenue Suite 3-CC-56,
Miami, FL, 33126
T 305-262-4556 | F 305-262-1160
Description: produced by the Swimwear Association of Florida, the largest swimwear tradeshow in the world

The Park (Formerly the Charlotte Merchandise Mart)
www.ppm-nc.com/index.php
800 Briar Creeek Road,
Charlotte, NC, 28205
T 704-333-7709
Description: Privately owned exposition center in the United States with over 100 shows and 1,000,000 visitors annually.

Trafik
www.trafiktradeshow.com
89 Fairlie St. Suite B/C,
Atlanta, GA, 30303
T 404-327-5755 | F 404-321-9939

Turkish Fashion Fabric Exhibition
www.turkishfabric.com
T 212-398-6241 | F 212-398-6244
itkibusa@aol.com
Description: represents a total of 51 major Turkish textile and fabric manufacturers

Make sure to verify all the information prior to attending. Visit only the shows which pertain to your particular genre. You don't want to waste time and money with trade shows that don't have what your looking for. Registration comes at a premium, not to mention travel and hotel accomodations. Some shows are cancelled due to poor attendance, and others have been around for years.

One of the larger shows for North America would definitely be *MAGIC* in Las Vegas. This is not to say that every supplier will be in attendance. The price to attend is modest but the price to have a booth with your own line can be very expensive.

When starting out, you may want to consider buying locally, and establish relationships with smaller companies which can provide that little extra for you.

Another great place to find suppliers is through the **trade consulate**. They are usually found in the government blue pages of the telephone directory. For example, let's assume that you want to import goods from Italy. Contact the Italian Consulate and ask to speak to the trade department. Let them know you are interested in importing from their country and want to get some info on suppliers there. They will most likely ask you to fax or email a request.

Try to be as specific as possible, as there are thousands of companies which are eager to get your business.

A sample request may include the following message: Interest in Men's Denim Wear, ready made.

That single line breaks down the selection, making it easier for the consulate to help you find exactly what you're looking for.

Today, the best place to find what you're looking for is through the Internet. Simply type, "Men's Italian Denim Manufacturer" in your preferred search engine. That will provide you with as many leads as you can handle—or more!

As you continue in business, there will be suppliers that come and those that go. Often, you can capitalize on the mistakes of others. Always keep your ear to the ground. You never know what deal may be awaiting you.

Chapter Seven

SIGNING THE LEASE

You will no doubt have to sign a lease or rental agreement binding you to the property you have chosen. This process usually begins by filling out an **offer to lease**. This is normally a one to three-page document outlining the key points discussed with the landlord and mutually agreed to, including the property address, the size, the date of commencement of the lease, rental rate, the parties involved, the lessee (you), and lessor (owner/landlord) and other details.

This is not the actual lease. The lease is usually twenty-plus pages or more detailing just about everything. It's important to note that all points in the offer will be spelled out legally in the actual lease, and is binding. In other words, the offer to lease is an extension of the actual lease, so it's important to read it and fill it out very carefully before signing.

The offer may be straightforward, but I recommend inserting a clause that states that your offer is subject to your (the lessee's) approval of and satisfaction with the actual lease, otherwise the offer becomes null and void. This way, you eliminate any surprises that may be in the lease itself.

Before I continue, I want to share my first encounter with signing a lease. I'd found a great spot, which required little work but had reasonable rates. The landlord seemed like a nice old man. We came to terms verbally and within three days I had a copy of the actual lease to sign. I took it to a lawyer for review. He began dissecting every sentence, crossing out and deleting words, etc. By the time he was done, he'd given the lease a total makeover.

Needless to say, this did not sit well with the landlord. He'd been using the same lease for over twenty years. His attitude was that it wasn't my place or right to change what isn't broken. He immediately called to cancel my offer and politely asked me to move on. However, this property was to good to pass. To make a long story short I signed the entire lease with no alternations and ended up staying at the same location for approximately ten years without any issues.

The moral of my story is that the agreement is simple. The landlord wants to rent you his or her location, and you want to be a tenant in the location. Sometimes squabbling over senseless details will lose sight of the real goal which is moving into a great location.

Most single-property landlords (owners) have a standard lease agreement that you can purchase from a supply store. One of the more important clauses that you should be aware of is the **demolition/sale clause**. Simply stated, if the building is sold, you're out, and if the landlord decides to renovate you're out.

The shopping mall lease or strip plaza lease may differ slightly. These will usually require more assurances from you personally, often called a **personal indemnifier**, and may have stricter rules which they enforce, such as set hours, late penalties, and a minimum to be spent on leasehold improvements, to name a few.

You will most likely be dealing with a management company, not an individual, so your personal charm and charisma won't have much effect. The corporations who own shopping malls usually own several properties. When you approach the desired mall, they may steer you to their less popular location.

I advise you to stick to your guns and push for the mall of your choice. If you're lucky, and have a proven track record, you may come across a mall which will take care of all the startup renovations in exchange for percentage rent. This is simple. They take a percentage of your gross sales, in the neighborhood of 10 to 15%.

When you sign a lease with a mall, I recommend that you insert a **guarantee sale clause**. Have a lawyer draw it up properly. What this insures is that if you don't meet a minimum sales requirement, you have a legal right to terminate the lease agreement. Most malls may not accept what sounds like an outlandish clause. But hold on a minute. Their clauses and requirements are outlandish as well. If they profess to have such a great location, bringing in crowds of shoppers they should back it up.

In closing this section, I want to leave you with an important reminder. Whatever is written, whether it is on an official-looking document or otherwise, is never the only option. This is all part of the negotiation process. You can try to change just about anything that does not sit well. Remember that you have nothing to lose. And, as always, if you don't ask, you'll never receive!

REAL ESTATE OR CLOTHING?

Often, when you've been at the same location for several years, you decide that a good idea is to purchase the building.

This may or may not be a good idea.

The most important factor to consider is that owning property is an entirely different business. Clothing is one type of business, and investing in real estate is another. It's true that you can make a lot of money in real estate, but it's also true that you can lose your shirt. Just like the clothing business, buying a property takes careful planning and market analysis.

The obvious advantage of owning your own building is that you have equity in the property, and one day you'll own it free and clear and can be at that location rent-free.

But, I always try to look at the disadvantages whenever I make a business decision. First, you need a large down payment to purchase a commercial building, sometimes as high as 40% of the value. If you're buying a property with a value of $400,000, a down payment as much as $160,000 or more may be required! Think about what you can do with that kind of money in the clothing business! You can literally set up a mini empire of three or four stores if you play your cards right.

Second, the area where the store is located may change over the years, and may not be as desirable as it used to be. This will make it more difficult to make a move. When you actually buy the property, it will usually anchor you to stay in that building.

Be careful!

This anchor effect can take its toll on your business.

I want to share a story of a friend who has gone through this scenario. He and his wife had a thriving clothing store. As time went on, they bought their location and had extra income from the apartment rentals on the second floor. Approximately two months into becoming a landlord, the roof almost caved in. They spent several thousand dollars on repairs. To make matters worse, the upstairs tenants moved out, leaving behind a disaster (watch the movie *Pacific Heights* with Micheal Keaton, you'll understand).

This real estate investment soon began to be a full-time business. My friends got through their struggles and continued the clothing store they had begun. After several years, the area began to change drastically with dollar stores appearing on every corner. That should have been a sign to move, but they did not.

To make a long story short, their business began to suffer and was never able to regain momentum.

A smart move would have been to rent out their existing location and move their business to a more desirable area, thus having rental income as well as a strong business. This is why you must understand from the beginning that one business is different from the other. When you attempt to integrate the two, it may cause harm to both ventures.

Never forget that a business should be treated as a business! Don't let your emotions get involved in your decision making process.

SEE SAMPLE LEASE IN APPENDIX.

Chapter Eight

HIRING EMPLOYEES

Hiring Beauty or Brains

You see it all the time—good looking people working in the fashion industry.

The media is what influences us all, everything from how we eat, what we drive, and in this case what we wear. Most of us are told what's in fashion, and this takes control on the way we think.

Selling clothing is about giving your customer the sense of looking better, sad to say, but if you walk into a store and the entire staff is overweight, poorly groomed, and wearing a beat up old track suit that they normally wear to kick around the house, you may have second thoughts about buying.

Fashionable clothing gives you the sense of belonging and provides that feeling, albeit short lived, that makes you feel good about yourself. We all hear the old cliche that when a woman gets depressed, 9 out of 10 times they go shopping. Why? It's because this holds true to some extent. The media has brainwashed everyone into wanting to look better by wearing certain brands and using certain make up. Just look at the number of Beauty magazines on the news stands. As a business person it's your job to capitalize on this.

Lets get back to hiring beauty versus brains. Here we need to apply common sense once again. If you were going to hire a manager, keyholder, or someone for any position of importance, it would be wise to hire the more competent person, not the better looking.

However the sad truth is that a beautiful person makes for a much better sales person than the ugly duckling. Why do you think that all bartenders and waitresses in the social scene are gorgeous? People tend to order more, don't take my word for it, just ask.

Let's look at a common scenario in the fashion world. A young male with raging testosterone tries on a pair of pants, comes out of the changing room and isn't sure about the fit.

The beautiful salesgirl comes over and tells him how great he looks, and he replies, "You think so, but the fit seems strange. I'm not used to it."

She replies, "Oh, I think it makes your behind look sexy," and she chuckles.

He smiles and says, "Really? You think so?" And she says, "Oh yes, most definitely!"

Seems ridiculous, right? As corny as it sounds, it works. I have been witness to it for over 10 years. This is why I always say, do not reinvent the wheel. Simply use what's been working for centuries.

Now, a compliment from anyone, beautiful or not, does go a long way. The point here, plain and simple, is to hire the right person in order to maximize sales.

Be very careful when hiring. A business cannot simply hire the most beautiful people on the planet without justifiable reasons. It's against the law.

Hooters (the restaurant chain) has had problems, in both Canada and the US, hiring girls based on their breast size.

The criteria you have for hiring may vary dramatically depending on the type of store you have. If you're selling bridal gowns, for example, then this entire section need not apply. It would be wise to hire a mature and knowledgeable person rather than picking someone based on looks alone.

To anyone reading this book who feels that my methods may seem a bit crude, I say to them, "Wake up, this is reality!" Try to keep our personal views outside of the business and use what works.

This book is designed to help you in business. As far as my personal views on the subject, that's an entirely different book. I treat everyone with the same respect, regardless of weight, color, or looks. In today's world, it's important to take advantage of the system, and let it work for you not against you.

Lou Perlman, who managed the *Backstreet Boys, Brittany Spears* and *NSYNC* (to name a few), was by no means a candidate for *Mr. Universe*, but it didn't stop him from exploiting these kids and making millions of dollars in the process, for them and for himself.

Be proud of who you are and treat everyone the same way you would want to be treated the results are astounding.

EMPLOYEE TRAINING

This next section has been taken directly out of my employee manual. It contains valuable information that has enabled my staff to function better in a fast-paced retail environment. I have included comments for each section.

The most effective way to train a new staff member is to personally provide a mini crash course. Having your employees read a book will only do so much—assuming they read it, and assuming they understand it if they do. The rest is up to you to make sure that your store policies are enforced.

If you have no rules or regulations in place, your business will undoubtedly turn into shambles. I have revised this manual five times since it was first written.

However, <u>it is important to note that what works for me may not work for you.</u> Everyone, and every business is different. Use my advice as a guideline and add your own twist, reflecting your needs, so it is tailored to your business.

SET GUIDLINES AND FOLLOW THEM

I use a point system in which a point is given to any employee who breaks the rules. If five points are accumulated within a month's time, their employment is terminated. I know that sounds harsh, but when your staff begins to exceed twenty-five, polices must be in place and enforced.

Don't expect staff to memorize the rules, but rather to know the rules and practice them. It will not happen overnight, so be patient.

Every time you witness poor efforts, make notes and include them in your manuals revisions. This may not have much significance when you're starting out, but when it's time to expand you'll appreciate having order among your trusted employees. If you promote or move an employee from one store to another, it's a lot easier for that employee if the rules are the same in all your stores.

McDonalds, which has over 35000 locations worldwide, has a manual called THE BIBLE. It is so detailed that it enables a 16 year old to open and run a multi million dollar location from start to finish. Their manual is over 1000 pages. Now do you see the importance?

EMPLOYEE MANUAL

INTRODUCTION

This manual was designed as a general outline to the company's rules and policies. To properly understand this manual, all contents should be verbally elaborated to you by management.

The following pages are from years of trial and error and are not meant to discourage you but to create a pleasant enviroment at the workplace for both you and your fellow employees.

PRIORITIES IN ORDER

1. BE ALERT, KEEP YOUR EYE'S OPEN

A youth market is what our product generally sells to. Usually between the ages of 18 to 25. Unfortunately the theft ratio is higher than normal for this age bracket, so our number one priority is to keep your eyes open for theft. Ask your manager for helpful tips on how to position yourself throughout the store.

This may appear to be bizarre to most retailers since the beginning of time the number one rule has been customer service. Again every business will have its own criteria. I was running a very busy off price denim store. The concept was designed as a self-serve shop.

2. CUSTOMER SERVICE

Although we have designed our prices to sell themselves, it is vital that each and every customer receive the best that you have to offer as a salesperson. Honesty, courteous, and helpful service is the right company image that we like to project. Treat all customers, as you would like to be treated yourself.

PLEASE do not bring any personal problems to the workplace, as it will reflect on customers.

3. PRESENTATION

Making sure the merchandise is properly in order is very important. Presentation is a big part of selling. Ask your manager for assistance. Proper folding and colour coordination is key. Chores such as tagging, labeling and cleaning are not on the list of priorities.

Most of the large clothing chains hire companies to merchandise their clothing. Think about it for a moment, isn't beautifully hung and folded clothing more appealing to the eye? Nobody wants to feel they are buying left overs (unless you are discounting). Visit your local mall to get ideas that may inspire you to merchandise like a pro.

MISCELLANEOUS DUTIES

- Sweep and vacuum daily
- Replace garbage (spray with Lysol) enquire on pick up days if applicable
- All shirts and jackets are to be buttoned and zipped up
- Make sure every item has a price tag (regular and sale)
- Any item with a flaw is to be placed in a bag and labeled with the defect.
- Use proper hanger for items i.e. don't use large jacket hangers on small ladies tops
- Make sure a security tag is on every item
- Make sure all shelves are stocked
- Pinning jeans for hemming (ask how)
- Windex, dust and wipe everything needed

The reason for having noted each and every chore is to ensure that your entire staffs know full well the duties required. This way you avoid any miscommunication. I find it crucial to have every detail outlined as easy as possible. So simple in fact that a grade school student will understand.

PRODUCT KNOWLEDGE

Product knowledge is essential to sell.

- Get to know everything you carry.
- Where is it made?
- How does it fit?
- What sizes do we have in stock?
- What is the background on the designer?
- What material is it made from?

The best way to sell any article of clothing is to have as much product knowledge as possible. Most designer labels are inflated in price, therefore it is important to justify why the price is what it is.

Each and every time a new batch of clothing arrives it should be inspected and discussed. If and when the store has no customers have your staff try everything on. What better way to sell something when there is first hand knowledge on how it fits? Let your staff in on any history that may become useful in the selling process. An expensive shirt may have been hand made in Italy, this will make anybody buying feel more comfortable in spending a larger price tag. Availability will help sales tremendously. Let's say a customer tries on a pant, which fits small, you may have lost a sale if there are no other sizes in stock. Product knowledge would have avoided this. Remember don't try selling red when blue is in stock.

CUSTOMER POLICIES

There are a maximum of 3 items per changing room at one time.

All bags, big purses, knapsacks etc. are to be kept outside the changing room or behind the cashier area.

I have touched on this subject earlier, the most common area for theft is the changing room, have a sign posted and no customer will get insulted when asked to keep their bag outside the change room.

The bathroom is off limits and for employee use only.

If your store allows it great, however most locations have their bathroom next to the stockroom area. It would be wise to ask any customer no matter how urgent to go to a nearby restaurant. Why risk a potential problem, furthermore it will take you time away from the sales floor to accompany them.

No smoking

Although it has been passed as a law that smoking is prohibited, you'd be surprised how many try, especially your own staff on those cold winter months to smoke in the backroom. Smoking will leave a foul odour to clothing not to mention discolour your walls.

No pets allowed in the store

I hate to have written this statement, as I am an animal lover. Unfortunately some pet owners are careless. It is annoying for other customers to have a peaceful shopping experience when there is a dog sniffing their crotch. Not to mention a possible bathroom break in the middle of the aisle. Once again post a sign by the door.

EMPLOYEE POLICIES

Greet every customer with a "hello" or "hi"

Most customers are walking into an unknown environment. The best icebreaker is a greeting upon entering. It doesn't matter when their head is down or if they walk in talking to their friend on a cell phone. A simple hello goes a long way. So do it each and every time.

Do not stand with arms crossed or lean your body somewhere.

I'm not sure who popularized this stance. However it is uninviting. If you walked into a store and had an employee with their arms crossed and leaning on the counter would you ask for assistance much less want to buy anything? I think not. Proper posture will project the right body language, and is often more powerful than words.

Do not make empty promises as to how clothing will turn out after washing or drying.

You won't believe how many customers will ask a question like. "How should I wash these jeans?" we have all owned and washed jeans since we were children, yet this question will haunt you. I had a customer walk through my door enraged that his jeans had shrunk 2 inches. I'm not exactly sure how they were washed; however he blamed the salesperson at the time for giving him improper washing instructions. I always suggest cold rinse hang to dry and fold inside out. This will avoid changes with denim. All other items should be washed as per label instructions. The point is, do not have your staff give a white lie to make the sale. It may cost more in the end as well as have an unhappy customer. Remember, as a professional you must take responsibility for your staff.

Do not use the telephone while customers are in the store.

We've all have witnessed this scene before. You need assistance but the person behind the counter is on the telephone talking to his or her friend about their plans for the evening. Enforce a strict policy, which is if at any time there is a customer in the store the telephone is off limits for personal use. If you are already on the telephone and a customer walks in, it's simple, GET OFF THE PHONE. Get the message. If a personal call comes through while a customer is in the store, let them know you'll call back later. This is not up for any negotiations. I remember calling my own store and my employee putting me on hold while she ended her personal call, I was waiting for several minutes????

Keep all store information confidential

Your staff will be privileged to all that goes on in the store. Information can be harmful to your business if it got into the wrong hands. Your business is your livelihood; it is what puts food on the table. A part time employee may not realize the potential danger in discussing private business matters with a friend or customer. I was eager to carry a certain label, which was slowly becoming very popular. At a staff meeting it was agreed that we should carry the line for next season. One of my staff members had begun letting every customer know of our plans. To make a long story short a competitor got wind of this information and beat me to it. He had convinced the supplier to an exclusive contract allowing his location to be the only one to carry the line in the area. The line took off as expected and I was left out in the cold. The moral of the story is to keep your staff on a need to know basis when it comes to certain matters.

There are no set times for breaks

Unless you have enough staff, I don't advise having set times for breaks. The reason is obvious when it is busy there is no break when nobody is in the store go ahead. I had an employee take a break by leaving my store to go visit her boyfriend at a nearby mall. She arrived forty minutes later blaming traffic and the length of time it took to find parking. Common sense remember.

Always notify your co-worker when leaving the sales floor

Teamwork is the name of the game. It's courteous and good practice to advise anyone on your shift you are leaving the sales floor area. Perhaps for a stock room check or a bathroom break. Don't assume you made eye contact, all it takes is a simply hand signal. This will assure who ever is left on the floor that they must reposition themselves accordingly.

Smoke break

For some odd reason smokers tend to smoke in company. I'm not sure what the reason is however as a business owner it is important to be on the alert. On more than one occasion do I recall driving up to my store with 3 employees standing out front inhaling their nicotine fix. This projects the wrong image to your would be customers. Further more, smokers tend to inhale their last "drag" as they walk into the store leaving the entrance with a foul odour. Set limits or better yet don't hire smokers.

Do not answer questions falsely.

This is a common salesman trait. When you don't know, do not pretend you do. When an employee is representing your business a strong suggestion would be to "tell the truth the whole truth and nothing but the truth". If a customer inquires on a new item, why should the salesperson make up a little white lie? Why not admit this is a new item and I am not 100% sure. This will make the customer feel more at ease and trust the salesman.

Ease up on the music

Have the stereo under lock and key. Otherwise on a regular 8-hour shift, 2 hours will be spent fiddling around with music and CD's. I kid you not. When your staff begins to feel that comfort, the stereo will be continuously misused. I once had an employee turn on the stereo before the lights. It becomes a disease. The music should only serve as background music to create a certain mood. It is not there for the amusement of your staff. They are on the clock getting paid by the hour.

Empty changing rooms

After every customer tries on clothing it is important to clear the changing room of any clothes that might have been left behind. This will enable you to know if the same number of items that have entered have come out. Also it is not a pretty site for the next person to walk into a messy room either. The most important reason we don't want to have clothes in the room while customers are shopping is their size may be in the room and not on the sales floor.

THE TELEPHONE

The telephone is not to be used for personal calls when customers are present in the store. If a call is for someone else take a message.

ANSWERING THE TELEPHONE

The most commonly asked questions are location (where we are located) directions and hours of operation.

Have this information readily available especially for new staff. A good idea would be to have this information written by the telephone for easy access.

MERCHANDISE INFORMATION

My policy was to not give information over the telephone. The reason being I would rather they come in person? Since clothing is purchased on impulse the chances of that customer buying something else are more than likely. Do not mislead anyone by lying and then trying to sell them something else. This is known as "bait and switch" and it is illegal. It will not only annoy but lose that customer for good. Should the customer become frustrated, let them know it is company policy and you are simply an employee following orders.

Always apologize and say you're busy if a customer begins with the 1001 questions. Be abrupt but polite.

Keep your eyes on the store if on the telephone.

A hard habit to break is when you're on the telephone and feel the need to stare out the window in the opposite direction of the sales floor. Anyone in the store can be robbing you blind.

I realize I sound overly paranoid but I had to be.

DEALING WITH CUSTOMERS

Help wondering customers by assisting, point out where brands are, different sections, sizes, etc.

You will hopefully know your store like the back of your hand, customers will not. When a customer is walking through your doors he/she is unaware of the set up. So it will be important to greet and give a general outlay of the store. This will help direct the shopper in the right direction. Be readily available for assistance. Most of the time shoppers need a few minutes to feel out the environment. Be accommodating.

When asked on a price of a garment, always give the retail price first then the sale price. It makes it seem as a greater value.

This will not apply to everyone only the discount set up or when you have marked down an item. It does not matter how much money you have everybody wants to save money. If I know I'm saving a few bucks it may persuade me further into making that buy. A good rule of thumb is to emphasis the fact that it's on sale.

Alterations

I advise every store to offer alterations. It's not only profitable but also provides a convenient service that your customer will love. However don't take it too lightly, pinning a garment incorrectly can be costly. You will need to replace the item at your expense as well as being stuck with your newly altered item, which nobody will want. Write all alterations on the invoice or have a separate alteration tag. Make sure the customer brings this in at the time of pick up, if not have the customer show proof of ID and have them sign your copy of the alteration slip. A good rule of thumb is to pin items longer than shorter (they can always be adjusted if need be later).

Exchange policy

Due to the fact that we run a discount operation, we do not offer the luxury of any exchange and especially a refund, although we do make the odd exception for size. However we do not want to contradict store policy. Always ask our manager to authorize when need be.

Just about every major retailer offers exchanges and refunds. Smaller businesses may offer exchanges only. I did not. The policy you set forth in your store will be entirely up to you. Some suppliers may work well with returns others will not. Generally selling regular goods at regular prices will almost require you to exchange. If not, customers may be reluctant to shop and go next door. It provides peace of mind knowing they can come back for an exchange. It's unfortunate that the consumer has taken advantage of the system. I recall watching a talk show on the subject, where a women would buy all her children clothing and return it all at the end of each season for new merchandise (months later), another women would find used sneakers in a Goodwill shop and return them to get a new pair, claiming they were defective. I'll bet you didn't know that certain stores offer a lifetime return policy. That's right, LIFETIME! They don't advertise this but if you bring a garment even a year or two later they will accept the return. So decide when to put your foot down.

MANAGER/KEYHOLDER OPENING AND CLOSING

When entering the store you must key in your alarm code.

This area will be given to a responsible and trustworthy staff member. I advise you to use a key that cannot be duplicated without ID such as a brand called Medico. Better safe than sorry. Next you will provide each key holder with his/her own personal access code. Alarm monitoring companies will be able to tell you who used the alarm and when. A good idea would be to order a read or print out every month. It's a statement that will have all the entry and exit activity. So you will know exactly who and when each of your key holders accessed the system. Show your key holder this report it avoids misuse. It will surely keep them honest.

Turn on and turn off all electrical devices.

This will include lights, alarm tag system, computer, stereo equipment, answering machine, stereo etc.

Forgetting to turn off electrical equipment can become costly. Have a checklist made for all new key holders. If you want to keep lights on your window display or signage, have them on a timer. There is no need to have lights on in the middle of the night. Furthermore having strong spotlights on can discolour clothing over time.

Sweep and vacuum

A clothing store should be kept spotless at all times. Would you feel comfortable buying clothing from a dirty location? This chore should be part of your daily routine.

Training staff

As a manager it is your job to have the staff below you do their job properly. A well-liked boss goes a long way. If you instill fear it will cause employees to lose concentration and make costly mistakes.

Handling customers

Every time there's a problem the first person on the list will be the manager. If that's you act professional at all times. There is never the need to bring personal feelings into the situation at hand. Always try to accommodate your unhappy shopper. You'd be surprised to know how much can be accomplished when the diplomatic approach is used.

INTRODUCTION TO THE CASHIER POSITION

Being a cashier is a big responsibility; taking care of each transaction with precision is vital to the company's financial well-being. The following section is designed to help you get a general understanding to how this company would like its cashier to operate. It's a proven formula which anyone who can apply common sense to will function with ease. Any and all points discussed should be verbally elaborated to you in training from management. The key to success as a cashier comes from being confident and focused. Remember getting nervous will always contribute to error.

TRANSACTION PROCEDURE IN ORDER

1. Add items and give total to customer immediately
2. Swipe card or take cash
3. While the transaction is processing ask customer to fill out a mailing list form or enter their information into the system

4. Fill out the receipt
5. Detach security tags
6. Bag merchandise with a smile

I have designed this method over the years for a reason. It should be followed in order. As mentioned previously shopping for fashion is mostly an impulse reaction. The customer does not buy out of necessity but out of desire. As a cashier the key is to make sure the sale closes. Often times when a transaction is taking too long the shopper will change his or her mind. They may choose to buy only one top instead of two or to pass altogether. I have been witness to this on several occasions. Once the cash is received or the card swiped, you can breathe easy. Keep in mind this is not a race but a priority system. Do not make the customer become impatient it is wise to have them fill out a customer profile while you process the sale. This should be done each and every time. This will be your best way to build a clientele base.

This is a sample client card.

CUSTOMER PROFILE

NAME_____ DATE_____

ADDRESS_____ APT. _____

CITY_____ ZIP CODE _____

PHONE ( ) _____ FAX ( ) _____

EMAIL _____

BIRTH MONTH Jan Feb Mar Apr May Jun Jul Aug Sep Oct Nov Dec (please circle one)

PERFERRED BRANDS _____

SIZE RANGE: Waist _____ Shirt _____ Dress _____ Shoe _____.

You can modify the profile to your own specs. Try to make certain it is legible and to ensure it is as complete as possible. I strongly advise the use of a computer for your database. It will save you a tremendous amount of time and money. The date will let you know how old the customer has been in the data base. If a client hasn't been around for a couple of years chances are they are not stopping by anytime soon. With the address make certain the info is correct, a letter misspelled or a number off can result in a return. The telephone number is useful to call to add that personal touch. The fax is generally used for the people who are at work the advantage here is no postage fees and there may be more than one person reading it. The email is perhaps the most valuable information you can get as it is totally free and it can be forwarded to many others as well. The birth month is used to perhaps send a special message or offering to your customer on his or her special month. Brand preference may help for those customers that are brand loyal and only wear one or two labels. The size range will come in handy when you are over stocked in a particular size. You can customize your sales promo to specific clients. This is just one tool to help bring clients through the door. There are computer programs designed to cater to your every need. I will discuss promoting in detail in the later section on advertising.

IMPORTANT NOTES FOR THE CASHIER

Accepting payment methods are Visa MasterCard and Interact (debit Card) We prefer to accept interact (debit) so be sure to mention it.

The debit card is the most widely used card. As you know the funds are taken directly out of the customers account. The service charge is only pennies for both user and merchant. When asked if you accept Visa tell them yes and always mention Debit as well. A simple comment can save you expensive percentage points.

No checks or foreign currency

There are services allowing you to accept and authorize the use of personal Checks. However I strongly believe you will not lose any sales by not accepting Checks. It also contributes to cashier error. This is not a widely used method of payment any longer. Those few dinosaurs still walking around with a check book will always have cash or plastic in hand. You are a merchant not a banker as such don't make it practice to accept currency outside your country. It will be harder to note authenticity and the current rate of exchange. If your store is located in a tourist area you may want to take extra steps in insuring you don't get ripped off.

No call in telephone credit card authorizations

Accepting card numbers over the telephone is against visa rules. You may have seen television infomercials allowing you to call in with a credit card, but they have a special merchant account set up which requires a large security deposit on their end. But did you know that if a caller decides to refuse the transaction at any time the charges would be reversed. That's right there is really no protection for the merchant unless the actual card has been swiped or imprinted along with the signature. Something I always find amusing is when a customer walks in with someone else's credit card and an authorization note. Under Visa international rule the only person allowed to use the card is the person to whom it is issued. NO EXCEPTION. Not the son or the daughter or even the nanny. However it is important you familiarize yourself with credit card rules and regulations. There are always updated rules and regulations. So do your best to stay informed and pass the information to the staff.

Have a cash float.

Your cash float is a consistent amount you leave in the till for change. Small bills and coins are fine. Just make sure to know what the float is every time to avoid error. It is the responsibility of the last person on cash to notify the manager if change is running low. The last thing you want is a busy rush and there is no change. Sure you can run across the street to the closest convenience store but this will surely irritate the shopper.

One cashier at one time

There should only be one cashier per shift. The reason is simple. If there is any discrepancy over a transaction or funds are missing, you need only point the finger at one person.

Receipts

Your invoices or receipts should be numbered in sequence. So make certain they are used in order. It makes for easy accounting and tracing a transaction in question.

Terminal assistance

Always keep a phone number of the credit card service centre handy. You should also have the merchant account number on file.

Price tags off garments

From time to time price tags will tend to separate from the garment. It is the cashier's job to make certain that the tag belong to the correct article. One of the oldest scams is a price tag switch. If you are using a computer system this may not be an issue however for those of you writing up manual invoices it would be wise to give some more attention to this area. If you are unsure go to the rack and try to match the item with another or ask management for help.

Empty the till of cash when it reaches a certain limit.

Although plastic is the preferred method of payment. There is always the good old green "cash". For security reasons I recommend empting out the till once it reaches a certain amount. That amount is entirely up to your discretion. Again this should become routine. It is common practice for most. When the funds are collected they should be put in a safe or an office under lock and key. If the manager is collecting there should be a slip indicating how much was taken to avoid a miscount.

Check it twice.

When there is a large purchase, it would be wise to do the math twice. It will only take a few seconds but can save hundreds of dollars in mistakes. Even a computer invoice should be carefully looked at for any kind of errors.

Return policy

Every company will have their own return policy. So it is important to have proper signage posted and have the policy clearly posted on all invoices. Please do not waste valuable company time going into a 45-minute discussion as to why! Let this type of customer know you are only the employee following orders.

Tax-exempt customers

In most of North America native Indians are exempt from taxes. They will always provide you with a card that contains a photo and number. Write as much info as possible including their name and ID number. There are other exceptions including diplomats. They too will have a card with a name and a number, follow the same instructions. Don't be fooled into a fellow business owner telling you he or she is exempt because they have a vendor permit number. This permit is only used to purchase resale goods through a wholesaler. Not to buy their spouse a new top for the weekend. When in doubt ask your accountant or bookkeeper, they will provide you with the most up to date information regarding these matters.

CREDIT CARDS

MasterCard / Visa

You must make sure of the following:

1. The back of the card has a signature

2. Hold card until transaction is approved
3. Make certain customers signature matches the card's signature
4. Take an imprint if the magnetic stripe fails
5. Have the customer sign the copy!!!!!!

Check for fraudulent cards

It will be up to management to know all there is on credit card fraud. Each year credit card companies lose hundreds of millions of dollars to fraud. There is more than one way this is done but as a retailer you can do your part to ensure this does not happen to you. The following is a quick checklist on what to look for:

Make certain the numbers that appear on the terminal match the numbers on the card.

Look for the hologram on each card.

Make sure the signature has not been tampered with. It will read VOID if it has.

The first 4 digits of the card are embossed on the card.

That the card name matches the cardholder, example a card barring the name Tiffany Smith should not be in the hands of a 250 pound male standing six feet tall.

Look for easy shoppers those that are piling up goods by the cash without trying anything on.

There is a great deal involved in stopping credit card fraud. Always read any new info posted in newsletters detailing the latest ways crooks have come up with scamming the system.

A manual imprint must be taken if card does not swipe.

The customer's card does not swipe, so you do what is called a manual entry by keying in each number into the terminal. At this point make certain to imprint the card with the imprinter provided. Have the customer sign both copies.

If the terminal reads, "hold card call centre"

Normally this would indicate there is a problem. Either the card has gone over the limit or it has been cancelled. Don't panic, the best advise here is to let the customer know of the situation. The last thing we want is a potential crime. If the customer is legit they will be glad to verify themselves with a Visa representative and sort out any problem. If however the customer is committing a fraudulent act they may decide to make a hasty exit. At this time it is wise to call the card centre and notify them of the problem. They may ask you to cut the card in half and mail it in. They may also take it a step further and ask for a description of the bandit. Try to answer as truthfully as possible. Keep in mind you are dealing with criminals here and your life is much more valuable than a credit card transaction.

When using part Visa and part MasterCard for the same transaction simply enter each amount separately.

That's right! You can combine different methods of payment for the same transaction. Part cash part plastic or one plastic with another. Some customers become rather peculiar when it comes to payment. Who cares? So long as you are closing the sale.

Terminal connected to your phone line

It is important to keep the telephone line free when a transaction is being processed. So stay off the telephone! Some systems may not allow you to run a card if your telephone answering service is holding messages. So clear all messages and retry. The odd time an error may occur in the network system putting a freeze on your terminal. Call customer service ASAP. It may only last several minutes. It may be as simple as turning the terminal off and back on again, allowing it to reset itself. This need not apply if there is a dedicated line for terminal transactions. Unfortunately it will cost you the same as a regular line.

Always confirm the price with the customer before swiping the card.

You've heard the old line "the only certainty in life is death and taxes". However some customers are still astonished when sales tax is added to the final total. A good habit to practice is to always let the customer know the total before swiping the card. I've had some upset shoppers in the past. It may also avoid the entire refund process.

At the end of each day you must CLOSE THE BATCH

In order to wire the days transactions into your bank account you will need to key in what's called a **batch closing**. Your bank will take you through the necessary steps, as each system is different. Please note that different institutions have different names for this process.

INTERACT/DEBIT CARDS

Card must swipe with terminal- No manual entry is allowed

Unlike credit cards debit cards will require a swipe through the terminal. This is a security feature. If the card does not swipe there is no way to complete the sale.

Once the amount is entered – Hand the pin pad to customer for authorization – while processing hand card back immediately

Another security feature is the time limit for pin number entry. After a certain length of time the terminal will expire and the card will need to be swiped again. So if the customer hands you the card and decides to wonder get their attention and let them know there is a time limit.

Note not all cards are set up to make store purchases

The bank must provide access for the debit card to work at a store otherwise it may only be valid for cash withdrawals. The terminal should read, "Card not supported".

Some companies offer their customer's the convenience of cash withdrawals at the point of sale. I do not recommend this service, as it will add to the level of error from your employees.

I hope this has given you some insight as to the importance of being the cashier. Believe it or not large chains have over one million dollars in cashier error annually, even with their multi million dollar computer systems. Keep in mind at the end of the day it will more than likely be an 18 year high student distracted by the cute guy that just walked in. This will ultimately become your responsibility to ensure proper training.

CONCLUSION

The information contained in this manual hopefully has given you enough insight as to how this company's staff should operate. You should study it until it becomes committed to memory and is second nature.

This manual should have been elaborated to you in training. Remember that everyone is subject to an evaluation. So if a fellow employee is not complying with any rules and policies or there is a conflict with staff, then it is your job to bring it to the attention of management.

All additional efforts to this company will not go unnoticed. Opportunities are available for who ever are interested.

There you have it my manual, which I personally wrote after years of trial and error. Obviously this pertained to my business and the type of staff I employed. Feel free to alter it as you see fit.

FUNNY EXCUSES FOR NOT BEING ABLE TO WORK

I just couldn't resist letting you in on some of the wacky excuses my employees have given me for not showing up for work.

Remember that most of my staff are part-timers, still in school. I'm sure in the very near future you will have your own hilarious stories.

The phone call:

"Hi, I just missed my bus, do you still want me to come in?"

The note was always a laugh. I'd show up and find a note wedged between the doors with comments like, "I had an emergency doctor's appointment." Or, "I forgot I had an exam at school today. Will call later, I promise."

The 3 AM phone call:

"It's John Doe. I can't come in tomorrow. Problems man! F**K!!!!!" Then the line went dead. (And yes, he was still alive.)

The call from the mother letting me know that her twenty-five-year-old child was sick with a fever and could not make it to work today.

The worried suburban mother who no longer wanted her twenty-seven-year-old daughter driving twenty minutes into the dangerous downtown area.

Calling a manager who didn't show up was a riot.

On one occasion my store was actaully closed for several hours before I knew what was going on. This guy was actually asleep. When he was called to the phone by his sister; he immediately gave me the, "Ahh, I'm in bed suffering from migraines, its baddddd, didn't you get my message?"

The new employee who quit after not getting her paycheck exactly seven days after she started. She thought that our entire operation was a scam!

Be sure to do background checks on everyone you consider. Better to be safe than sorry.

SEE APPENDIX FOR SAMPLE APPLICATION FORM

Chapter Nine

CREATIVE ADVERTISING

As I've mentioned previously, advertising is essential to any company's well being. Unless you're in a busy mall, you need to set up a formula for your advertising budget; one which best suits your needs.

It's a simple equation: The more you advertise, the more people will come.

More people translates to more sales.

That's it.

Even a preschooler can understand that.

Let's look at the different choices. I've tried and tested almost everything. I'll share my findings with you.

The best source of promotion is **your own customer**. A satisfied customer base, who talk to their friends, may take time to acquire (if you're new), but the results are by far the best.

Each customer profile will vary according to what you're selling. The profile should include the customer's name, address, telephone, fax (if they have one), and email. Try to keep as much info as possible, including spending habits, brand preferences, sizing, and birthdays.

That's right birthdays. Wouldn't it be nice if your customer received a birthday card giving them a discount on their very special day?

If you've been in business for a while and have, let's say, a thousand customers in your database, that's a thousand birthdays. Even if only a third take advantage of this special saving offer, that's over three hundred and thirty three extra sales a year. I'm sure that the rest of the postcards you send out will not only remind your customer that the store is still around, but will also generate some appreciation as well.

In addition to birthdays, you can send out a post card or letter inviting your customer to an upcoming sale or promotion, or to let the eager shopper know that new merchandise is arriving. Try to get one of the labels you carry to subsidize the cost of the mailing, afterall your selling their product line. Before email, I made certain to send out a new flyer every month. Over the years, I perfected what works and what doesn't with my customers.

You should do the same.

I expect that most of you will use **email**, which saves postage and printing materials, not to mention the labor involved in putting stamps and address labels on mailings. As effective and cost effective as emails are, I don't recommend sending one out every week. This will annoy customers, and be perceived as Spam. In time the ads will lose their strength and be overlooked.

Before sending an email, be sure the customer agrees to receive it. If the email is viewed as Spam, you'll drive the customer away instead of bringing him or her into the store.

Magazine print ads might seem to be a high profile way to increase public awareness on your business, but these ads are also high priced; very expensive. Forget nationally-distributed magazines. Try to stick to local, more affordable, magazines.

Be careful about using new magazines, which are just starting out. They have little or no readership and more than likely will be going out of business soon. I'm not a fan of magazines, because they target a wide array of potential customers, not all of whom will be interested in what you offer. Try to use a magazine whose readership targets a specific demographic. The large magazine companies will tell you that most businesses that advertise with them are already known and well established and have a national reach with their product.

Why anyone like you or me would spend several thousand dollars in a national magazine is beyond comprehension. Only a very small percentage of its readers will make their way into your store.

Calvin Klein, Ralph Lauren, and other major labels spend millions in print ads, but their motives are much different than yours. For them, it's all about brand awareness. They have a brand to promote and need to maintain broad public awareness of their name. The more people see their names in magazines, the more everyone will think their brand is the must have.

For you, the single or multiple shop owner, this is not the way to go. However, if you reach a certain level of success and want to have a national magazine ad for your store, so you can frame it and show it to your grand kids some day, there are a few questions you should ask.

How many subscribers does the magazine have? This will determine how many issues are going to be sold, guaranteed. Magazines set their advertising rates based on their subscription size. That's why they offer such great deals to lure subscribers, like 60% off the news stand price, or a free video or gift of some kind. Ask for their rate card. You'll note that there are different rates. Prices for advertising space will vary according to the size of the ad, the positioning of the ad (i.e. back covers and the first pages cost more), the time of the year, or the issue itself (they may charge a premium to advertise in December (Christmas issue), or in their fashion buyer's guide issue), and the number of issues you book at one time. A company which books ads for an entire year will most certainly receive the best price.

I recommend checking out the competition. This will give you a general idea of what and how much to advertise. Try and get your hands on a few back issues. If you find the same stores advertising month after month, that usually means their ads are working.

An effective way to cut costs on print ads is to set up your own **ad agency**. I'm not suggesting another full-time operation. Simply set up a company under another name, for example, ABC AD GROUP. Make up some stationary with a company logo and submit it to whoever you are interested in advertising with. They should immediately give you anywhere from 10 to 20% off regular rates. Ask if they offer sell-off space. This is when they have extra space available that didn't sell. This is a perfect opportunity to snatch up some real savings.

When they send an ad rep to come and see you, the rep will have all these fancy charts and graphs telling you how many people will see the ad. They may offer a substantial savings from what's written in their charts.

The bottom line is that you have to do some research. The salesman's job is just that—to sell.

Don't be a fool.

Why are they offering you, the first time small guy who they don't care for, a discount?

Television falls into the same category as national magazines, if not worse. It's a great medium, but simply too expensive for the little guy to afford.

There are production costs. Thousands of dollars can be spent on the simplest of commercials.

Booking space on your favorite channel is another costly affair. Getting ads into the right time slot can consume the entire advertising budget, if not more.

A late-night slot is more affordable, but who cares? You'll have nothing but unemployed deadbeats channel surfing through all those infomercials. Networks consider prime time to be between 7 to 11 PM. Monday to Friday, so this will be the most expensive time slot—by far.

There are however, effective ways to have an advertisment on TV for a fraction of the cost.

The first way is the **channel listing station**. This is the channel that lists all the TV shows and times. This channel has space allocated for advertising, but it's offered at a fraction of the cost of a regular commercial. Their advertising department will assist you in designing and writing dialogue for the spot.

This type of channel serves a local community and may prove effective if you're selling the right product.

Another way to receive on-air mention is to **sponsor** an on-air personality with clothing for a local program. They will usually mention the name of the store and may show your business logo on the screen. This is great exposure for the buck. Be sure not to let the on-air personality keep the clothing (you'd be surprised). If you establish a good relationship with the program, they may consider doing a segment on your store. The best part is the cost. Zero.

That's right. They'll spend up to fifteen minutes talking about your store, for free. They may even decide to interview you on air. What a great way to get your fifteen minutes of fame!

Radio can be a cost-effective alternative. It's one of the lower-priced mediums, but still has reach. Get a feel for who your customer will be and decide on which station to advertise with. When you create your customer profiles, you can ask which station they prefer to listen to. That profiling will also tell you which radio station to use for music in your store, if you have music.

Again, let your competition do the homework. Don't spend hard-earned money on experimenting.

When you've decided which station to use, call the station (dial 411 to get their number) and ask to speak to the sales department. They'll connect you to a rep who will more than likely come to see you in person, bearing a leather-bound folder with all those stats and figures.

This is a good time to turn on the negotiating power. Don't fall for the salesman's charm. They're going to try to sell you a package. It will usually be a six-month to a year contract. That will give you a tremendous per spot saving on your ad, but that shouldn't be your concern. The first ad or series of ads should always be considered a test run. When the spots show signs of success, then you may consider signing a long-term contract.

Something to keep in mind with a contract is that if for any reason you must break the deal, they will pro-rate the commercials already aired and bill you. Simply put, they will charge you for the spots used at a premium, as if they were used on a spot by spot basis. That's why they always offer discounts on their posted rates. If anyone cancels the contract, the price will increase to the regular published book rates.

Be sure to mention something worthwhile in the ads, like the store address, website, phone number, or a special price offer.

It's a complete waste of money to mention clothing and brands and nothing else.

Anyone with half a brain is sick and tired of those loud, obnoxious, spots shouting things like, "GIANT WAREHOUSE SALE THIS WEEKEND...SAVE, SAVE, SAVE!" It's been done to death and doesn't work anymore.

Newspaper ads are a great way to attract business. There are many options, from community to local papers, and also multicultural papers.

Always try to define your customer and seek out the competition.

You may be surprised to learn that members of the Asian community are huge shoppers for designer goods. Ads in the local Chinese paper can give you fantastic results. Costs run much less than other citywide papers.

A small four inch by four inch ad in the local paper can cost only several hundred dollars, but increase sales by several thousand.

Once again, be careful of pushy sales people whose only goal is to get a contract signed. A newspaper or magazine may entice you to run an ad in a special edition or section of some sort. Questions you want answered are what other stores are advertising, and what their ads look like. The last thing you want is to spend your advertising dollars, only to have the competition beat your advertised prices.

Should the salesperson tell you it's classified or top secret, express your concerns and threaten to cancel the spot. You'd be surprised how fast this works.

Some community papers have a shopping section where they do articles about local businesses. You may even find such a section in a major daily paper. Pay attention to what the area newspapers do.

Find out who's in charge of that section, send them a package, and invite them to visit your shop. Include photos, brands, prices, and anything which makes you unique. Sometimes you're not even required to advertise with the paper.

The best approach is to offer to take the writer to lunch or dinner, introducing yourself as a nice, warm-hearted person. If you win them over with your charm, it may well be worth the few bucks and hour or so of your time.

THE INTERNET

When I started, the Internet was in its infancy. Had it been around in full swing when I began, my business might have taken a different turn.

I'll never forget a customer who asked me if I'd considered having a web presence. My response was immediate. "Who would use the Internet (certainly not my customers)?"

She responded; "That's what people said about television, years ago."

I wish I'd listened to her. She was absolutely right. The world has become a small place thanks to the World Wide Web. It can either be used to sell or as a tool to promote your business.

Most people are on their computer daily now, so it would be wise to take advantage of what's going on around us. I've dedicated an entire section on how to bring your business to life on the Internet later in this book.

DOOR-TO-DOOR FLYERS

This is a very inexpensive way to get the word out. Most companies will design, print, and distribute flyers, providing all those services under the same roof.

The only problem is the target market you're trying to reach. Let's use our common sense. If the ad is going to thousands of homes, how many of those homes will be potential customers? The last thing you want is to spend thousands of dollars only to have grandma call your store asking whether you sell support pantyhose.

Flyers are more effective when you hand them out at a particular event, like a fashion show, school, or any other social event.

If you're selling nightclub wear to a youth market, a great idea would be to walk into a club and speak to the manager or owner. Ask them if they'll allow you to hand out flyers at the door as patrons leave. They may have their own door people give them out for you. Put some in the bathrooms. Have a lot on hand, as they will often get ruined or thrown out.

How do we get the rich and powerful owner to agree to this? The best solution would be to offer the owner either half price on everything in the store or a certain amount of clothing for free. Of course, do this only if it's working for you. It may seem like a high price to pay, but when you consider all the potential shoppers in a nightclub, it's definitely an option worth considering. If that fails, hire a couple of kids to put your flyers on the nearby cars.

CLUB AND VALUE PACKS

We've all gotten them at one time or another; those thick envelopes stuffed with all kinds of coupons for everything from alumium siding to $2 off on fish n chips.

As I said in the paragraph on flyers, it's all about the target audience. Unless the coupons are all related to fashion, and are being sent to specific customers who have some interest in the fashion world, I strongly recommend you save your money.

FASHION SHOWS

At one point or another in your clothing career, someone or some group will approach you, asking you to offer them clothing for a fashion show, usually a school or fund-raising event.

I did a few of those when I started out, but found they were more of a headache then anything else. The clothing was often returned damaged, or was missing completely. Sure, you may have a contract stating that the association is responsible for the clothing you lend them, but see how far that gets you. It will not be as easy as you think. Remember that the people wearing and showing your clothing are mostly wannabe models seeking their fifteen minutes of fame. The last thing on their minds is you or the care of the clothing they're wearing.

Yellow Pages/Directories

Unless you have multiple locations, it just does not make any sense to spend extra money on a bold ad in the Yellow Pages. Believe me when I tell you that anyone looking up your company name will go through each and every name to find it.

Directories, on the other hand, may prove to be more beneficial. For example, if someone is putting together a fashion directory that will be either distributed or inserted in a local paper, each and every person looking through it will have some interest in fashion. Those are the people you want to reach.

This is time to let your creative side take control. Highlight the brands you carry, offer a discount with mention of the ad, free gift with purchase, a website with more info, or anything that will motivate a potential shopper to check out your store.

Price is always a factor, of course. Should the price of a directory listing seem higher than you thought, pass it up. Remember, it's important to not get emotionally attached to a decision you may decide to change on a whim.

Business Cards

This has always been a tried and true formula. I have personally given out thousands of cards over the years, with not the greatest of success. However, it comes down to timing. If you're selling evening dresses and you happen to hand a card to a possible client who happens to have an important engagement coming up, chances are you have a potential sale.

I'd like to share a little idea that I tried and had great results with. I designed business-size cards with the brands I carried stating,

WITH THIS CARD, RECEIVE ANY JEAN FOR $59.99

I also inserted authorized by_____ and expiration date_____, which were left blank and written out manually. That gave customers a sense that the card was actually authorized by someone at the company and not some mass produced ad.

I passed these cards around to some busybody friends and made them this offer: For every card with your name used for a purchase, they'd receive $10 cash, or $15 in store credit. The results were fantastic. It's a great way to advertise for little money and no effort.

FRIENDS

It's important to note that friends are most likely your worst customers. Nobody is loyal! The faster you understand this, the better off you'll be.

I've had my own very dear friends shop for the same product at another store and pay higher prices.

Why?

There are many reasons why this could happen. Clothing, for the most part, is bought on impulse, so if your friends were at another mall and something caught their eye, chances are they'd just buy it without putting much thought into it.

Depending on the individual, they may feel that coming to your store puts them in an awkward position, almost feeling obligated to buy. Often, they simply forget. Clothing is such as huge market that your store can get lost in the shuffle.

YOUR OWN STORE

Your store itself can serve as an excellent forum for promoting.

Eye catching signage in the window may bring in business. I recommend using something that looks a little different than the rest—you've seen one you've seen them all.

Big red signs that proclaim, "SALE!" Or, "Up to 50% off the entire store!" are not that effective.

Hand-made signs that have a clear message are the way to go. Think about it. If you saw a hand-made sign, wouldn't it catch your eye more than a standard store-bought sign?

The reason is that your eye is so accustomed to the same old signs at every turn that they begin to become dull and lifeless.

In Toronto, *Honest Ed's* is a famous retailer who uses hand made signs for years with great success. A great example of effective signage is:

BUY ANY ITEM & RECEIVE 2ND ITEM FOR HALF PRICE!

This method sometimes discourages retailers, who say that there's no room for profit. Depending on what you sell, the real reason for pushing customers to buy two or more items is to clear your inventory and create some cash flow to purchase new and exciting products.

Don't always look at what your profits are. When you do this, it will hold you back from turning over unwanted stock.

The interior of the store is just as important.

Note: Treat every customer as if they were foreigners and don't know how to read or speak the language. Don't assume because you and your staff get it that the rest of the world will. Have items on a separate rolling rack with a sale sign on them, or put a sale bin in the corner.

Let's say you have a high-end boutique with expensive dresses. I challenge you to do the following:

Put the dress you want to sell **behind the counter** on a hanger and watch how many customers inquire about it. The reason is that they feel it's been sold or it's for someone else, and the feeling of losing out drives people insane. A good response would be to say, "Well it was on hold but if you want to try it on, I think I can arrange it."

Have small accessories placed by the cashier's counter. These are called **POS items**. (Point of sale).

Most of what sells is bought on impulse. Have jewelery, scarves, gloves, hats, wallets, perfumes, ties, and such displayed at the point of sale. POS items are anything that may add to the purchase. Impulse buying, remember?

A great idea would be to discount an accessory with the purchase of anything else in the store. It's a small idea, but can grow to huge profits. Let's do some math. It's important that you understand and believe in the system, because otherwise your staff definitely will not. Let's say that for every ten buyers you successfully sell two add-ons, and let's assume that there's a $10 profit for every add-on. Now lets assume there are an average of twenty buyers a day, 365 days a year. That's 7,300 buyers. Using the 20% theory, that means that the total add-ons sold would be 1,460. With a profit of $10 per unit, that's a whopping $14,600 in extra profit at the end of the year! That can cover rent or one hell of a vacation!

Promos need to be enticing, otherwise every customer will pass. Try to spark a deal with your suppliers on small items that are collecting dust in their warehouse. Also, there must be some incentive for your staff and cashiers to push the add-on. Offer them a prize or a cash bonus for the most add-ons sold at the end of the month.

Have staff wear what's in stock. You'll be amazed by the number of customers who'll want to try on something simply because staff is wearing it.

If you have to go so far as letting the staff wear clothes from store inventory while working, it's worth it, but not recommended. Better to have them purchase it at a substancial discount.

The last thing you want is to have a customer try on a garment with bad body odor. Not only will you lose that sale, but any other as well.

Make sure what the staff wears is available. If a salesperson tells a customer it was in stock last month, that won't mean much, and certainly won't sell anything.

I once heard that at *Sears* every manager had to make certain that every stock item was available, otherwise it was grounds for dismissal. I don't know whether this is true or not, but it makes a great point. If it's not in stock you will lose a sale.

Almost as effective are **mannequins**. They've been around as long as stores have been open. The same principals apply. The shopper can visualize what an outfit will look like. It's important to dress the mannequin with as much care and as many accessories as possible. Why sell a skirt and blouse when you can sell an entire business suit, equipped with a purse and jewelery?

Have prices visible. When a customer is looking at an item, price can become the deciding factor. Most people, including myself, can't be bothered to ask a clerk who's on the phone behind the counter what the price is. I will simply move on.

If you're having a sale, it's important to **slash** the regular price tag as well. The sign on the wall will often be overlooked.

Shuffle clothing around. Surprisingly, something so simply will give the illusion to regular customers that new merchandise have arrived. Often, an item at the back of the store will seem new and exciting when it's displayed at the front of the store.

Again don't take my word for it; just try it.

I've been giving you my own experiences in the retail world. I know it works.

Conversation is another great way to let your customer know what's happening in the store, whether it's a promo or new arrival.

We've lost the human touch in how we do business today. You and your staff are in the same four walls day after day. Your customer is not.

It's important to guide everyone in the right direction. I once purchased an overstock in a particular style of pants, they were all the same colour and for some reason they weren't selling. I'm not sure why. They were a beautiful cut and fabric.

I put my sales charm to the limit. I had decided to push this one pant to each and every customer. It worked. I single-handedly sold thirty identical pairs of pants! They were even the same size!

The point is that using a personal touch goes a long way. Remember, people are told what is in style. They don't know unless they're told. Often that extra push goes a very long way.

Create a frenzy. That's easier said than done, but if you can attract a crowd, it will increase sales, hands down. People don't want to be left out. If there's a crowd, it will attract more people to come in and see what all the fuss is about.

Another technique is to sell some items as **a loss leader**. That's when you sell an item for cost or below cost, in the hope of attracting customers who presumably will buy other products once they're in the store. Supermarkets use this technique. They often sell milk, Pampers, toilet paper, etc.; items everyone needs, which will bring in hordes of shoppers—and how often does someone enter a supermarket and buy just one thing? I never could understand why anyone would drive to a supermarket and wait in the check-out line for a long time to simply save a buck or two, but they do.

Again, remember the way the mind works, people will go to great lengths to save. If all else fails, offer free cookies and coffee to everyone who walks in, people love the word free.

If you carry brand names, **keep all the magazine ads handy**, whether it's an ad or a celebrity wearing the brand. You'd be surprised how many customers will want what they see being glamorized in a magazine.

Remember the O.J. Simpson trial? Sales for his *Ford Bronco* went through the roof, as did the judge's lap top computer, which he used during the trial, and which appeared on TV. Don't fight it, give people what they want.

Celebrity Endorsement

If you want exposure, have a local TV news reporter or a highly visible media person wear your clothing. Make sure it's worn on the air. If possible, get a mention. This won't necessarily cause hordes of customers to stampede through your doors, but it will definitely give your store better name recognition and will make sales a tad easier.

Just think. You can tell a customer that this is the same shirt that a reporter or anchor for Channel 2 wore last night.

Large corporations spend millions of dollars on celebrity endorsement but, as I've said, this kind of marketing is geared more towards a product or brand name, not to a single or multiple location store.

I have a friend whose family sells men's formal wear. It just so happened that Jay Thomas, a not so famous actor, purchased a tie from the store and wore it on *The Late Show* with David Letterman. As the story goes, Dave, being a tie enthusiast, asked Jay where he got the tie. To everyone's surprise, he mentioned the name of the store on the air, in front of millions of viewers. Needless to say, it made my friend's dad a local celebrity. I'm sure his business picked up, as well.

I've always said you can have billions of dollars but never achieve the attention of a celebrity. If your fortunate enough to befriend a celeb, take advantage of that relatonship. The smallest detail such as a signed picture hanging in your store wall will do wonders for your store image.

WHAT NOT TO DO

A tried and true method used by car and stereo dealers. In the advertising world it's called **bait and switch.** Essentially, what happens is a great deal is advertised on say, a DVD player, but when you get there the salesman politely tells you they're sold out, but they have a comparable DVD player for the same price or perhaps another model for a slightly higher price. It always works.

However, I should note that this practice is shunned upon and is considered illegal in some places. If you've really sold out of the item on sale, and had more than one or two when you ran the ad, then it makes sense to tell a customer what else is available, but don't advertise something you don't have or only have a few of.

After some consumer backlash, some companies were forced to list the number of items available at each store. This avoids wasting a customers time.

I've given you some examples of the do's and don'ts of the advertising world. Hopefully some of my ideas will inspire you to come up with ideas of your own. The most important thing to remember is that it's not just about one element, but it's a combination of everything. Including staff, inventory, location, cleanliness, and everything else I discuss in this book.

Read on, and take notes if you have to, but I recommend reading everything twice so that you just get it. That's the whole basis of this book—easy and common sense.

Chapter Ten

CREATIVE SELLING

&

HELPFUL WAYS TO INCREASE SALES

Choose the most unwanted article of clothing in your store. Let's stop and think for a moment. The first person took the time to design and produce it. The second person chose it during the store buying process. I have to figure there is a third. THAT'S YOUR CUSTOMER!!!!!

Throughout this book, you will pick up information that will assist you in selling all that inventory. Common sense. I know by now I must sound somewhat repetitive, but I don't mind, it will ensure that my point gets across. You'll thank me for it later. The best advice I can give you to sell your product begins with the salesperson. We have all walked into a store and have been pestered by that pushy salesperson. It usually becomes annoying and doesn't make for a pleasant shopping experience.

That said, it is important to treat each and every customer as you would like to be treated. Sounds simple right? But guess what, it's not. Over time a salesperson will have to endure repetitive behaviour from customers and believe me when I tell you that it will take its toll on anyone over time. Have a proper training program in place and create your own employee manual to suit your needs. Another great idea is to have a professional come in to train your staff. Also, show the staff an instructional video.

To prove my point further I'd like to share with you my first visit to Las Vegas. For those of you who have never been, Las Vegas offers exceptional service pratically everywhere you go. It is a haven for making money with good reason. I was stunned on my first visit. Walking on the grounds outside my hotel I asked my friend, "How can I get my staff to become so professional?" To which he replied, "That's how!" and pointed to a giant building adjacent to the hotel with a larger than life sign that read "EMPLOYEE TRAINING CENTER." I could only imagine what an investment the casinos make in training their employees.

This proves just how important it is to have your staff properly trained. In doing so it will not only provide a professional enviroment required to succeed but will ultimately increase sales.

The following is a list of pointers that will increase sales GUARANTEED. Incorporate everything in this book, along with this list and, as always, a little common sense, and sales will dramatically increase.

Send out advertisements regularly

Keep the momentum going. If your location has traffic flow, it is important to keep it there. Promote your business on a regular basis. At the very least, once a month. The more your sales increase so should your advertising budget. Remember large corporations advertise for a reason.

Hire more staff

The more sales staff on the floor, the faster the merchandise will sell. It's rather simple, the more you can attend to the needs of your shopper, the more he or she will part with their hard earned cash.

Have staff wear what you sell

This is a fantastic way to sell your product. Visually seeing how the clothing looks on a real-life person will by far produce the best results. This is the whole basis of runway fashion shows. Buyers make their decisions based on the way the garment looks, moves, and stands out on a model. I do recommend offering all your staff (who have been working at least a month) a substantial discount, say 50% off on all clothing in their size, which they will wear in the store. It's kind of like an employee uniform which will increase sales and won't cost much. Try to have whatever they are wearing in stock, otherwise this method is pointless.

Have mannequin displays

As with wearing the clothing, mannequins offer almost the same visual effect. Dress them up as much as possible along with accessories. Garments on a mannequin stand a much better chance of selling than being folded on a shelf or hung on a rack. Although they are somewhat pricey, I recommend using as many as you can in window and in-store displays. Try to change them on a regular basis, and never refuse to remove a garment off a mannequin if there is a customer interested in buying that garment.

Make certain everything is priced

As I already mentioned in the book, if a garment is not priced, chances are most customers won't bother asking for its price. I have found over the years that having a individual price tag on the garment will increase sales guaranteed.

Be courteous

It is important to note that during the normal course of business, you will begin to overlook the fact on how it functions. A customer is bringing his or her money and is willing to part with it in your location. So it is extremely important that you never overlook this fact regardless of how much time passes and how successful you become. It is even harder for your part-time employees to grasp this concept. Practice being courteous on a regular basis and it will pay for itself in the long run, and provide you with repeat and loyal customers, I promise you.

Product knowledge

Clothing for the most part has seen dramatic increases in prices over the years and with good reason, people are buying them. However I find it helpful to have a general knowledge as to why the garment has arrived at the price it has. Try to find out as much as possible. Who designed it? Where is it made? What fabrics have they used? How difficult is it to produce such a design? These, along with any other answers to questions, will help in selling and justifying the prices, making customers feel comfortable spending more than they would normally spend on average.

Rotate stock

This is a very simple technique which will provide the illusion that you have new merchandise. Move stock around from the rear of the store to the front and you'll be amazed by the reaction of customers who were in your store just days before. The idea here is to make it seem as though new merchandise has arrived. I can recall getting compliments on clothing I'd wear from my old and unwanted section. I began thinking as to why shoppers would be interested in clothing I had sitting in the back of my store which never got a second glance. Then it hit me, the reason is that the merchandise was thought to have no life on the sales floor. Afterwards, I soon began shifting old inventory in the new arrivals section as well as matching some of the old items with the new. The results were more than satisfactory. I recommend rotating stock at least once every couple of weeks.

Door crashers

It seems to have become a gimmick these days, but door crasher specials are a tried and tested formula that work (if done correctly). Offer a staple item, such as a basic t-shirt in multple colours at a very reduced price, say cost. Have them in plain view so that the moment any shopper passes through your door, they will be visable. In addition, don't forget to mention the incredible deal. Years ago, I struck a deal with a local belt manufacturer who offered me belts at the cost of his materials only. This was to keep his employees working on the off-peak times. I then offered his belts at half the regular price as a door crasher and took it a little further by offering an additional 50% off with any purchase. The results were phenomenal. To put it simply, the sales at the end of the year increased by several thousand dollars – all because of one item.

Know the inventory

It is vital to know what inventory is on hand, otherwise you will be trying to sell items which are out of stock and at this point, it will become difficult to persuade your client into something else. Whenever possible, have the staff go through the merchandise to find out what is on hand and what is not. This knowledge provides for a great salesperson. Have a general idea of all sizes available.

Offer a no hassle return policy

We've seen it time and time again on those annoying infomercials, *"if you are not completely satisfied, simply return the item within 30 days for a full refund... no questions asked."* This is the line that probably convinces everyone to pick up the phone and order. But did you know that the reason they offer this money back guarantee is that approximately 10% of the shoppers actually return the item? Can you believe it? Most people can't be bothered with repacking the item, visiting the post office and sending it back to the vendor. The same holds true for clothing. The more at ease the customer is about the sale, the easier they will part with their money. I did not offer refunds in my business (as it was a discount outlet) and I do recall losing a sale or two. Use your judgment and offer whatever policy your business can sustain.

Send out birthday promotions

Try to collect as much data on clients as possible, including their birthday. Offer them a special discount for the entire month of their birthday, why limit it to just one day? It will be a sale you probably would not have made. Furthermore, you are reminding your customer you still exist and I am certain they will appreciate the gesture. If possible, have staff call past customers. This provides a great personal touch that is lacking in today's world. If this is not possible, an email or postcard will do. This may not mean much when starting out, but if you have hundreds of clients, that translates to hundreds of birthdays over time which translates to... you guessed it, thousands of dollars in sales.

Point of sale items

These are the small add-on items next to the cash register. Hats, gloves, jewelery, watches and sunglasses are just a few items that will entice shoppers into spending a few extra bucks. Clothing is mostly an impulse purchase. I always appreciate the larger chains that have a organized line up to pay forcing each shopper to go through a maze of items before reaching the cash register. I can guarantee using this simple set up adds a great percentage to their overall revenue.

Keep shelves full and neat

Have you ever walked into a store where the shelves were half empty and not many sizes were available? I am sure you felt less than enthusiastic to shop. Now try to remember walking into a store such as the Gap, where the store seems full of life. All sizes and colours are in stock and everything is neatly displayed. Huge difference, right? And with good reason. I cannot stress enough on how important it is to have the store visually appealing to customers. Cleanliness, presentation and an abundance of inventory are all factors which will increase sales.

Have less quantity, more variety

This is a no brainer. The more variety you have, the easier it will be to sell more merchandise to one customer. I have walked into stores which had multiples of everything. Needless to say, the selection was less than desirable. It makes more sense to have the same amount of stock with more variety. This will not only keep the shopper in the store longer but will provide them with options, and sometimes a choice between two items will result in the temptation to purchase both. It happens all the time.

Smile

The power of a smile goes a long way. When a customer walks through the doors, it is important to make sure they feel that they are in a pleasant enviroment. A simple smile and a greeting will do that. Otherwise, should the customer feel uneasy, they will exit sooner than they should, resulting in no sale and perhaps no desire to return. Keep in mind, clothing is a repeat business so it is vital to maintain clientele. Each and every person walking through the door can buy something, return to buy some more, and better yet, bring another customer through your door.

These are but a fraction of techniques to help improve overall sales. Every clothing store has a life of its own as well as its own personality and it will be your job to define what works and what doesn't.

Chapter Eleven

THE INTERNET AND EBAY

The Internet has become the largest communication and marketing medium in the world.

I read somewhere that most companies who are actually showing a profit, other than porn, are those servicing the websites—hosting, designing, and maintaining, but that assumes that the business is trying to make a profit entirely on the Internet. It would be wise to take advantage of all the web has to offer including marketing your small business.

To start I assume everyone will have a computer and internet access. The next step is to build a website.

Contact a web designer to create a website. Most companies offer a one-stop shop. They'll arrange everything from start to finish.

The basics of a website are company logo, address, an "about us" page, maps, brands, prices, etc. When you sit down with a web designer and discuss how much to spend and how much is needed, they will tell you how much time and money will be required to make it happen.

You want a web site that will stand out from the crowd, but always remember to keep it simple with as much relevant information as possible. There are very fancy sites out there that require longer than normal load up times. This is due in part by fancy graphics that don't actually do anything other than annoy a potential customer that is attempting to access information on the store or store products.

When meeting with a web designer compile a list of your favourite websites to reference from. This will give the desginer a look and feel of what you are after as well as knowing if they are able to do such work.

Be sure to ask the cost of each item they recommend. There will be a design and setup fee, and then an ongoing hosting charge to keep the site on line, and maintenance charges to update it as needed, for example when you want to promote a special sale.

The site will need constant maintenance as new items arrive and sales are made. Keep customers informed by changing the home page regularly.

The important thing is not to go into creating a web site blind. The setup expense and ongoing cost has to fit within the advertising budget.

Once the site is up and running, traffic will depend on how much the site is advertised. The more visible the site the more it will cost. There are different ways to optimize your sites ranking on various search engines.

On most search engines, sites that have top ranking usually pay a premium to be there. Paying for position makes sense—assuming you can afford it. People get tired easily when they're faced with scrolling through hundreds of pages, especially when the information they need is usually found on the first or second page.

There are two reasons for your store to have an online presence. To have information about your location including any special sales you offer, or you can sell directly online, or both.

If providing information to local clientele is all you desire than search engine ranking won't be a priority and shouldn't break the bank.

Selling online is another matter entirely. When you sell online, the market, quite literally, is the world. It's entirely different than having a retail store or several locations.

You must have up-to-the-minute inventory listings on everything you carry. There are also different rules and regulations for doing credit card transactions online.

Once again, scout the competition, don't reinvent the wheel. Jot down a few ideas from other sites and ask your web designer what it will cost to have a similar version. A great idea would be to link up with as many sites as possible.

The easiest route is to pitch your idea for an online clothing store to someone or to a company who will set up and maintain the site for a share of the profits. After all, computers are not an easy venture. Many hours can be spent creating and maintaining a site, and to track and fulfill orders. It's not a small undertaking.

Although online shopping has increased dramatically, some people are still reluctant to buy an article of clothing without first trying it on, feeling the texture, and so forth.

I know of businesses that spent several thousand dollars to have their site on a search engine, but when you clicked on it, there was nothing there but flashy icons and colors moving around. These businesses paid good money for their web presence, but there was nothing on their sites that had any value.

The key to spending advertising dollars is to have customers come through your doors, not to have them stare at a screen with your logo moving from side to side. There's no point having a web site if it has no useful content.

In the end, promoting your site will cost just as much as any other form of advertising.

Links with other sites can be cost-effective. The object here is to barter. Ask companies to include links to your site from theirs, in exchange for your site having a link to their site. The more links the better. That way everyone helps generate traffic for themselves and everyone who links with them.

Banners are box-like advertising icons that are usually in plain view when you open a web site. The prices for banner placement on vary from site to site. The more popular the site, the more it will cost. How do they determine that a site is popular? The way most companies sell their banner advertising space is by the number of hits they've receive.

Be careful! A hit is not always what it seems. When you click on a site, that's considered a hit. However, hits are also measured by each new page you open on the site, so if you click on ten pages on one site, it's considered that the site has had ten hits. The reality is that just one person is visiting that site, so the true amount visitors is only one.

There are site tracking services which will provide a weekly report of how many hits your site received, and break it down into how many visits to your home page, and how many page views of the other pages of the site. Ask your site designer whether his or her company offers or can refer you to such a service.

As an example of the value of such a tracking service, someone who clicks on ten pages of a site is more interested in what that site offers that someone who looks at the home page and moves on, so those ten hits mean more than a single hit by someone who took one look at the home page and decided they weren't interested in looking further.

For God's sake have something interesting to sell! There are so many people trying to make a buck on the Internet that whatever anyone desires is available.

Ask yourself, "What am I going to do that sets me apart from the rest?"

If the answer is nothing, I would seriously consider not setting up shop in the first place. Offer brands everyone wants at a discounted price or perhaps offer items which are sold out in stores, be creative otherwise you'll have spent a fortune with nothing to show for it.

Due to the overwelming popularity of the net website designing and hosting have become far less expensive than they were years ago. There are companies offering complete construction of a website for as little as a few hundred dollars as long as you use them to host the site with a monthly fee starting at $10. So as you can see there should be no excuse as to why your small business should have some kind of web presence.

DO IT YOURSELF

There are also sites that provide ready made templates that simply require you to drag and drop text and images. The result is a professional looking website in a few hours.

There are several services to choose from. Check out the following:

www.1and1.com

www.wix.com

www.monstertemplate.com

www.godaddy.com

OPTIMIZE YOUR WEBSITE

Use the following as a checklist when either hiring or building your own site. Some of the terminology may be difficult to grasp at first but it is important to implement as many strategies as possible to increase the visibility and ranking of your website.

1. Use Keywords and Phrases within the **copy** of each page. I recommend at least 2-3 times on a short page and 4-6 times on a long page.

2. Use the Keywords or phrases **within the first 50-100 words**. This will yield better results with search engines.

3. Keep the **Title Tag under 65 characters**. Search engines don't display more than this, thus having more is rather pointless.

4. Use the **Meta Description**. This will increase the click-through rate.

5. Have a shorter URL. They tend to perform better within search engines.

6. Choose keywords that are **the same** or **similar** to the name of the site.

7. Use **hyphens** instead of underscores to link words.

8. Tag each image with a **name**. Use keywords that best describe the image (Who, What, When, Where). Use <alt> in the description of the photo.

9. Increase the time it takes for your site to load. In as little as 5 seconds a visitor will decide to exit the site and move on.

10. Exchange **links** with other websites and blogs that have similar subject matter and themes.

11. Set up Google Alerts www.google.com/alerts to help find what it is you are looking for. Use it for the business name or a clothing brand you carry. When it pops up on the web, you will receive an email alert. Bookmark each alert as it may come in handy when trying to close a sale with a not so informed customer.

Wow... that's a lot of information to digest. Don't let it discourage you. What's important is that you are aware of what is needed to optimize any website. By applying most of these techniques you will no doubt have an incredible launching pad that will drive thousands of potentials clients to your business

I am sure by the time of this writing there may be a few other tips ad tricks out there. So stay informed and add whatever new methods are made available.

eBay

This site is great to compliment your existing site.

You've heard about it over and over, for good reason. There are millions of users, world wide, buying and selling everything from cars to computers. And, you guessed it, clothing.

Did you know that every three seconds an article of clothing is sold on *eBay*? It is safe to say that whatever label or article of clothing you key in, something will pop up. It's as easy as child's play.

eBay is constantly growing, and the potential is fantastic. There are over 100 million registered users (as of this writing) and the numbers keep growing daily.

Here's how it works. They structure each sale in the form of an auction. An item is listed at a starting price, usually for a seven day period, giving everyone the chance to view what you have for sale. There is also the option for three, five, or ten-day auction periods.

You need to make some choices, like the category you're marketing in, and provide a detailed description of what you're selling. The more information provided, the better. Interested buyers place bids, and the highest bidder ends up purchasing the product.

Sounds simple right?

All you need to get started is Internet access, and a digital camera or use photos off the web if possible but make sure they accurately depict the item you are selling. Most cell phones are equipped with high resolution cameras.

You need to familiarize yourself with a few terms. Some of the most common are:

Feedback. *eBay* is a community and works on the honor system. Every time you buy or sell, both the buyer and seller have the option to leave feedback, either positive, neutral, or negative. The more positive feedback you receive, the higher your feedback rating will increase. This gives anyone attempting to do business with you an insight on how transactions are conducted.

If someone is new or has poor feedback, it will affect their success. That's why it's so important to maintain professionalism and good service.

eBay has strict rules and regulations, which they uphold. Anyone disregarding the rules will be suspended.

Every user has the option to respond to any feedback, which may require an explanation.

How much does it cost?

There's a small **insertion fee**. Check the site for current rates. The folks at *eBay* are so nice that if your item doesn't sell, they give you the option to re-list. If at that point it does sell, they'll credit the insertion fee back to your account only after the item sells.

There is also a *final value* **fee**, added only when you sell your item. The amounts are very reasonable. Check eBay for current rates as they are subject to change without notice.

Chances are that anything you have to sell is already selling on *eBay*. A good idea would be to key in whatever it is you have for sale using their search engine to see what prices are being asked for similar items.

Don't get discouraged by the low prices. It's the final price that interests you. Find an item and click on *Items you're watching*. This will keep the results you're looking for on file.

This is totally free, so don't sweat it. *eBay* also gives you the option to view items for sale by what's newly listed, what's ending soonest, and the highest and lowest price. This feature will come in handy when searching for an item that has hundreds of pages of listings.

Once you've decided what to sell, you'll have many decisions to make to help sell your item. The first is the photo of the item. When selling clothing, it's important to light and display your item properly. The first photo is free. Each additional photo costs a few cents. I recommend taking more than one picture. Showing the front, back, and possibly a close up of the label will increase sales dramatically.

A great idea would be to use a mannequin. The better the item is displayed, the better chance it has to sell. Always check out the competition to get ideas. You may be selling exactly the same item as many others. You may decide to use your competitor's photo (simply save it on your computer by right clicking the mouse and use it for your own listing).

Next is the **description** of your item. *eBay* shoppers have become accustomed to having an abundance of information about what they're buying.

I highly recommend providing as much information as possible. Otherwise, you'll be subject to a high volume of email questions which should have been answered in the listing.

Bold print, highlight, and gallery options are all designed to help your item get noticed. I personally never use the extra features, as the cost of my product doesn't allow for it. Fees can eat up items selling for $20 or less, and before you know it there's no profit left for yourself.

Buy it Now is a feature which allows anyone to buy items without having to wait for auctions to end. The price is usually higher than the auction price, but it won't matter to those who are eager to buy. The cost of adding that feature is only a few cents.

Once the item has been listed and sold, *eBay* will instruct you on the **check out** process via email, as well as on the site itself.

You'll need to send an invoice instructing the buyer what their total is, including shipping, handling, and taxes if applicable. Sales tax is usually applicable if you are shipping the item within the same state or province you do business from.

The buyer has the option of sending payment in the form you desire. I recommend you use all that are offered.

The preferred method of payment is called **PayPal**. It's an online banking system (which happens to be owned by *eBay*) which enables all who register to send and receive funds from anywhere in the world. All it takes is a credit card and a couple of minutes. It's free to sign up.

One of the reasons it's preferred is that it protects the buyer from any misrepresentation from *eBay* sellers. This means that if your customer feels you were misleading, or the merchandise never arrives, *PayPal* will reverse the funds to the buyer.

Of course there is a small transaction fee involved.

The biggest advantage is that the funds are directly deposited into your account the instant the transaction is complete.

Some untrusting dinosaurs may elect to send a check through snail mail (internet term for post mail), but checks may take several days to arrive and clear. I don't advise accepting personal checks, as this will take much longer than expected to clear. Do not ship the item until you've received payment!

If several days have passed and the buyer hasn't sent payment, you have the option of sending a *payment reminder* through the *ebay* website.

After repeated attempts to receive your payment go unanswered, I recommend re-listing your item and filing for a *non-paying bidder* through *eBay* to retrieve your insertion and final value fees. This is done by right clicking on the item which will then allow you to chose the *Non Payment* option.

This is a very basic example of how to sell your item on *eBay*. Once you do some research, give it a try. You won't be disappointed.

I was reluctant to give it a try. I began with a few items and was pleased, not by the price they sold for, but rather by what was selling. I'd decided to sell some old stock. I even sold my personal collection of used ties! I soon began putting my premium goods on the site and had tremendous results.

It helped that I'm from Canada, and the auction currency is set in US funds.

The emails began pouring in, with eager buyers wanting to know more. Within a year, I turned what was an innocent test into a full-time business. Whether you're looking for full or part-time results, *eBay* is a great avenue to move new or unwanted goods. There are many books on the market that can help you.

I recommend fiddling around on the site yourself, first. Become familiar with the terms. Then, if need be, pick up a book, learn from someone else's expertise on the subject, and apply it to your needs.

eBay has made using their system fun by providing audio and visual instructions. They even have an eBay university for the serious user.

eBay has a section at the top of the page titled **Site Map.** This will take you to a page with a series of headings, which will usually answer most of the common questions asked. I conclude this section this statement: THE BEST INFORMATION about eBay IS ON *eBay*!

Chapter Twelve

EXPANDING YOUR BUSINESS

Setting Up Multiple Locations

This section is designed for the ambitious business person. Once you've capitalized on one location and there is a surplus of inventory, you should have the itch to open another store.

Along with the benefit of becoming a much more profitable company, there are more dangers involved. If proper management isn't in place, you run the risk of harming the entire operation.

First things first, ask yourself whether you're financially able to open a second location.

Sure, everything that applied to opening the first location will hold true, only this time it may be slightly easier. You've probably built relationships with suppliers, allowing you to reduce costs on inventory. This, however, is step one of opening more than one location.

You can't physically be in two places at the same time so you need to put an organizational system into place. *McDonald's* (a multi-billion dollar franchise) has a system in place which allows for a 16-year-old to open and successfully operate a location so you should be able to do the same.

The key here is to properly train every employees to adhere to the rules and regulations you've implemented to achieve success at your first location.

Become super organized The weekly meeting won't cut it anymore. Have a Manager's Manual in addition to an Employee Manual. Outline an itemized breakdown of any and all procedures that staff must follow. The goal is to have the entire staff operate as though you were present.

Don't fall into the easy trap of feeling that something "is just common sense." While this may hold true for an owner, you'll quickly discover that it isn't as clear to the average employee.

Make notes about the smallest details. Update and revise constantly. This will relieve you of the burden of having to come up with an entire plan overnight. Don't discard input from the team. Remember, there is no "I" in team (a cliché, but true).

EXPANSION

The following list will assist you in the expansion process.

Keep the **same company name**. This will prove to be a wise choice for many reasons. First, it will cut costs on advertising. Using both locations for the same ad will cut expenses in half and allow promotion twice as much, whichever suits you best. There will also be a savings on printed materials like business cards, flyers, shopping bags, and signage. It will generally make life easier overall, not to mention projecting a more powerful company image.

Choose the new location wisely. When I set up my third location, I made the mistake of opening too close to my first store. A fifteen-minute drive wouldn't stop my customers from bouncing from one location to the next.

In the end, it made sense to have only one location for that particular area. I eventually turned my third store into an outlet with a new concept. Every item was $25 (buy four, get one free). I created an entirely new customer base from that idea.

Make certain the location is either **different or a considerable distance from your other locations.** Some will disagree with this. Some large chains have more than one location within blocks from one other. The reason is that they want to capture more of the market, preventing the competition from taking a slice of the pie. This will not apply to you, just not yet.

Companies like the Gap work with extremely high margins and can afford to keep a location open for years without making a profit. I highly doubt you can do the same.

Purchase wisely. The fact that there are now two locations to fill will sometimes motivate overbuying. Don't make the mistake of buying up large quantities of product only to have it sitting in the back stockroom. Remember, fashion trends change overnight so buy on a need to sell basis only.

Use **inventory transfer sheets.** This will enable you to keep track of merchandise being transferred from one location to another. Use inventory control software but ensure hardcopies of all paper work between all locations.

Shift merchandise. There are many reasons why a certain product will sell faster at certain locations. As time passes, you'll be able to identify what each location requires—what sells best at one location may not hold true for another.

Provide transfers. Let us assume a customer is interested in a particular size which is only available at onw location. Do you send them to the other location the same day?

Absolutely not!

Unless the customer is desperate and wants to go for a drive, have the item shipped by the next day. This is not only convenient, but also offers a valuable service. Always take the customer's contact information and call them when the item arrives as a simple reminder. Try and have them pay in advance, or at least a deposit. It may be difficult but worth asking for.

Give customers a two day grace period for pick up, otherwise I recommend placing the item back on the sales floor. Often, a customer will want to buy simply on impulse, so don't take it personally if they don't return. I've included a sample of what an inventory transfer sheet should look like. Feel free to alter it to your own specifications.

SAMPLE INVENTORY TRANSFER SHEET

COMPANY NAME
Address 1
Address 2
Telephone • Fax

STORE TRANSFER

TRANSFER NUMBER_____

SHIPPING STORE	RECEIVING STORE
DATE	SHIP VIA

ITEM NO.	DESCRIPTION	QUANTITY	PRICE	U/M	TOTAL
			TOTAL TRANSFER		
DATE RECEIVED		RECEIVED BY			

Managing inventory. It is one of the most important tasks to manage. This is where a computer system will come in handy. It can track how well an item is selling and how well it's selling at each location, right down to the size and color. This can be done manually, but it will be a more time-consuming hands-on approach.

The most important thing to consider is the communication between locations. An overview of the sales summary and a simple walkthrough will help identify what's moving and what's not.

Hire a district manager. His or her job will be to oversee all the locations. Store managers should report directly to the district manager. In the beginning, I recommend taking on this role yourself, as it will give you valuable insight on how each location is run.

A rule of thumb is to physically dedicate time to be in every store.

Combine expenses. Perhaps the greatest advantage to multiple locations, besides the extra cash flow, is the savings. Whenever possible, have all the expenses under one business name. When advertising, you can now have all the locations in the same ad. This will also allow for more ad space, or simply more ads. It's a win-win situation.

There will no longer be a need for security deposits, since your business now has a proven track record.

Having multiple locations will entitle savings, as most companies that you'll fo business with will offer discounts when setting up more than one account.

Hire a courier service. This will come in handy for transfers. Don't tie up an employee's time to go across town delivering an item to another location. Hire a local courier. I don't recommend the big boys like *FedEx* or *UPS* for this service. There are many reliable smaller couriers which offer same-day service for less than the hourly rate you'd be paying your own staff. Remember, the employee is paid by the hour. They may resent using their own vehicle and gas. I should mention they will take their sweet time. Trust me, it's not worth it. A local bicycle courier can make deliveries far less than the cost of regular mail.

Chapter Thirteen

OTHER USEFUL INFORMATION

FROM CONCEPT TO GARMENT

Ever wonder how clothing gets from an idea to a garment hanging on the rack? There is much more involved than you think. I will briefly take you through the entire process to provide a better understanding on how it all happens. The first person is the visionary, or the designer. This is the person who draws a sketch of their idea.

The next step is to source out fabric. This will be the material used to make the garment. Next, the designer begins what is called a pattern. This is simply a paper cut-out of how the fabric needs to be cut. Patterns are used for many seasons; what might change is the fabric.

Once the fabric has been chosen, it is brought to a cutting facility, along with the pattern design. Once the fabric is all cut out, it will be brought to a sewing facility. Most manufacturers do both procedures under the same roof.

Now the cut up fabric is sewn together to produce the actual garment. There are different methods used for manufacturing, which will affect the final cost. But for now, I am just giving you a general idea on the process.

As the garment is being assembled, labels and tags are being produced. The manufacturer is usually the one to attach the finishing. The garment is now complete, but it is not in the stores just yet.

Before the garment goes into mass production it will need to get graded. A professional will take accurate measurements in order to come up with how each size will be manufactured.

It is then delivered to a distribution company or wholesaler, sometimes one in the same. They now begin to fill in the orders, which were placed by retailers in the previous season. Once the items get shipped to the store, they are ready to be merchandised.

I have just given you months of development in about a page of writing. The process I have just discussed has many variables to it and at times gets more advanced, so does the entire process of producing clothing.

THEFT: WHAT WORKS, WHAT DOESN'T

As I have mentioned in my employee manual, clothing is a preferred item for thieves second only to electronics. In my career, I have experienced a great deal of theft by both consumers as well as employees. That's right, you have to worry and protect yourself against your very own staff. They have a much more elaborate term for this kind of theft, it's called internal theft or shrinkage.

Large corporations now include shrinkage into their equation. How pathetic is that? It is now considered the norm in day-to-day business.

Here are a few tips on what measures to take in order to protect yourself and your profits.

SURVEILLANCE CAMERAS

These are those little cameras tucked away in a corner somewhere. In a casino, the term is known as "the eye in the sky." The setup usually requires 1-4 cameras 1 monitor (a TV will do just fine) and 1 time-lapse digital recorder. The prices start in and around $1000 and may require professional installation. In my opinion, they serve only one purpose, to scare would-be thieves.

It is a great deterrent for the amateur, but does little to stop the pro. Think about it for a moment, if there is nobody manning the monitors, what good are they? Sure you can review the footage once the thieves are long gone, but by then it's too late. It may be an advantage stopping repeat offenders. It may also help reduce internal theft, but before you stick a hidden camera behind a mirror, consider if it is lawful.

The following is a list of several laws applicable to the use of surveillance equipment. First, you must post a sign making everyone aware that they are being recorded. Second, you cannot use listening devices, only visual. Third, there are restrictions as to where video cameras can be placed; a changing room or bathroom is a definite NO.

So check with local authorities for more information on the lawful usages of such devices.

Make the cameras as visible as possible, it's not a candid camera set, the goal is to let all would be thieves think twice about lifting valuable stock. A good habit is to keep a hard drive space enough for a thirty-day cycle. This is an adequate enough period in the event footage must be reviewed.

Technology is always on the move. There are systems set up through the Internet, which allow you to be watching the store while at home, or away with your smart phone or laptop computer. Talk to your security company for more details. This won't, however, do for you what it was intended to do...STOP THEFT. It's a question of what makes you sleep better at night.

As of this writing, digital equipment has become more economical for the average consumer. A good idea would be to fully investigate what makes more sense financially.

SECURITY TAGS

This is probably the most widely used form of theft prevention. Essentially a small electronic tag is pinned through clothing. If the tagged clothing passes through an antenna stationed by the door, an alarm will sound. This system can cost $1,500 and up. The price will vary on the type of system along with the number of tags purchased.

The package should include one antenna, one demagnetizer, one alarm ringer, plus tags with pins. There are many different tags available from small to large size as well as ink filled tags. They range in price starting at about a dollar each. The advantages with this system are the deterrent factor. They can serve as eyes behind your head.

Shoplifters will think twice when tags are visible so don't try hiding them underneath garments. The goal is to keep customers honest. The disadvantages of this system are many.

Garments can easily be damaged when pins are being applied so it is extremely important that your staff be properly trained to install them. Try to insert through the seam or the stitch of the garment. Ink-filled tags may be more costly and cause more damage. They are designed to leak if pulled on or mishandled. What good is the garment if it has been stained with ink? Why take the chance to have an accident happen.

Professional thieves know how to pry off the tags with ease. When wrapped tightly or covered by certain materials, the ringer may not function properly. It may be a good idea to install a dual antenna by the door. This setup will double the signal strength, however, this system will be more expensive.

Here is a situation that happened to me. A customer walked in purchased an item walked out the door and the alarm sounded. I asked her to come back inside believing I had left the tag on. The tag was taken off, but yet the alarm kept ringing each time the customer walked by the antenna. I began questioning this sweet innocent looking girl. I also pointed out that if she indeed had taken something by mistake it would certainly show up on camera. She insisted on her innocence and became insulted from my accusations. I tried to appeal to her good nature by letting her know we all make mistakes and that I will not call authorities.

To make a long story short She left and there was nothing I could do besides call the police (I did not). First, the law does not entitle me to obligate anyone into emptying his or her pockets; I could wind up getting sued. Second, if she had indeed taken something she probably would have never shown her face again (she did not). There are some situations you'd rather avoid. I'd rather lose one item and get rid of an unwanted customer for life. As for the video recording, it didn't show much.

Sometimes I'll walk into a store and the alarm will sound for now reason. There may be something in my pockets, or something to do with my phone and radio waves. What do I know technology isn't perfect?

ANOTHER COMICAL EMPLOYEE STORY

A rather amusing story to tell before moving on; I had my demagnetizers lost twice by employees. Keep in mind that it has significant weight and is a twelve by twelve square unit. I discovered that the magnet units were accidentally placed in the customer's shopping bag at the point of sale. At a price of several hundred dollars, it makes sense to bolt it down with screws. Before shopping around, know that there are companies out there providing these systems on a rent to own (or lease) basis. This comes in handy when working with a limited budget.

WIRE AND LOCK SYSTEMS

For very expensive articles, certain stores have elected to use special hangers that lock with a key or they are wired into a ground unit, which doesn't allow for the item to go very far. They are typically used for big ticket items such as leather jackets or furs. They work great also for after hours in the event of a break in. The problem is that if some potential customer decides he or she may want to try the item on they may lose interest or not bother for some salesperson to unlock it.

POST SIGNAGE

Posting a simple sign in plain view stating *"Shoplifters will be prosecuted to the fullest extent of the law"* will do more than you think. It triggers the subconscious into becoming a model citizen. Sounds like voodoo magic, well consider that large department stores used to play background music with subliminal messages encouraging customers to spend and not steal.

There should be another sign posted by the changing room stating a maximum number of items allowed in the room at one time. Also, a sign letting everyone know large bags and backpacks are not allowed into the changing room area.

I laugh at stores that allow people to use the change room entering with huge bags big enough to stuff a winter coat in. That's a potential disaster waiting to happen.

THE STAFF

This is your first line of defense. All the high tech gadgetry in the world will not be as effective as your own staff. The proper training is essential (see my employee training manual) to ensure theft prevention. Have employee's eyes always in view of customers. Have them assist customers at the changing room area making sure each article is accounted for. Let other staff members know when you're leaving the floor. Have a policy in place and enforce it. Have all customers leave large bags in the front of the store possibly behind the counter.

Always ask customers if they require assistance. This lets them know you're on the ball.

Hire more staff for those busy weekend rushes. One day's salary is equivalent to one item stolen.

Don't allow customers to continue to browse with shopping bags even after a purchase has been made.

These are just a few examples of how to recruit your staff into watchdogs.

INTERNAL THEFT

Gone are the days of checking bags and purses on the way out at the end of a shift. Today's thief is much more advanced. After working somewhere for several months, or even weeks, a staff member will easily come to recognize the system.

Defend yourself as best possible. Do a background check. Many are hired without a reference call ever made. Do your homework on whomever you're considering to hire. Never hire friends or relatives. As time passes, co-workers tend to become chummy. When this begins to happen, changing shifts would be appropriate. If you do decide to use cameras, make employees aware. Store the recording device in a safe and undisclosed location, preferably under lock and key.

Don't let staff know of your travel plans, have them believe you can show up at any time. It's best to have everyone on their toes at all times. Have a snitch on your side. OK, maybe this is a tad extreme, but having someone loyal to you can do nothing but good. Occasionally ask questions to see responses (i.e., "where did that red shirt go?" Or "didn't we have a size 6 in this?") You get the idea. This will remind them that you are aware of the smallest of details. Inevitably there is only so much that can be done.

Try to not have emotional ties with staff. Remember they are working for you. If it's friends you seek, go to the local bar or better still join a social network online.

The following is a list of additional random pointers to help reduce the overall shrinkage in your business:

- Have locks on changing rooms
- Whenever possible, hire more staff
- Keep only 1 of each size on the floor the rest in a stock room
- Keep all shopping bags behind cash counter
- Do inventory counts regularly
- Pay staff commissions on sales
- Avoid using friends on the same shift
- Make certain each garment has a security tag
- Clear changing rooms immediately after use
- Avoid phone use when customers are browsing
- Change camera surveillance tapes regularly
- Remove any view obstructing racks, shelves etc.

- Install angled mirrors, providing an entire view of the sales floor
- Have small accessories under lock and key
- Have keys with management only
- Install hidden cameras in stock room
- Keep stock organized (neat)
- Offer large employee discounts
- Have customers fill out and sign refund slip
- Have management do random garbage bag checks
- Be friendly and treat everyone with respect

COMPUTERS FRIEND OR FOE?

Do I computerize my store? The answer seems obvious in today's fast-paced world. What business can live without one? Your personal situation will determine whether it is right for you or not. I will outline how a computer can function within the clothing business.

Inventory management is perhaps the most common reason to computerize. Programs designed with retail clothing in mind allow you to keep track of each item in the store right down to the size and color on hand. Essentially, what happens is that each time a sale is put through the computer, it will automatically delete it from the inventory, thus allowing you to know what is in and what is out. It will go so far as to prompt you when an item is low on inventory, providing ample time to restock.

Basic accounting is another great feature. It will keep track of all your purchases and expenses as well as company payroll. Everything can be found with ease. Think about how easy it is to hand in sales figures to the accountant with the touch of a button. However, I still recommend you always do a physical count. Remember what the computer tells you will not always be accurate to what's on hand.

Customer profile is my personal favorite. This can be set up to your own specifications. You can create a mailing list to inform customers of upcoming events, such as sales or new arrivals. Simply enter their info and keep it on file. I recommend collecting email addresses. This will save you thousands of dollars in postage and printing materials. However, it lacks in the personal touch of a birthday card or direct phone call.

Another great feature is customer profiling. Say you have an overstock in size 4 dresses. Pull up every potential customer and target them directly with a personal invite.

With all this info on hand you can also create a profile giving each customer points with every purchase. These are some of the benefits of using a computer. I feel this feature alone is worth the money.

Staff scheduling can be formatted allowing you to keep track of employee hours.

Signage is another great way to make use of a computer. You can instantly turn a rack into a sale rack with a simple sign.

Another great feature will outline **peak sales times** that will tell you which times during the day are the busiest on average based on previous sales. If 12 to 4 are your peak sales times, you may consider having an additional part-timer come in only on those hours. It is a great way to cut costs. The only disadvantage here is with clothing it is at times unpredictable. You can get a rush first thing in the morning or at the end of the day.

Keeping staff honest is another great advantage, every item is accounted for and every sale must be entered. The system is so smart that it will record all transactions, which have been voided. For example, let us say a trustworthy employee decides to enter a sale, put the cash in his or her pocket and then void the transaction. The computer will tell you when and by whom the transaction was deleted. There are also many security clearances enabling some staff members to do more than others.

There are constantly new upgrades for programs so do some research before buying. I recommend sticking to the big boys, such as *Apple* or *Microsoft*. They usually back up their product and have an excellent support team. Here are a few links to help get you started;

www.vigilant.com
www.retailanywhere.com
www.capterra.com
www.vendhq.com
www.posnation.com
www.merchantos.com
www.zingcheckout.com

You may think you are saving with a small independent programmer, but in the end you'll end up spending more than you bargained for. Some programs only allow you to rent their software and charge per terminal used while others may charge a flat fee and an annual upgrade fee.

Pay for only what your business needs. Why spend the money on all the bells and whistles when you may only need one bell. I have personally gone through 3 different systems with no luck.

Here are just some of the common problems to anticipate.

Delays in stocking the racks are very common due to the amount of time needed to enter each item. Remember the computer only knows what you tell it. You may also be spending more money in computer programming. The call from your staff will happen several times a day, especially from someone new. The receipt printer is jammed what do I do? I hit enter several times and nothing has happened. I can't find this item on the system. The list goes on.

Slowing down the rush, especially on a sale day will often deter a customer from waiting around for your computer problem to get solved.

As you may be aware downloading off the Internet has become extremely popular as of late. My advice is to ban the staff from any unauthorized use of the Internet as you are run the risk of catching a virus.

The last thing we want is for all your records to be ruined because a part-timer decided to illegally download the latest track from Britney Spears.

But good luck on this one.

IF IT'S NOT ON THE COMPUTER IT CAN'T EXIST?

I will end this section with a couple hilarious computer stories and how they don't always make our lives easier.

I recently went shopping at *Radio Shack* for some speakers. They were on display, but the computer read they were out of stock. So I physically pointed them out to the salesperson that appeared to be in his late 40s. He seemed confused.

After spending several minutes trying to sort it out, I recommended he write up a manual receipt and enter the item once he sorted out the problem. Still confused, he called his manager who made matters worse. Needless to say, I could not buy the speakers, which were staring at me four feet away.

My other story takes place in a restaurant. I had decided on an ice cream dish when I asked the waitress to combine 2 flavors. She replied she could not. Puzzled, I asked why. Her response was that the computer would not allow her to order it that way.

The morals of my stories are simple: do not make the computer take over your common senses.

PREPARING FOR THE BIG SALE

What's to prepare? That's what I always thought. I couldn't have been more mistaken. Not properly preparing for the big sale will result in loss of sales, irritated customers, and frustrated staff. It's important to organize ahead of time.

I could never understand what the big deal was on a sale day. My customers' shopping habits always had me confused. For some reason, I always got rid of the unwanted stock which had been lying in some boxes in the stockroom.

It's important to fill the shelves with as much stock as possible. Create special sale racks with odd sizes, weird colors, or even damaged and returned goods. Use something that you're overstocked in to create a door crasher. Have it all out on the sales floor.

You don't want the customer to feel as though he or she missed out on anything, which is why half-empty racks are not a good idea. There won't be time to restock in the midst of the frenzy of a successful sale.

Have plenty of supplies handy. Shopping bags, proper change in the till, and pens (which often go missing) should be in abundance at the cash counter. The last thing you want is to have the cashier hold up the line because their out of quarters, or he or she can't find a pen so the customer can sign a credit card receipt.

Hire additional staff. Although they may not have experience, it won't matter. Have them man the changing room area, or have them fold all day long. The regular staff will see to the needs of potential buyers. It's worth the extra couple of bucks in wages in order to produce more sales. Many part-timers will work for clothing instead of cash.

Have plenty of legible signage everywhere. If items aren't marked, most shoppers won't bother asking what the price is.

Schedule lunches and breaks. On a busy sale day, there won't be time to follow the normal routine of having a cigarette break every half hour. A good idea would be to have a supply of water and snacks handy.

Don't be afraid to keep the capacity to a maximum. If the store becomes overcrowded, have customers form a line outside the door. Nobody wants to shop in an overcrowded environment.

Extend an invitation to friends and family the day before the sale since there will be no time to provide the same attention they receive on a regular day, and we all know how easily they'll get offended.

Always make notes for the next time. The key is to have the sale run as efficiently as possible. More important, we want the customers to come back!

MY THEORY ON DISCOUNTING

Having come from an off-price environment, I consider myself to be an expert on the subject of branding and the effects of discounting.

I can sum it up in one word: VISIBILITY.

The more the product is visible, the more it will sell. Most brand-name distributors are concerned that their regular buyers will not buy at regular prices should an outlet be selling the name at a lower price. Nothing could be further from the truth. The fact is, most shoppers who buy at a discount will not buy at regular prices, EVER! Discount items are usually a season or two old. The regular customer will always want to keep current with the latest and greatest. They're completely different customers.

It's actually healthy for a brand to be offered at a discount. This will introduce an entirely new customer. To prove my point, we've seen large discount outlets sprouting up just about everywhere you turn. Most are corporately owned by the brands themselves.

Do you think brands like *Nike* and *Tommy Hilfiger* would consider opening discount outlets all over North America if they thought it would harm their sales? Most of the negative reaction to discounting comes from other retailers.

USEFUL BUYING TIPS

This next section could save you thousands of dollars over the years.

Read it very carfully.

You've already been told that the buying is just as important as the selling. The reason I may repeat myself at times is so you never forget. Hopefully, you'll thank me for it later. Over the years I have developed a craft for negotiating with whomever I do business with. One of my favourite tactics is NO MATTER WHAT the circumstance, ask for a discount on the set price. Sounds simple right?

Now let's examine it a little more. Lets assume you've chosen several items at the supplier's for a price of $50 each.

Step 1: Always ask right then and there for a discount, regardless of who your dealing with. It's 3 seconds out of your life. Remember, we're blocking out pride here, it's only business. So let us assume you get a modest 3% discount bringing the item down to $48.50. Take it a little further by asking if there is any possible way to to bring the price even lower if perhaps you decide to purchase a larger quantity. I realize it may seem as though your pushing it, but who cares? You're not trying to get married here. The name of the game is saving money. Now you decide to buy 25 pieces totaling $1,212.50.

Step 2: Even though you have agreed to purchase the items at a set price, the next goal is to shave an additional $112.50, making it an even $1,100 total price. Always act humble. Leave your leased *Mercedes* at home.

No matter how small or large the company is, you may catch the supplier at the right time. You don't know if they are in dire need for the cash. They may have a sizable payment to make for new merchandise, plans for expansion or maybe the supplier is about to propose to his girlfriend and will be visiting *Tiffany's* that weekend.

The key is not to do this once and awhile, but to do this each and every time. You'll be amazed how much you will actually save over the years. It will surprise you. Make this a habit.

Chapter Fourteen

BECOMING AN IMPORTER

Once you've mastered the art of retail, you may decide to cut the middle man and buy directly from the source. This road will most likely lead to importing different clothing lines from around the globe.

At first, the idea of importing may seem overwhelming. Don't let that discourage you. I started bringing in products from South America and Hong Kong when I was only nineteen. I didn't know a thing about importing.

One thing to always remember: You're entitled to do whatever any other company is doing. Nobody is special, or has special privileges, for that matter. We (North America) live in a free enterprise society, which means we can conduct any business we wish, as long as it's within legal limits.

There are important factors to consider before making the journey across the big sea. First, are you in a financial position to do so? When you consider the high cost of an airline ticket, hotel accommodations, and general expenditures, those costs may ultimately kill off any profits.

I recommend incorporating a vacation into a business trip. Just don't leak this information to your better half! They may not appreciate it (unless, of course, they're also a business partner).

If you're planning a vacation anyway (and I strongly recommend you do), why not take it in a place that has industry? Especially clothing.

There are many exotic destinations that offer great buys on all kinds of product. South American countries like Venezuela, Mexico, Columbia, and Brazil offer great product. There's an entire new world to be discovered in the Orient. China, Korea, and Thailand offer prices that you must see to believe. Then there's the almighty Europe, particularly Italy and France, the

Mecca of the fashion universe. Here is the crème de la crème of everything under the sun with regards to fashion. You may pay top dollar, but you'll have the competitive edge needed to be ahead of everyone else.

I recommend doing some homework before departing. Search the Internet for manufacturers which produce products of interest to you. You can easily contact them through email for further details.

You'll be pleasantly surprised to learn that they will often greet you with open arms. Remember, some countries are not in the same economy as America. Once you become a big enough buyer, they may decide to invite you over from time to time, all expenses paid. Just like a casino. But let's not get ahead of ourselves just yet.

We'll look at importing and decide if it's right for you. I'll also include my own real life experiences, which may encourage or discourage you, depending on the type of person you are.

Getting Started

Freight forwarder, customs broker, letter of credit, telegraphic transfer, rate of exchange, quota restrictions, duties, and permits, are just some of the terms you'll hear every day if you become an importer. These words may sound foreign but, just like everything else in business, in time they'll become second nature to you.

I'll share my humble beginnings of importing as a business experience. Looking back, it seems as though I was a preschooler. My goal is that after reading the next few pages, I will at the very least have given you an general understanding of how the system works. More important, I hope this makes certain that most of you don't make the same mistakes I've made.

The first experience I ever had in importing was during a vacation to sunny Mexico. My friend and I had fun wheeling and dealing with the street merchants, who were selling everything from hand-made towels to marble chessboards. The silver jewelery seemed to be the biggest hit among the vacationers.

I had little knowledge of jewelery or how large the market was. Asking around, I realized that there was a big demand for this type of product back home. I decided to bring some back home with me.

Prices from one vendor to the next varied dramatically. This led me to believe that the source of the jewellery would have the best price. After becoming friendly with the hotel staff, (and a little financial persuasion) they led me to an area outside of the city where the street merchants went to buy their goods.

Not only were the prices incredibly low, but there was much more selection to choose from. When I promised to return for future buys, the little old lady behind the counter offered me great deals, and advice on which items were the best sellers.

Who knows, she could have been lying, but what did I know? I was only nineteen. I purchased a bag full and returned home with them. I began selling them like hot cakes. (Who started that expression? Do hot cakes really sell that fast?) Soon afterward, I thought of importing them on a larger scale.

That turned out to be a disaster. There were all these different laws, rules, and regulations to follow. I just wanted to bring over some goods and resell them. What's the harm in that? Apparently, the government saw harm. That discouraged my dream so much so that I gave up entirely on the custom jewelery business.

Later, I went from silver to watches. My motto was that everybody needs a watch. I strongly believed that the best way to succeed was to import directly. I was wrong.

After sifting through some magazine ads, I noticed someone selling a directory of manufacturers of watches. I wrote to each and every address.

About a month later, my mailbox was flooded with brochures on the different selections offered. The only problem was there was a minimum to buy. After careful consideration I made my choice. I ordered samples of everything, and made a international money order, which I sent to this company in Hong Kong, and sent in my order.

My order was supposed to arrive in six to eight weeks. It did not. I tried to call, but there was nobody there who spoke English. I wrote, and waited almost two weeks for a response. They assured me that my samples had been sent. Christmas was rapidly approaching and I didn't want to miss out on the season, so stupid me went ahead and placed my full order. The box did arrive before Christmas but was held up at the border. I got a notice that there was proper documentation to be provided and taxes owing.

After making inquires, I called a customs broker, who handled everything for a small fee. The excitement of opening my package was indescribable—my first shipment as an importer!

I WAS DEVESTATED!

The watches were oversized and looked nothing like the photos in the catalogue. Furthermore, they appeared to be of poor quality.

What was I to do? I had no choice but to try to sell this mistake from Hong Kong (not that there is anything wrong with Hong Kong). I visited every store in the local area. The response was not favorable, to say the least. One vendor was nice enough to direct me to Chinatown (in my very own city), where there were many watch wholesalers.

What a rude awakening! I was stunned by the prices there! Every watch was selling for well below my actual cost. I knew I was in trouble. I desperately decided to unload whatever I had. That meant knocking on every door, including family and friends.

This was an even bigger wake-up call. Nobody will buy something just to support your dreams, most of all friends and family, if you set up shop with this in mind I urge you to reconsider.

To make a long story short, I was stuck with my watches for months before unloading them all. Take every experience as a blessing.

I began buying a variety of watches from Chinatown and made a nifty little profit.

THIRD TIMES A CHARM

My next adventure in importing gets a little more exciting. A friend had vacationed in Venezuela. On his return, he called me over to show off all the clothing he'd purchased at incredibly low prices. I couldn't believe my eyes. I thought my friend was full of BS, but I knew what kind of person he was, I knew he would never buy all that clothing unless the prices were truly low.

I decided to take a trip to Venezuela. What did I have to lose? In the worst-case scenario, I'd soak up some rays and sip on some pina coladas.

The trip proved to be more than I had expected. The entire Venesuelan city of Margarita Island was full of stores with designer labels at discounted prices.

Why?

Margarita Island a duty-free city, and is considered a place which doesn't affect the regular market, i.e. the US and Canada. Therefore, most manufacturers didn't have a problem sending their overstock and seconds there.

I felt like a kid in a candy store. I didn't know where to begin. Every store had something worth buying. I didn't care about duties and taxes! The deals were so great that I couldn't lose.

I began buying up everything I could afford and bringing them back to my resort. The boxes started piling up in my room. The entire resort thought I was a tad shady, but I didn't care. I was thinking of the dollars to be made on my return home. When the end of my trip was near, a representative of the tour package told me I might have a problem sending all those boxes on the airplane. I began to panic, frantically making calls to everyone with no results.

But, luckily for me, the hotel food wasn't the greatest, so my friend and I walked over to the pizzeria next door to take our chances. As luck would have it, we began talking to the old man who owned the restaurant. We explained our situation and asked what his thoughts were. He began to laugh, telling us that anything is possible as long as you're willing to pay for it.

I thought he was off his rocker. How could money influence a major airport, not to mention an airline company? But one phone call was all it took to arrange for my boxes to pass through local customs and be placed on the airplane.

Of course this service had a price, but it was well worth it. Had I gone through the airline I would have had to pay approximately $5usd per extra kilo, and I had ten giant boxes.

You're probably asking yourself why didn't I approach *FedEx*, *UPS*, or some other type of shipping company. I did, with poor results. They had restrictions on the size of carton used, and a long list of regulations. The cost would have eaten all my profits.

The merchandise arrived, but to my surprise was held at the border. I provided them all my invoices. They were nice enough to explain that I needed to clear commercial merchandise by either filling out Canada Customs forms, or that (the easier way) I could hire a customs broker. After careful consideration I opted for the broker route. The forms were a tad to stressful for me at the time.

These are just three of my early real life experiences of importing from foreign countries. They by no means should set the standard on the do's and don'ts of importing, but I thought you might learn a thing or two of reading on what a naive little kid did to try to make a buck.

Since then, I've been importing from various countries on a regular basis. There's an Old Italian saying, usually translated as "the entire world is a town." Once you begin to travel, you'll realize how true this is. Each and every country imports and exports products, everything from food to cars to, and you guessed it, clothing. Everything is within reach. Believe it or not, you don't even have to leave your home, thanks to the marvels of modern technology.

How do I find merchandise to import?

Years ago, finding merchandise was a painstaking process. The only way was to pack a bag and hit the road. With the Internet, all this has changed.

Almost any product from any country is accessible on the net. If it isn't, I don't recommend doing business with them. Simply use your favourite search engine. www.Google.com or www.Yahoo.com do great for me. Type in whatever you're looking for and, presto!, the screen will be filled with valuable new contacts.

Do not run right out and give all your business to the first company on the web page! Spend a few hours doing research! It's well worth it.

Once you've found something interesting, visit them in person or have them ship samples for you to work with. Pictures will not always give you the best idea of what you're buying.

If the manufacturer or wholesaler is reluctant to send samples, I would seriously consider moving on. If they expect a company or individual to place a large order, without viewing the merchandise, they're either very busy and don't need the business, or are completely shady. Either way, I consider that a clear signal to steer clear of doing business with them.

If you're buying clearance product, invest in a trip for viewing. The only problem is by the time you book a trip and get there, the goods may be gone. They may very well have never been there. How do you really know? Once you arrive, they may steer you towards another deal.

Another version of bait and switch.

I've been in this situation in the past. After a long exhausting trip, you feel the need to buy something simply to make the trip worthwhile.

This is a mistake!

Don't hesitate to put your tail between your legs and come home empty-handed.

Use that hard-earned money to buy product that will sell.

International trade shows are a great way to find merchandise from all four corners of the globe, all under one roof.

Perhaps the largest is the *MAGIC* show in Vegas, where you'll find tons of merchandise. The best part is that samples are there for the viewing. It's like one giant flea market. Each supplier has a booth set up to display his or her products.

A word of advice: Keep written notes about all the suppliers which are of interest to you, because by the end of the day you're sure to lose track of who was who, and who offered what. A good idea wold be to write directly on the business card or pamphlet provided.

Another great way to find overseas suppliers is to contact the consulates of the countries of interest. Ask to speak to the trade department. They may ask you to formally submit a request, in the form of a letter or fax. They will supply you with a list of manufacturers who want to do business in your country.

Once you have a list, go through the same procedure as before. There's no guarantee that every company will be 100% reputable.

Keep your nose in current affairs. Look through the designer magazines and see what's hot. Usually European or Asian trends take time before they make their way to the US and Canada.

COMPANY IMAGE

If you plan on dealing with overseas suppliers, I recommend having the right company image. Project the notion that the company is larger than it actually is. Remember, we're talking about overseas; they don't have a clue about the amount of business you can provide.

When attempting to bring in a well-known label, chances are they'll require proof that you can handle the amount of business they're after. Manufacturers often prefer to align themselves with wholesalers of well-established lines. They're not willing to take a chance on a newcomer.

Even if you BS your way into convincing them that you have what it takes, they may still require a minimum amount of sales per year. If you don't meet the quota, it's more than likely that the contract will be terminated

I do not recommend falsifying documents! This practice is not only immoral but also is illegal. The truth will come out, eventually. I'm simply saying to bend the truth.

It's much easier to obtain a contract with a new line, one which has not yet gained recognition. Such a line will often be more flexible to deal with.

A professional letterhead works miracles. I recommend using more than one address, if possible. Or use the heading, Head Office. This signifies that the company has more than one location.

The fax number and email address are vital. When sending any kind of correspondence, be sure to personally sign each document. Instead of signing the letters John Doe, President, (or CEO), it will be more effective to use Head Buyer, or Senior Buyer. Those titles automatically translate to sales in the minds of the companies you're attempting to do business with. If possible, always have someone else answer the phone line and transfer calls to you. Virtual secretary services are available for a modest monthly fee.

Fake it 'til you make it sounds a tad dishonest, but you're not attempting to defraud anyone. You simply want the opportunity to prove yourself.

Let's examine some of the most common companies you'll have a use for.

FRIEGHT FORWARDER

This is the company which will handle transportation. A term also referred to as logistics. When importing from another nation, there will be different modes of transporting goods to where you reside. Airplanes, ships, trucks, or a combination of the three are the most common methods. The freight forwarder will manage all methods of transportation. Basically, they're connected to all the transport companies around the globe.

For example, if you're importing from Italy and live in the US, your freight forwarder will be linked up with an Italian counterpart. Simply tell them where you're buying from, and they'll put you in contact with who to use in the area.

At that point, let the supplier know which company will be handling the shipment. The supplier, in turn, will contact the shipping company when the order is ready. Often, a supplier will be familiar with local transport companies, so don't be afraid to ask whether they're reputable.

Sometimes a fright forwarder will shop around for the best rate, but not the best service. If the supplier is in a remote part of town, you may be limited in who you can use.

When your order is ready, it will be placed with whichever method of transport you've chosen. Depending on the time of year, the shipment may be held, waiting for the next available space. Remember, you're not the only one bringing in goods.

Once the shipment arrives, it will be placed in a bonded warehouse until it clear customs.

Sure, you can always call *FedEx*, but their rates are much pricey. They specialize is fast service, usually for small packages or documents.

For importing, we want a freight forwarder to accommodate the size of our business and to always shop around for the best deal. Prices vary from one company to the next. The small guy can usually provide a better price, but what's vital to your business is the level of service that is provided.

A large company may seem professional from the exterior, but they can always pawn you off to a rookie who just got promoted to service. Do your homework. When you find a company that looks after your needs, stick with them.

AIR VS. SEA

When shipping from overseas, the rates will vary dramatically between air and sea. For obvious reasons, air is much more expensive. This doesn't mean that you automatically go with sea. That will depend on the size of the order and how fast you need the goods.

For example, from Europe to the US, a ship can take four to six weeks to arrive, while the same shipment by air will usually arrive in four to six days, if not sooner.

The method used for determining shipping rates can be quite mind boggling. It's a combination of size and weight. Ask the freight forwarder what the difference in price is between the two.

At this point, look at the shipping costs in relation to the cost of the items. For example, suppose you buy 2,000 T-shirts, and the total cost of shipping is $2,000, or $1.00 per unit. It would be a good idea to add $1 to the price for every t-shirt. When spread out, that's not so bad.

When you ship by sea, they usually put your shipment in a shipping container of either twenty-foot or forty-foot size. If your order doesn't fill an entire container (when starting it most likely won't), you'll have to share space with other cargo destined for the same place. This may cause an additional delay.

It will be difficult to get an exact delivery date when you ship by sea. The vessel can run into severe weather conditions, among other possible delays. I've heard stories where containers have been completely blown off the ship by strong waves.

There's also the possibility that garments may suffer water damage. If you're importing sensitive items like lingerie, you may consider air. The biggest reason that you will most likely choose to go with air is the time factor, which includes greater certainty of the delivery date.

Weigh all the variables. Merchandise will make money only when it's in your possession, not when it's battling tough seas. If, on the other hand, you're a wholesaler and have already filled the orders, then there's no real hurry. You might as well save a couple bucks.

Be certain to purchase adequate insurance for each shipment. This can be also done through your frieght forwarder.

TRUCKING

Almost always, there will be a need for a truck. Trucks are about the only way mechandise gets from the supplier to the airport (or seaport), and from the airport to your doorstep.

Truck rates are the least expensive. When a shipment arrives, you have the option to have it delivered to your door, or do an airport pickup.

My advice is to have them deliver.

Regardless of whether you own your own truck or not, who wants to load and unload heavy boxes? For an extra couple of bucks, it's not worth the aggravation. You're running a business and have much more important issues to contend with. This is the core principal to a popular financial term called "opportunity costs" which essentially means that it will cost you more money to take care of running a small errand than doing what is more important.

If you're transporting a very large shipment and require an 18-wheeler or tractor-trailer, you'll need to assure that you have adequate space for the truck to do a radius turn on your premises. This is actually a problem you want to have. It means you're importing in a very big way.

THE FINAL TOTAL IS?

If you're a stickler for hidden costs and fees, then I recommend asking a freight forwarder and customs broker for exact amounts. They will always include additional fees such as fuel tax, disbursements, and surcharges, to name a few. When working with a tight budget, the last thing anyone wants is to have merchandise sitting in a warehouse because they're short on funds. I should also mention that merchandise left unclaimed in a warehouse space will be subject to charges after a few days have passed. This charge will be considered a storage fee. Rates will vary.

QUOTA RESTRICTIONS

Whether you're traveling in person or searching the web, you may come across out-of-this-world deals.

But, when importing, you may be surprised to learn that there's a quota restriction on certain items. This is a way for the government to help control their homeland industry. For example, if you intend to import leather shoes from a South American country, there may be a restriction. The reason is that your country doesn't want to ruin resident shoemakers who cannot possibly compete with overseas prices, from nations where the economy is much different and are able to provide better prices.

Items such as electronics don't have this problem, because over 90% of all consumer electronics are made outside the US and Canada. Check with your government, as the regulations and restrictions are constantly changing.

COUNTRY OF ORIGIN

When importing from other nations, the law requires that there be a label in each garment stating where it was made, for example, *Made in China*.

Check with the local office of consumer affairs. There are certain guidelines to which all importers must adhere. For one thing, the label must stay on after a certain number of washes. Any supplier will know this and have proper labels. However, I've seen some manufacturers try to cut corners by using paper stickers as a substitute. If the shipment is inspected and paper labels are found, they may require that proper labels be inserted prior to selling. This is not as important when importing as when selling. In the past, some manufacturers have pulled the wool over the consumers eyes, for example, making the sole of a shoe in Italy and the rest (the upper portion) in South America.

As a consumer you are led to believe that the entire shoe was made in Italy, and thus are happy to pay more for it.

Watch for evasive tags that read *"Styled in Italy,"* on products which were made in China.

Don't get me wrong. I'm not trying to tell you that because an item is made in Italy or Paris it's automatically better in quality. It is a matter of people's perception, and that's the basis of the entire fashion industry.

LICENSING

This will vary, depending on where you live. The best advice I can give you is to contact the customs branch office nearest you for exact details. It's not much to worry about. In Canada, an importer's ID number used to be required, but now they've incorporated everything under one business number.

For all government listings check the BLUE pages in your phone book.

IMPORTING A WELL KNOWN BRAND

As you know, any brand which has any kind of notoriety (brand name recognition) will undoubtedly have an importer representing the line, though some designers handle their own distribution.

It will be more than difficult to take over an existing line unless you present a considerably better offer. More important, the manufacturers will want to see your credentials that demonstrate you can back up your claims.

Let's assume that you're bringing in a not-so-well-known name, but you feel it has enormous potential. The first and most important question you may be asked is, "What are your intentions for this line?" That is, they want to know how you will market, faciltate, and sell their product. Be prepared, a slick business plan outlining as much details as possible will broden your chances in securing the product line.

The second question they may ask is what kind of sales volume you anticipate. I hate that question. In Canada, we have a relatively small fashion market. Toronto, Montreal, Vancouver, and maybe Edmonton make up for most of the fashion market. That's it! Four cities are almost the entire fashion market for the entire country. Many states in the US have more cities than that!

Don't get discouraged! The goal should be to get started. Don't make any promises until you've had ample time to study the market. Why should you commit to a large order that's uncertain? You want to know what you're getting, and be as certain as possible that you can sell it (without having to do a "blow-out sale!" to clear all the left over inventory!).

Have the manufacturer provide a set or two of samples. Once you're armed with the actual merchandise, its much easier to do your homework. Try to deal with a company that's been around for at least a couple of seasons. The last thing you want is to get started and the company doesn't produce the merchandise—or simply goes out of business! I've seen it happen on more than one occasion.

Today, everyone and their mother wants to produce a fashion line, but the bottom line is that it takes money.

Now that you've decided to carry a line, do some simple arithmetic. You want to know as accurately as possible what the merchandise will cost, the total landed cost, purchase price, shipping, duties, etc. Once you've done the calculations, add at least 30%. This will be the profit margin, which has to pay its share of the rent, employee salaries, and other business expenses before it becomes the net profit.

You need to mark up the merchandise at least that much, or it will be difficult to turn a profit at the end of the day. Then add 10% for agencies or sales reps, and then multiply it by 2.2. This will give you the retail cost. For example, if you purchase an item from the manufacturer for $10, adding 30% brings it to $13. Adding 10% for agency/rep fees brings it to $14.30. Multiply that figure by 2.2 and the final retail price to the consumer will be in and around $31.46. Obviously it won't be priced at such an oddball amount, at this point it would be wise to come up with a suggested retail price of say $35.

Now that you're prepared, it's much easier to know the market. If similar brands are selling well below this price, you may have a problem. If their prices are higher you're in luck. It means you can add a little extra to your original total.

GET IT IN WRITING

The next step is the contract agreement, which I discuss under Exclusivity Agreements. You may want to know what measures the company will take to promote their line. Ask whether they have a marketing fund in place. They may ask each importer to contribute. Who knows, you may even get your name in fine print in a magazine ad! I don't recommend spending a dollar here. You're testing unknown waters, especially when the line is relatively unknown.

Nothing is special any more. Unless you have major advertising dollars behind you, no one will care much about another clothing line. Large companies may offer a drop-ship program, which will save you thousands of dollars in warehousing costs. I will discuss in the section titled Wholesale.

IMPORTING YOUR OWN LABEL

In today's fast-changing world, it makes no sense to sit by a note pad and sketch drawings, believing you're about to become the next *Versace* or *Calvin Klien*. The truth of the matter is that almost everything has been done. Today, it's all about distribution and branding. If the product is in enough stores, it will have more exposure, which assures more sales.

Manufacturers are fully aware of the market and have in-house designers to create products which they offer to companies which want to sell using their own label.

Let's say, for example, that you're going to use your own name, Jane Doe Designs. The funny thing is that there already is a Jane Doe line out there. Do a search for labels that may have a similar name. This may prove to be a conflict and can become a potential law suite in the making.

Once you've decided on the type of line, check out different manufacturing houses as potential sources. They'll show you a complete range of patterns or ready made products available for production. You provide them with labels, they put them on the garments, and away you go—instant clothing line! It's as simple as that.

There's no need to do the designing yourself. Don't be afraid to alter designs to suit the needs of your clients.

The same rules apply when importing. You still want to research the price points and stores you want your line to be in. The next step is wholesale, which I will discuss in another chapter.

IMPORTING FOR USE AS A PRIVATE LABEL

Once you familiarize yourself with the world of importing, the opportunities are endless. Don't limit yourself to one or two lines. If you have a handle on a great manufacturer, you can produce private label merchandise. Essentially, you're providing clothing for a particular store and putting their name on the label. That's much like producing your own line.

Check out a larger company; say a chain or department store. They will each have their own label in the store right next to the well known brands. For another example, think of designer lines like *Bebe* or *Harry Rosen*. You don't think they produce everything themselves do you?

Approach the department or chain stores and offer them samples of your product. With any luck you may get a test order. The margins are not as much as in normal wholesale, but the volume will usually compensate.

Be extremely cautious with orders from larger chains. More than likely you will have exact specifications to adhere to. Your order may be rejected if any of the garments are off-spec in any way—and guess who's stuck holding the bag?

There may also be a cancellation date, which means that the company has the right to cancel the order if the product doesn't arrive by a certain date.

A great way to avoid many potential problems of such situations is to have the manufacturer work with you on the order. Increase the manufacturer's price and make him a partner, if you can. This will avoid using your own money and lower the risk.

EXCLUSIVITY AGREEMENTS

When importing a brand name line, or your own line, for that matter, it's important that you have something on paper which gives you rights that protect you from others trying to cut in on your territory.

When bringing in a brand name, they'll usually have their own contractual agreement drawn up, which you must abide by.

The larger the brand, the larger the contract.

Brands like *Tommy Hilfiger*, will more than likely use more than one distributor. Men's wear, ladies wear, jean wear, fragrances, and underwear will usually (but not always) have different distributors. The agreement will always be pending on your performance. If sales or certain prior commitments are not met, they'll find a replacement for you faster than you can blink.

Some friends of mine had an exclusive line from Italy. It started innocently enough with a few shirts. After more than eight years of hard work, the line was everywhere you turned. It was considered one of the hottest lines the city. The company expanded into a 1,000-piece collection. That's gigantic, by industry standards.

To make a short story a little shorter, they lost the line. One day they received a phone call from overseas, calling the partners in for an emergency meeting. Upon arrival they were met with the company's executives and the soon-to-be new distributors.

It seems the manufacturers were given a more lucrative offer, one which they accepted unbeknownst to the original distributors.

Imagine that after eight or nine long years building a line from scratch, you have it taken away with no warning and no possibility of appeal. A line that was feeding the mouths of three families stopped dead in its tracks.

There's a valuable lesson here. Don't put all your eggs in one basket, and make sure the contract is ironclad. Either way it's always a risk.

In the movie business, they say you're only as good as your last picture. In the clothing business they say you're only as good as your last season. What's hot today most likely won't be tomorrow.

LAWYERS IN THE MIX

I want to bring up the subject of lawyers. You may feel that it's absolutely imperative that you hire a lawyer to represent you in agreements and such, but the bottom line is that they won't save you should the mother company decide to cut you off.

In my opinion, lawyers don't always serve their purpose. They have become salesman of time. Billing clients every chance they get. They somehow always manage to extend their services for months battling with the other side for a matter which can be settled in a matter of a week. Remember once you have provided them with the large retainer fee, most of the time they will try to use that up as much as possible. I could go on about lawyers and my misirable experiences, but that would be a book on its own.

Most situations can be resolved over a cup of coffee. Unfortunately when served with a legal situation you will have no choice but to take on the services of a professional.

How Much Do I Buy?

Now that you've decided what line to import, it's important to protect yourself financially. Don't run the risk of bringing in overstock. That's a risky venture.

Years ago, when the market was presumably better, importers had an abundance of stock on hand, and for good reason—almost everything sold. Today, most importers base the quantities they produce on the orders they have. They may add 10 to 15% more for repeat orders, but that's it.

I recommend starting small and working your way up. After a few seasons, it will be easier to know your customers' buying habits and be able to meet them more easily.

Buy Direct From Importer

The signs almost everywhere you turn. The reality in today's market is that many retailers are importing themselves and retailing directly to the customer. Retailers know the value of saving and passing it along. The sad part is that this phrase has lost its luster through overuse.

Consumers aren't falling for sales gimmicks anymore. If you're providing your customer with value, that's enough to sustain any business. Don't be fooled into believing that importing an item will automatically make it more appealing to your customer.

Customs Broker

It's easy and fun to prepare documentation for customs. Okay, I lied. Its boring and complicated. This should not be where to focus your time and energy. For about 1 to 2% of the value of the shipment or a flat fee, a customs broker can handle everything for you. And believe me when I tell you that it's well worth it!

Customs brokers are somewhat like airport porters. You tip the porters, and they get you right through customs. Well not always. The same goes for customs brokers. They usually clear hundreds of items weekly. Believe it or not, it's more difficult to import clothing than a car. The reason is that on top of the duties you must pay, there is provincial tax for Canada, and permits. The permits come directly from Ottawa, our nation's capital. A seperate permit is required for every fabric type in the garment, so if your jacket contains cotton, nylon and polyester you will need three permits. The permits are usually processed in a couple of hours, unless they're backed up.

Your broker can give you exact rates for everything prior to you spending your cash.

FOB (Freight On Board or Free On Board)

When getting quotes, you may see these letters after the price, for example, $100, FOB Italy.

Simply put, the supplier is quoting you the price of the merchandise while it's still in Italy. All shipping duties and surcharges will be extra.

CURRENCY

In any country, you'll be dealing in their currency. Most of Europe has converted to the Euro. If you haven't bought currency in the past, now is the time to familiarize yourself.

Prices will vary from bank to bank, but don't travel the entire city looking for the best rate. Rates are pretty much the same anywhere you go. Remember that prices will vary between buying and selling. Buy only what is required. Otherwise, you'll wind up losing when you sell it back.

Don't be surprised if suppliers in the Orient or South America require US funds. Their currency is not as stable as the US dollar, so they prefer payment in dollars from the good old US of A.

Those who buy and sell currency for a living are called currency traders. Don't get stuck in that trap. Whenever a shipment is waiting overseas, send payment immediately. Time is money, and we don't have the luxury of sitting around waiting for the dollar to fluctuate in your favour.

If we knew where the dollar was heading, we wouldn't be in the clothing industry. We'd be sipping champagne cocktails while making millions trading currency.

A business associate of mine purchased a large deal overseas, and had everyone, including myself, interested. Unfortunately, his greed got the better of him. His banker told him that the Lira (Italian currency at the time) was on the decline and he should hold out for a few more days. The Lira had actually increased, leaving my associate in a jam. His potential buyers pulled out of their commitments to him, leaving him with a warehouse full of goods at a high price and nobody to sell to—all because he wanted to make a couple of extra dollars on the currency.

Methods Of Payment

Wire/telegraphic transfer is the most common way to send money overseas. It's just like Western Union, except that you're using your own bank. Funds are transferred from your bank to your suppliers through the banking system.

Obtain information on the supplier, like the name of their bank, its address, their account number, beneficiary, and a swift number. The supplier will provide this information for you. The fees can range up to $50 or more, depending on who you bank with.

I don't recommend using this method unless you are familiar with the business in question. Once the money is sucked out of your account, it's gone, and is extremely difficult to get back.

Beware of scam artists. The Internet has spawned a new breed of cyber criminals. They pose as legitimate businesses, but in fact are out to bilk you out of your money. It almost happened to me. A company was selling video equipment, which I needed, on the web at a fantastic price. The only method of payment they offered was western union, sent to one specific location. Through email, they told me to wire the funds there in my best friend's name, to secure the funds. Once I received the merchandise, I would change the beneficiary name to the seller's name. After I sent a few emails asking for more details and explanation of why they wanted to do it that way, I got the feeling that this was a setup. Regardless of the name on the wire, they would have found a way to extract that money, either with a phoney ID or by using someone on the inside. I should mention that unlike the US and Canada many countries can get almost anything done if the price is right.

Another person alerted me, advising me that his personal information had been compromised. They'd been using his email and contact information, posing as someone else in order to scam would-be shoppers.

This sort of thing happens all the time, but don't let this discourage you. Wire transfer is a tried and true method that's been around for years. Just try your best to do a background check with the company your dealing with. The best soluton is to have refrences, believe it or not other companies are willing to provide vital information on the ligitimacy of business' overseas.

Letter of Credit, called L/C for short. This is a somewhat complicated method which insures that you're getting what you pay for.

These are the basics of how it works.

The bank will open a letter of credit between you and your supplier and their bank. The letter will outline each and every item to be shipped, and specify when it should arrive. It will contain a stipulation that once the shipment arrives, it will need to pass inspection by you, by a third party company, or through a sample that was obtained prior to the LC setup. Once the goods pass inspection they will be released, as will the funds to your supplier.

This can get a bit messy, because the supplier will need to absorb the shipping costs up front, until he gets paid, and you have the option of refusing the merchandise.

There's a fine line between what the merchandise is and what it was supposed to be. Most suppliers need the business and will agree. They understand your position and don't want to scare off a potential client.

The cost of an LC can range from several hundred dollars and up. The reason for that cost is obvious. There's much more work involved.

Certified check is a widely accepted form of payment for local transactions, but is not commonly used for international trading.

What happens is that the bank takes the funds from your account (debits the account) and the funds are placed in a new separate account until the check is deposited from the supplier.

The fee is nominal, usually under $10 or so. Try to sweet-talk the teller. They may not even charge you.

Bank draft/money order is an easy and painless way to send money. The difference is the amount ordered. This method is preferred by most local suppliers, but is uncommon when dealing with overseas sources. The fees are minimal; anywhere from $4 to $8. Drafts are considered as good as cash, but you're still going to need courier services to get the funds to your supplier.

Traveler's checks are a great way to transfer funds when you're physically there. All banks offer them, in either Canadian or US funds. A signature is required twice, once when receiving them from the teller and again when redeeming them. They're a safe and secure way to conduct business, but remember that they're considered valuable on the black market as is, without the second signature.

The cost is approximately 1 to 1.5% of the value. When dealing with large amounts, that can become costly.

I recommend you discuss the different accounts available to you with your banker. Some accounts allow you the privilege of buying traveler's checks without any cost. These accounts usually have a modest monthly service fee.

Credit Cards are a safe and easy method. If you intend on spending more than your credit limit, simply make a payment over and above what you think you'll be spending on the card. This will instantly bump up the available credit amount. I do recommend using a bank transfer, otherwise a check may require several days to clear. An added bonus to using a credit card is it may intitle you to bonus points.

Cash is always king, but in the business world this simply is a term used when paying upfront or upon delivery. With any of the methods I've just described. I strongly advise you to stir clear away from any supplier asking for actual cash in a brief case. This is trouble waiting to happen.

These are just some of the different methods of payments when conducting business overseas. Most suppliers will tell you what forms of payment they accept, and what they prefer.

As with anything else in business, nothing is written in stone. If, for whatever reason, you don't feel comfortable or are having second thoughts, insist on whatever makes you feel more secure. As the buyer, you always have the power.

Should you ever come across a scam artist overseas, contact Interpol immediately. They're the international police, who deal with this sort of problem everyday. They're always grateful when someone gives them the information they need to shut down a scam operation or anything that tries to skirt the law or cheat any overseas buisness.

GREY MARKET IMPORTING

Although it sounds a bit shady, the definition of gray market importing is that you're bringing in a brand name product which you may not have the rights to sell.

That doesn't necessarily mean it's illegal. Get in touch with a copyright and infringement lawyer. They'll advise you on your legal rights.

If you're traveling and come across a great deal on a hot label, you may want to consider importing it on your own. The most important document you'll want to obtain is an invoice, which states that the vendor is a licensed or authorized dealer for the brand. Often, quantities are sold to jobbers. They literally buy by the pound—thousands of items are sold at one unit price, usually for pennies on the dollar.

The issue here is that most of these buys are supposed to be exported to a third world country or someplace where the regular market won't be affected by the sale of these goods.

The merchandise doesn't always go where it is intended. They make it appear as though the shipment has been exported, to its original destination but in fact has been re-routed to another location, sometimes the shipment never leaves the country where it was manufactured. This type of conduct usually is short lived as manufacturers will catch on fairly quickly as to where the merchandise is eventually sold.

The Problem..

If the exact same product is sold at half price at a discount store, how can the regularly priced merchandise stand a chance?

What supposedly happens next is that sales decline for the regular market. This creates a chain reaction, destroying the brand's image. This is the argument posed by the manufacturers. Since I come from the discount world, I tend to disagree. The fact that the goods are offered for sale doesn't mean that you can't get into legal issues with the brand name itself.

You may be asking yourself, "But how will I know?"

The larger and better-known the brand, the more likely you are to have a problem, but that shouldn't stop you from investigating a little further. As you will undoubtedly learn, not everyone you do business will be on the up and up.

Let's say you are away and a opportunity is too good to pass up, but you can't get in touch with a lawyer, so you go ahead and purchase the deal. Importing is the least of your worries as long as you're paying the proper duties and taxes. Custom agents can care less what's inside the boxes (unless they're knockoffs or counterfeits).

Now that you have the goods in your possession, use caution. If you purchase 2,000 *Tommy Hilfiger* T-shirts, I wouldn't recommend displaying them for all to see. The best advice I can give you is to contact your lawyer and do a search to find out if the brand has been registered. More than likely it will be.

Don't advertise. It will create unwanted attention. You may be asking yourself, "What's the big deal anyway? I bought these items legitimately, so what can they do?" Seek professional advise!

"You haven't been in business until you've been sued"

ANONYMOUS BILLIONAIRE

Counterfeit Merchandise

There is a huge difference between grey market and counterfeit goods—otherwise known as knockoffs.

The terms are used when a manufacturer copies a brand almost to the letter and tries to pass it off as an original garment at a very reduced price. Most of these products come from overseas, usually, but not limited to, Asia.

Clothing is not the only target. DVD's, video games, handbags, music CDs, and even medicine are among the most popular items found on the black market.

Should you decide to buy and sell such products, the legal ramifications could be more than costly. For starters, the owners of the brand have the legal right to come into your store with police officers and seize everything in sight. They may also decide to take legal action against you personally, stating that their business has suffered as a direct result of your store carrying fraudulent merchandise.

At this time, seek legal advice! Most of the time, the goal is simply to remove the merchandise from the store. Taking every storeowner to court would wind up costing more in legal fees.

At the end of the day, their lawyers have to prove that the merchandise was purchased by you knowing it was counterfeit, which is difficult if not an impossible task. But this is still no excuse.

When traveling or on the Internet, it's difficult to know exactly what you're buying. Therefore, the only true way around this risk is to purchase everything from an authorized source.

What To Do Next?

The reason you decide to import, hopefully, will be to either save money or to bring in an exclusive product. Whatever the reasons, importing will certainly enable you to grow at a rapid pace.

Now that you have an importing business, the next step is to distribute the product. The easiest way is to hire a wholesaler and hope for the best. However, were going to assume that you will take on wholesaling yourself. The next chapter will provide guidelines on how to effectively reach other stores across the entire country.

A word to the wise: Don't run before you can walk. Grow at a pace that is manageable.

Chapter Fifteen

THE WORLD ACCORDING TO WHOLESALE

" I would rather receive a 1% return on the efforts of one hundred men than a 100% return on my own efforts ."

J. Paul Getty – Billionaire

Wholesaling can be more profitable with less of a workload. The problem is getting there. It's more difficult to set up a distribution network than a simple retail outlet, the experience in the retail world will undoubtly have provided you with the fundamentals on how the business works.

In this section, you'll come across topics which I've discussed in the retail part of this book. That shouldn't stop you from reading it again with more attention! After all, even if you have no wholesale ambitions (at this point) it pays to know how wholesalers work—and the more you read this book the more it will inspire and add something new to your clothing venture.

In order to succeed in the wholesale game, you must develop a different outlook on your product. Typically, the markup will be dramatically reduced from that of retail. Generally, a 30% markup is the standard, unless you design, develop, and manufacture everything yourself.

I'm going to assume that you already have merchandise on hand, or soon to be on its way. It's now time for the selling. Hiring a sales rep or agency is by far the easiest route.

Sales Rep/Agency

When retailing, you may remember getting those pesky 9 AM calls from sales agents trying to sell everything you didn't need or want. Now it's time to capitalize on their pushiness.

A sales agent is usually someone who can talk your ear off, is always excited, and can sell ice to an Eskimo. If you don't find those qualities, I suggest moving on. An agent should represent the line in the best possible way. If they're not excited, no one else will be either.

Scouting A Rep

The easiest way would be to use someone whom you may have been in contact with in the past (through your retail business) and with whom you've developed some kind of rapport. If no such person is available, ask around. A good, solid reputation goes a long way in this business. If you're still out of luck, visit a local trade show. This will provide you with a ton of leads. Make sure you chose wisely. For example, if you're selling jean wear, don't chose a rep in the bathing suit department. The reason should be obvious! What kind of clientele can they have to service your needs? You want to choose wisely. Here are some questions to ask:

- **What does your client base consist of?** More specifically, what type of product do they carry, and will it coexist with your line?
- **What price points do you carry?** There's no sense wasting time trying to sell a $200 product when your agent has been selling $20 items. He or she will not properly facilitate the line. More specifically their customers will not be in the market for such high priced merchandise.
- **How many years have you been with the same lines?** Although it may seem harsh, the truth of the matter is that reps are like gypsies. They'll move from one hot line to the next, leaving you high and dry. Don't take it

personally. There's not much you can do. If you find that the rep in question has changed lines twenty times in the past two years, you may want to reconsider.

- **How many other lines do they carry?** It's definitely impressive to find a showroom full of different product. However, I find that your line can get lost in the shuffle. If the rep is not willing to push your line, then you may as well forget it. Often, new, aggressive reps are exactly what it takes. If they're working with one or two lines, they're more likely putting their focus on your label.

- **Do they work the trade shows?** Depending on your vision, it may be very important to have your label out there at trade shows for the whole world to see. The more exposure the better. Some agents don't set up at shows any longer. The reasons are many. They may feel they have a large client base and don't require new accounts wasting their time. Or, quite simply, they don't want to spend their money on the cost of the show.

- **How large is their client base?** It's a question of quality, not quantity. If an agent has over 300 accounts on their roster, I can guarantee you that more than half are duds, meaning that they're poor payers. I would rather have sixty to eighty good-paying accounts as opposed to 300 slow or non-paying accounts.

- **Where is their office located?** If they're in a distant and remote area, it may be difficult for clients to visit. Unless they pick up a sample bag and hit the road, they aren't doing the job you want and need.

These are just some of the questions you want to ask prior to hiring anyone. Why stop there? If you have other concerns, don't be afraid to ask.

If you're still finding it difficult, you may want to place a classified ad in any of the trade magazines. You'd be surprised at the response. The ad should read something like this:

Seeking Rep/Agent for exciting new denim line from LA. All territories available. Contact (your name) at (insert email and phone number) or Fax resume to (fax number)

In Canada, some agents belong to CAWS, the Canadian Association of Wholesale Sales Representatives. For more information visit their website at www.caws.ca

They offer a service that will send a message to all of their members outlining your need for an agency. The cost is somewhat pricey. It's about $500, but when you stop and think how direct and effective it could be, I think it's well worth it.

YOU'RE HIRED

Now that you've made your mind up on a rep, it's wise to cover all the legal grounds. Most agencies have their own contracts set up, outlining territories, commissions, and durations.

Should you be distributing a well-known label, I recommend having your own contract set up by a lawyer. This will protect you in the event that the agency produces poor results. The standard commissions paid to agencies are 10%. This will include their expenses. Keep in mind that commissions must be paid for all orders written up within a certain timeframe, even though the customer is behind on payment. It will be your job to screen buyers (more on this later).

Depending on the size of the agency, the territory will most likely cover an entire city. Some reps handle more than they can chew, wanting an entire city but only servicing a sector or small pocket.

Familiarize yourself with the agency's roster. That will provide a clearer picture of where they've been.

I hired a rep who signed up for the entire city, but only worked the northern region. My product wasn't in the core of the city, where it would have had the most exposure.

Always leave yourself a loophole in a contract giving you the freedom to change agencies at will.

You may have noticed that I have been using both the words rep and agency. The Rep is housed under an agency, both do the exact same thing and most times are one in the same. Whatever the term is shouldn't concern you as long as you don't exceed the 10% fees.

OFFER INCENTIVES

Just like an employee, the more money someone stands to make, the harder they'll try. Have a system set up where when the rep reaches a target amount in sales, he or she gets a bonus of some kind. An example would be to pay an additional 3-4 % on all sales exceeding the projected amount. A scale system also works well. The following should give you an idea on what I mean.

Sales Amount	Commission
$0.00 - $10 000	10%
$10 001 - $30 000	15%
$30 001 - $50 000	18%
$50 001 - $100 000	22%

The amount of commission you can offer will vary based on how much room you have to play with.

GO NATIONAL IN A WEEK!

Depending on the size of your bank account, you may want to launch your line nationally, within a week. It's easier than you think. In the same way you found your current rep, do the same for the rest of the country. A new set of samples for each agency will be required to ship out.

The orders may begin to flow in, but you need to be able to back those orders financially, and be prepared to handle more as your business grows. The "more" is due to the fact that the business will need to carry on as usual, even though there may be monies outstanding (Accounts receivable).

It's even more important that you acquire proper management skills before you take on the wholesale world.

If you're inexperienced, that may result in poor customer service. Mistakes on orders, invoicing blunders, and delayed shipping all affect the end result. In today's fast-paced world, business owners have little or no patience with or mercy for your inexperience. I recommend starting with one agency and based on that success seek others.

PREPARATION MEETS OPPORTUNITY

THE NEXT STEPS

Now that agencies are in place, organize yourself with the proper tools to assure quality distribution. I've chosen a few documents which you may want to use. By all means modify them to suit your needs.

THE ORDER FORM

Print your own purchase order forms. They'll serve as a guideline that your agencies must adhere to. There's no need to print and send out thousands of copies, as merchandise may change, and so will the agency.

A must on the PO (purchase order) form are the following:

Date. There should be a date the order was signed, as well as a delivery date requested by the buyer. Not all companies want their order shipped the next day.

Method of shipping. Unless specified by the purchaser, use the same company each time. The more volume you do with a courier the more benefits it may have.

Sold to. That's the legal company name and complete address, so you know where to send an invoice.

Ship to. Many companies have an office or more than one location, so it's wise to have a section for a separate shipping address.

Terms. This way there is no miscommunication on what was decided.

Agency. This will come in handy when accounting comes into play. Assuming you have different agencies set up in varies areas, this section allows you easy verification as to who sold what.

Authorized signature. This verifies that an order has been made. This is so important because orders are often signed months before shipping takes place. You'd be amazed how many customers will forget their orders, or change their minds, for that matter. Once they sign the order, it becomes a legally binding contract—but try to collect.

The description and **size scale** will vary, depending on what you're selling. Some larger companies may have their own forms, which you must adhere to. Be sure to read each company's form thoroughly, as they may have special instructions set aside for all shipments destined to their stores. Failure to comply may result in the order being rejected and sent back to you, which means no sale. Once the damage has been done, chances are slim to none that they will give you a second chance.

Cancellation dates are among the most important items on a PO. If the order doesn't arrive by a specified date, the company has the right to refuse the shipment. If, for whatever reason, it's within a few days, always call the buyer ahead of time and ask for an extension. More often than not, they'll accommodate you, but make sure it's in writing. Circumstances will always arise, and most businesses understand this, but try your best not to make it a habit.

SAMPLE PURCHASE ORDER FORM 1

COMPANY NAME
Address 1
Address 2
Telephone • Fax

PURCHASE ORDER

DATE: _____

SOLD TO: _____

SHIP TO: _____

DATE SHIPPED	SHIPPED VIA	TERMS	AGENT							
MODEL/ARTICLE	DESCRIPTION	26 XS	27 S	28 M	29 L	30 XL	31 XXL	32	33	34	36	38	QTY.	UNIT PRICE	TOTAL

SUB-TOTAL $
TAX $
TOTAL $

IMPORTANT
No return of merchandise will be accepted without authorization. Every claim must be made within 5 days following the receipt of merchandise.

AUTHORIZED BY

SAMPLE PURCHASE ORDER 2

CREDIT

Unfortunately we live on credit. This pains me. We as suppliers must pay for everything we manufacture or wholesale and have to give our merchandise to complete strangers for up to ninety days without seeing a dime.

Sounds unfair, right?

Well, we can't change the industry standard. However, we can protect ourselves.

The first document for all businesses seeking credit should be a **credit application**. This will provide the necessary information to do a background check. Have them include as much information as possible. Later, I'll discuss using a factor company to take on the financing for you. For now, we will assume that all the screening will take place in-house.

The following is a sample credit application. Feel free to modify.

SAMPLE CREDIT APPLICATION
COMPANY NAME
ADDRESS 1
ADDRESS 2
TELEPHONE • FAX

Credit Application

Company Name:_____ Date:_____

Mailing Address:_____ City:_____

Province:_____ Country:_____ Postal code:_____

Telephone Number:_____ Fax Number:_____

Date Business Started:_____ E-Mail Address:_____

Bank:_____ Address:_____

Telephone Number:_____ Contact:_____ Fax Number:_____

Provincial Tax Lic. #_____

CURRENT TRADE REFERENCES   (Please list Four (4) and include addresses and telephone numbers)

1) Firm:_____

(   )_____

2) Firm:_____

(   )_____

3) Firm:_____

(   )_____

4) Firm:_____

(   )_____

Appl. Submitted By:_____ Title:_____

Don't Stop There

Now that you've armed yourself with this information, it's time to put it to use. I recommend sending a **reference letter** to all those trade references by fax, email, or regular mail. Don't be shy. This is common practice in the wholesale game.

SAMPLE REFERENCE LETTER

COMPANY NAME
Address 1
Address 2
Telephone • Fax

Date: _____ /20

RE:

Attention Manager:

Your name has been submitted as a trade reference by the above. We would appreciate the benefit of your experience with this account.

Sold Since : _____

Terms : _____

Amount Owing : _____

Amount past due : _____ 1-30 _____ 31-60 _____ 61-90 _____ 90+

Average payment record : _____ 30 _____ 60 _____ 90 _____ 90-120

PDC'S Requested   Yes   No

NSF Cheques ?   Yes   No

Comments : _____

Any information provided will be treated in strict confidence. (For credit purposes only) If we can reciprocate in a similar capacity, please contact us.

Sincerely

If you just can't wait, I advise you to call directly for faster results, but this practice is not recommended. You may be perceived as interrupting, or may bothersome, for that matter. However, this will provide vital insight as to the buying habits of the account in question.

CREDIT THROUGH A FACTOR COMPANY

As I've mentioned time and time again, this business is built on credit, so to effectively capitalize on the system we must use every possible resource in order to eliminate would-be deadbeats.

There are companies who offer a service known as **factoring**. This is a fancy term for credit or finance. Here's how it works. The factor (finance) company will insure all your orders, but there are strict criteria that must be followed in order for this to happen.

Each and every client-seeking credit must fill out an application, which will be sent back for processing, along with the order. This won't take more than twenty-four hours.

At this time the factor company will advise you whether they deem the company worthy of credit. They reach their decisions based on the previous track record of the buyer. Spending habits, timely payments, and what's outstanding all play a part in the approval process. Often, what happens is that the buyer will qualify only for a portion of the total order, which means that the finance company will insure only up to a certain limit. The rest is up to you.

The cost for this privilege is approximately 1.5% of your total sales (rates can vary from company to company). The truth of the matter is that unless you have sales well into the millions, it may not be worth the expense. I recommend financing yourself as much as possible. Do as much homework on buyers as possible. Use credit reporting companies like *Equifax, Experian,* and *TransUnion* to provide you with enough information to make the right decision.

Most factoring companies use *Equifax* and base their information on the *Equifax* report to make their decisions.

There's always risk involved, however. If one or two accounts burn you at the end of the year, chalk it up as a loss. I'm almost positive that the price of a factor company will far exceed that of a couple of bad accounts.

The key ingredient here is to have sellable merchandise. The reason is that when your customers sell their first order, they'll come back for more.

If you're selling nothing but duds, then it will be more than difficult to get repeat business.

Don't let greed get in the way. If you have a large order from some company who just doesn't have the right credentials I would give it some serious thought before shipping anything.

TRY NOT TO BURY YOURSELF

I have a friend in the furniture manufacturing business who supplies, among many others, *Wal-Mart*. He can't believe the volume they go through. He has enough business solely through *Wal-Mart* to sell to them exclusively and keep the same level of sales he's been doing supplying hundreds of smaller companies.

I asked him why he didn't sell to *Wal-Mart* exclusively. It's guaranteed sales and less headaches.

He replied that this was true, but *Wal-Mart* could decide to change suppliers at any time, and then where would he be?

All those little accounts who've been keeping my friend alive for the past twenty years would be gone. My friend would have to start all over again.

The moral of this story is simple. What seems to be a good idea might become a bad idea rather quickly. Assess each and every move carefully.

GOVERNMENT DOCUMENTS

In Ontario (Canada), all businesses buying merchandise for retail sale must fill out a sales tax-exempt form. This will save them from paying tax to you, the wholesaler. .

Businesses must fill it out one time only. Once it's on file, it will serve as a blanket for all future buys. Often, this becomes a non-issue for most, overlooking the fact that it is required by law that it must be properly filled out. Under normal circumstances you may never have a problem, but in the event of an tax audit the government may request proof that all these businesses have indeed filled out the forms. Failure to produce the required forms may result in your company having to cough up all that tax money.

Whichever city you do business in, I'm almost positive there will be a similar form to have buyers fill out. Check with your local tax office for the proper information. Any accountant or bookkeeper will point you in the right direction. The easiest way would be to have your agency attach a signed copy with all the orders sent.

The following is a tax exempt form. Most tax offices should have a the newest downloadable version online.

```
                    ONTARIO RETAIL SALES TAX
                  PURCHASE EXEMPTION CERTIFICATE

                            Blanket  ☐

    Date: _____

    Business Name: _____

    Name of Person Authorizing the Purchase: _____

    Business Address: _____
                     _____

    Vendor Permit / IRP Cab Number (if applicable): _____

    Reason for Claiming Exemption: _____

    I am claiming the following exemption from Ontario retail sales tax under the provisions of the *Retail Sales
    Tax Act* on the purchase of taxable goods, taxable services, contracts of insurance or benefits plan:

    ○  Taxable Goods or Taxable Services Purchased for Resale

    ○  Machinery, Equipment, and/or Processing Material Purchased for Manufacturing

    ○  Equipment, Tools, and/or Machinery used by a Person Engaged in Farming or Fishing

    ○  Insurance/Benefit Plan

    ○  Religious, Charitable and Benevolent Organization

    ○  Hospital Equipment

    ○  Identity Card Type and Number_____

    ○  Other (please state exemption) _____

                              IMPORTANT

    The person buying the taxable goods or taxable services, or entering into a contract of insurance or benefits
    plan for which an exemption is claimed must complete this certificate and give it to the supplier. The supplier
    is to keep this form as stated in the regulations.

    Every person who makes a false statement on a Purchase Exemption Certificate or misuses the certificate
    is liable, if convicted, to a fine of not less than $1,000 and an amount of not more than double the amount of
    the tax that should have been paid, or that was evaded, or to imprisonment for a term of not more than two
    years, or both.
```

SHIPPING AND SUPPLIES

Hopefully, the packages will begin flowing out of your shipping doors. When this happens, it's wise to set up an account with a courier company. Shop around for the best prices, and, most of all, for the best service.

I recommend using the big boys, like *UPS* (www.ups.com) or *Canpar* (www.canpar.ca) most of the time. They offer exceptional service—except when things go wrong. .

Items can be tracked with a phone call or a click of the mouse. Most shipping companies offer online service for everything from printing labels to tracking packages. All the necessary supplies will be delivered to you free of charge. It may seem a bit overwhelming at first, but over time it will become child's play.

It's important to note that your clients will pay the shipping costs. No one escapes this, not even the larger companies. Try to have a price quote prior to shipping, so you can include this on your invoice with the package. Otherwise pass along the shipping cost once you have an accurate cost.

Be advised that packages will be picked up and delivered as usual until something goes wrong. I had a shipment go out in the rain, but when it arrived the buyer refused the shipment—with just cause. The boxes had been split open and the contents had severe water damage.

They were returned to me in different packaging, and sat in a warehouse until I resolved the issue with head office. I was furious. Not only did I lose a very large sale, but I also was without merchandise and received no compensation.

I tried to put in a claim. They had a supervisor contact me and took me through proper procedure which was detailed in fine print on the back of my bill of lading. It stated that all parcels must be of a certain thickness and must be properly wrapped with a certain lining etc., etc., etc.

I asked why wasn't I informed of this. I'd been using this company for more than two years. If the packages weren't up to code, they should have informed me of it sooner.

This was a rare situation. I don't want to discourage you, but it's always best to know what could happen. The last thing anyone wants is a surprise. Always buy insurance and bill the customer for it.

Shipping Supplies

The following is a list of items needed for shipping your merchandise.

Cardboard boxes are the standard for shipping clothing in large quantities. You'll need to find a good supplier. Places such as *Staples* may be okay for an order or two, but when volume orders are involved I recommend finding a manufacturer or distributor of boxes. They'll provide many shapes and sizes to suit your needs. They may also deliver. In the end, this will save you time and money. For more information visit these websites:

www.uline.ca

www.cartonneriemontreal.com

www.provincialpaper.com

Tape and a **tape gun** go a long way. This is perhaps the easiest way to seal the boxes once they are packed. Buy in bulk. Keep in mind that boxes will be tossed and turned, and stacked up in trucks and on planes, so it's vital that each shipment is properly sealed in order to assure it reaches its destination in the same condition as it was sent. Otherwise, the order can be rejected and sent back to you, costing you time and possibly a cancellation.

Labels are required on each box, just like an envelope's to and from addresses. In the early stages, simply print labels from any computer. There's no need to spend money on useless customized labels. In the end, they'll be discarded the moment they arrive.

Packing slips are placed inside or affixed on the outside of each and every box. They should outline what's inside. Be specific about quantity, size, colors, models, etc. This is to assure that when the merchandise is received, it can be properly allocated.

```
                           PACKING SLIP

                    FROM:  COMPANY NAME
                           ADDRESS
                           TELEPHONE • FAX

                    TO:    COMPANY NAME
                           ADDRESS
                           TELEPHONE • FAX


    DEPT.#: _____ ORDER # _____


    VENDOR/
    STYLE #: _____ QUANTITY: _____


    CARTON #: _____ OF _____ TOTAL NO. OF CARTONS
```

Miscellaneous items are not to be overlooked. This will vary, depending on your applications. Have plenty of stationary supplies, such as pens, markers, staple gun, scissors, and so on. They'll come in handy.

BACK ORDERS

This is a wholesalers dream—or is it? When you're selling merchandise, you'll get orders for items which are no longer available or are out of stock.

Now comes the question: Do we produce or import more goods, or do we simply tell our customer that we're out of stock?

The answer should become clear to you based on your customer's reactions.

If, after all shipments have all been delivered, within a week several stores call to place orders for more, you know you have a winner on your hands. At this point, find out how much time it will take for re-ordering.

Pass this information along to your customer. If they're willing to wait, and there's enough commitment, go ahead and place the order.

Other factors come into play. If the reorders are late in the season, customers may have a change of heart once the reorders arrive.

Timing is everything!

Most wholesalers carry some overstock for immediate delivery. The amount will vary. If you're a newcomer, I don't recommend stocking up. Once you've established yourself, it will become easier to know your buyer's spending habits and merchandise selection.

SUBSTITUTIONS

When an item is out of stock, suppliers often double up on what was ordered, or ship whatever they have on hand, to make up the total order. Sometimes you'll get away with this, more often you won't. I don't advise making this a practice for your business It will irritate clients, end up costing you money on shipping, and perhaps result in loss of future orders. This practice is second nature for overseas suppliers. They send whatever they have on hand, changing an order at will. After all, what are you really going to do once it has arrived, from thousands of miles away?

Of course they will ask you to send it back, but this is more of an hassle than anything else. Don't stand for this BS either. Have them credit you or send the merchandise back.

Why should you be stuck with merchandise you didn't order?

It pays to be personable. Let's say you're down to five units in broken sizes of one particular model when an order comes in. Why not make a call and let the customer know there are only five units left, which are available for a discounted price. What do you have to lose? I guarantee you making this a habit will move thousands of dollars of unwanted inventory every year.

Returns

On most of the purchase orders or invoices, there usually will be fine print outlining the return policy. For example, all claims must be made within five days of receipt of merchandise.

This may appear to be straightforward, but don't expect any of your accounts to take it too seriously. As a wholesaler, it's vital that any and all flawed items be accepted within a reasonable timeframe. Five days hardly constitutes as a reasonable time.

When an account calls for a return, you'll have to issue an **RA Number** (return authorization). They'll attach this number to the garment being sent back. I recommend using the customer's original invoice number, or creating a profile that will keep track of the returns in an easy format. At this point a credit must be issued for the return.

Whenever possible, try to replace the returned item with the same or a similar item. This will make it easier on the accounting, as well as in counting your inventory at the end of the season.

End Of The Season

It would be a dream to have zero inventory at the end of a season. Alas, this is but a dream.

There are a number of ways to clear end-of-season goods. For starters, offer the merchandise to your customers at 30 to 50% below the normal cost. The name of the game is to clear your stock and make room for next season's merchandise, not to make a profit. Make certain that you don't offer the goods too early in the season, as customers will come to expect this and hold off on ordering or reordering during the regular season.

Next, have a sample sale in your own office. Send personal invitations to friends, family, and neighboring businesses. You'll be amazed by the results.

Post some flyers and have some kid go door to door in the area. Sell the merchandise at wholesale prices.

Now that you're the bottom of the barrel, gather whatever's left and kiss it goodbye. Call up a jobber or discounter to purchase the rest at pennies on the dollar. It will no doubt break your heart.

Do not get emotional!

You don't want old inventory on hand! Use whatever money is generated to start fresh and buy new merchandise. Watch out for discounters who will use this opportunity to advertise your line, making the rest of your clients unhappy. I personally don't believe this is a bad idea, as it will create more exposure. If this should be of grave concern, I recommend selling to a larger company that's willing to not promote. They may go so far as to put it in specific stores far away from all your accounts, should you request this. The advantage here is that the remote location will not affect the regular accounts located in the city.

Another alternative is the cut the label name out of the garments. However, this will deter many from buying.

The beauty of these types of sales is that they are all COD.

Take the money and run.

Chapter Sixteen

CREATIVE FINANCING

In this chapter I will provide you with some strategic ways to raise and/or aquire funds to help your business grow.

If you can't beat them, join them. Take advantage of the wonderful world of credit. OPM (other people's money) is the basis of how most entrepreneurs operate these days, and why not?

There's no need to risk your own hard-earned money.

The traditional route is making a visit to the local bank or credit institution. Try to obtain a **revolving line of credit**. Think of it like a credit card without the piece of plastic card. This will enable you dip into it whenever it is required. This doesn't mean it's time to take a vacation. Misuse of credit can dig you a hole that you won't be able to climb out of.

The number one item on the bank's list is your financial statements for the past two or three years. The better the statements look, the more funds will be available to you.

If at all possible, try to obtain an unsecured credit line, which will not tie you up personally. Try to let the strength of the business stand on its own two feet.

Sadly, this is often extremely difficult. The banks have been burned one too many times in the past, so their caution is understandable.

The other option is to apply for a loan, either as a term loan or as a business improvement loan. Again, the banks will follow certain criteria. They'll look for, and ask you for, specifics.

I've been dealing with bankers (loan officers) for many years and have drawn one conclusion: They're all afraid of losing their jobs. That's why they shy away from lending whenever possible. It's true that loan officers are paid a commission based on how many loans they give out, but first they're expected to make sure that all the bases are covered. They won't last very long if borrowers begin to default on making payments.

That's why most business owners seeking funds hire a reputable accountant to formulate a business plan which adheres to the bank's requirements. That makes it easy for the loan officer to loosen his tie (and the bank's purse strings).

BUSINESS PLAN CONTENTS

The following is an outline of what should be included in a standard business plan. Try to provide as much information as possible. Include all relevant info.

PURPOSE

What's the reason for this plan? To provide start up funds, or to expand an existing business.? Be specific about how the funds will be used to expand or create your business.

FINANCING REQUIREMENTS

You should have a dollar amount in mind. If you approach any financial institution and say, "I want whatever you can give me," won't boil over well, as it will appear that not much planning has been done.

BUSINESS DESCRIPTION

In this section, include a company profile. Try to provide as much information as you can, for example, the year the company was established, the number of employees, costs and revenues, etc. Provide full background information on your existing business, like the size of your location and where it's situated.

The nature of the business seems obvious to you, but there may be a number of different readers of this plan at any given time, so it's important to write the description in a manner which will be comprehendible to everyone who sees it. They all have to understand what you're planning to do with their bank's money.

Include major suppliers, those you do business with on a day-to-day basis. How long have you been doing business with each supplier? The banks want to know that you've built up good relationships with other businesses, and that they've been in place long enough to be reliable.

MARKET DESCRIPTION

What's the market and geographic area served? Include the age bracket of your customers, and the area which you serve. If your business is located in New York, that doesn't mean you serve the entire New York City area. It's appropriate to narrow your service area down to a specific area.

Provide some insight about who your customers are, current as well as potential. Don't be afraid to jazz it up a little. Remember that the bank wants to feel comfortable lending you money. It's your job to assure this by providing as much valuable info as possible.

Provide some industry profile. The bank isn't in your line of work. They've never heard terms like double knit cotton or left hand weave washes. Try to provide stats on your market share.

Market trends. Include the changes you intend to make to keep up with the fast paced and ever-changing world of fashion. If you have an established business and are looking for expansion funding, you can tell the bank what you've done in the past to keep up with trends, and why that enabled you to make a profit.

The competition must never be overlooked. If you intend to open a denim shop in a mall where there will be another fifteen stores selling similar product, it would be wise to learn all you can about your competitors—before you even think about opening a store in that mall, much less approach a bank for a loan. Learn what product lines they carry and what their price points are.

More important, be able to demonstrate to the bank why you'll have a competitive advantage.

Describe your selling and advertising strategies. Include everything from how many flyers will be distributed to local residents and schools, to how you'll bring in an expert to train the staff on how to produce the best results in the retail environment. (Who knows, some banker might actually be impressed!)

Last, describe clearly what will set you apart from your competition, that is, why you'll succeed in spite of (or perhaps because of) what your competition is (or is not) doing.

What are the key success factors for your business? This is a broad question, so take the time to include whatever you think will make the difference.

Is it your expertise in the field?

Your prices?

Your product?

Your location?

Or maybe the big-boobed (okay, attractive and personable) staff you hired for sales?

Whatever it is, write it down

MANAGEMENT/OWNERSHIP DESCRIPTION

Include your experience in the field as well as your managerial experience.

This is one of the most important sections of this proposal. The reason is that one of the three most common reasons businesses fail is lack of managerial skills.

This does not rule you out if you went from working at a construction site to opening a clothing store, but it may persuade you to invest in hiring suitable and competent staff who have the expertise you didn't get in the construction business (or any other field). If so, include this in your plan.

When a fancy new restaurant opens, part of the success is how well-known the chef is. If he or she has reasonable notoriety in the community, it will undoubtedly increase the restaurant's chances for success. Likewise, if you hire a known expert to either run your store or train you and your staff, that looks good to the bank.

DESCRIBE WHY YOU'RE COMPETENT

Your competence may come from attending fashion design school, or because you've been working in the field for a number of years. Perhaps you're simply an entrepreneur. CEOs shift from one company to the next, from businesses that have nothing to do with each other. The reason is that the fundamentals of business are the same, no matter what the business may be. If you have proven management skills and experience, once you're put in any business environment, you'll learn how to adapt and excel.

REFERENCES

Include any and all people and companies with whom you've established a good relationship. Please note, however, that when using anyone as a reference, I advise you to call them first, advising them that you plan to use them, so they're prepared for the inquiry.

FINANCIAL DOCUMENTATION

Provide as much information as possible about your financials, past and present. It would be wise to include a forecast, or an updated financial statement (prepared by an accountant). It would be ideal to have it show that it can facilitate the loan in question.

ALSO INCLUDE:

Include any and all assets of partners and/or shareholders. This will give the bank an indication of your stability. Try to provide personal income statements.

The lease or offer to lease is a definite requirement if you need funds for any purpose. The bank will want to know that the lease doesn't expire in a year or so. A good rule of thumb is to have a five to ten-year lease, at the very least. Most of the larger leasing or management corporations will want you to sign personal indemnifiers, but try to avoid this at all costs. It's like signing your life away. As I've said, this is business we are conducting, so it's beyond comprehension why anyone would sign personally for more than a year. Anything can happen, from illness to the selling of your company.

The following is a common chart outlining expenses for any company. Adjust the items listed according to your needs. The banks will want some idea as to what and how much your disbursements will be.

NOTE: Do not show the same figures for each month, because that will appear to be (and is) unrealistic. Certain months require more expenses, for example more inventory and advertising in December (the holiday season).

Try to be as honest and true as possible.

CASH DISBURSEMENTS	Jan	Feb	Mar	Apr	May	Jun	Jul	Aug	Sep	Oct	Nov	Dec	Total
Purchases													
Accounting													
Legal Services													
Marketing													
Travel/Lodging													
Vehicle													
Salaries													
Rent													
Insurance													
Bank Charges													
Loan Payments													
Maintenance													
Loan Interest													
Telephone													
Office													
Courier													
Utilities													
Miscellaneous													
CASH SURPLUS													
CASH SALES													

USE YOUR OWN SUPPLIERS

Why not try to have your own supplier work with you? After all, it's their product you're selling.

Your supplier may be hesitant to give out any kind of credit, as they may have a large investment, which is already tied up in inventory.

One wrong move can be very costly especially for someone the size of a supplier. Still, once a relationship has been established it should be easier to set up some sort of arrangement in which the supplier can provide you with, at the very least, 30, 60, or 90 days of credit on the merchandise they ship to you. This is industry standard.

Sadly, if your contacts are overseas, it will more than likely be impossible to receive financial aid from them.

Often, a supplier is set up to move large quantities of stock, so one idea would be to jump on the clearance bandwagon. Ask whether they will allow you to sell any remaining inventory to the same jobber, or whether they can include your inventory with theirs and possibly get a credit for a future sale.

If you're dealing with a new and hungry supplier, they may be a lot more flexible in their response to your needs.

Once credit is established, it's important to remember the golden rule, which is "pay when you get paid." That sounds easy enough, but in business everyone overlooks the fact that they're running a business, not a personal relationship. If you're swamped with accounts receivable, it causes a chain reaction. Until you clear up your outstanding invoices, you pass the wait on to who ever is owed money. This may seem a little unfair, but life in the business world is definitely unfair.

It's a chain reaction. If the product you're selling is worth selling, your customer will need it to survive. However, use your judgement. Every wholesaler in the business will get burned for X amount of dollars a year, so take that into consideration when deciding how long the wait period will be. The last thing you want is for every supplier to blackball you within the industry. If that happens, you may not be able to continue.

The key is to always keep the lines of communication open. Don't avoid calls or letters. Simply explain the situation, and try to reach an understanding. After all, we're all in business and understand that this sort of stuff happens.

FRIENDS AND FAMILY

Everyone may get a chuckle at this one, since most family and friends are believed to be the last to be of any assistance. I've found this to be a myth. Most people only dream of having their own business, so when they see a friend or family member make a go of it, this usually ignites some type of fire. Most will interpret this as envy, but it's more of an opportunity for you, the businessman, to capitalize on their eagerness to become a part of something they're unable to do themselves.

You have now become his or her window for that extra buck everyone is yearning for. Try to be as professional as possible, and prepare a proper presentation.

Remember that to your rich uncle you're not little junior any more. You're a respectable business person and need to be perceived a such.

Provide whatever proof is necessary to put your investors at ease. Bank statements, tax returns, invoices, and perhaps a walk through your operation. Whatever reassurances they need to part with their hard-earned money.

It's important to note that you should never have any intention to scam or bilk any friend or family member out of even one dollar.

As you'll soon learn, most people are willing to part with money on the promise of a good return. However, they'll become your mortal enemy should there be any wrongdoing. All agreements should be outlined and explained thoroughly, and perhaps also explained in writing.

The last thing we want is Uncle Frank thinking he can come by and hang out in the store for eight hours a day, trying to hit on the staff and disrupting business.

I recommend keeping everyone at bay, in order to avoid any urge to be part of the day-to-day operations. Make this clear from the beginning. Their capital should only entitle them to a return on their investment, not a voice in the company's procedures and operations. You're the expert they trusted, so it's only fitting—and smart, for them.

Have some sort of schedule for the repayment of their investment, and provide a periodic report about how the progress is coming. A month-to-month statement may become costly, but your accountant should prepare a quarterly review of the business operations, which you can use to keep your investors informed. Your accountant should know how to put that information into the proper form for a report to investors.

OCCASIONAL USE

To make life somewhat easier, you can use investors only on a need-to-invest basis. For example, you may encounter a time when your operating funds are diminished, for any of many possible reasons, but you have an incredible opportunity to purchase a deal on a fantastic designer, which will guarantee that you can turn a nice profit. Use the investor's funds solely for the deal. Explain that their investment will be used solely for the purchase of that specific merchandise and nothing else. Their funds won't be used to pay overdue bills, renovations, or other risky expenses. As the merchandise sells, investment is returned.

This works exceptionally well with investors who don't want to tie up their money for a long period of time.

HOME EQUITY MORTGAGE

At the time of this writing, mortgage interest rates have never been lower. You can get a fixed-rate mortgage for less than 3 % interest.

There's no better place to save on borrowing funds than your own home. A $100,000 mortgage will cost approximately $500 a month. That's only $6,000 a year.

Just imagine how much profit can be generated by investing $100,000 in clothing in one year! A popular form of this type of investment is called a homeowner's equity line of credit. This allows you the benefit of being able to repay at any time, and pay interest only. Another advantage is that it's just that—a line of credit. You draw on the money as you need it, and pay only for the amount you've used, not the total amount available.

A disadvantage of using your personal funds, especially using your own home as collateral, is that if things go wrong it can get you divorced faster than commiting adultery. It's extremely important to make certain that the investment will, at the very least, pay back the principal borrowed.

I once borrowed $90,000 on my home to buy what I thought was a deal of a lifetime. Unfortunately, the contact was somewhat dishonest and the merchandise was far from what I expected. To make an aggravating long story short, I ended up taking a very long time to sell off the less than desirable stock. It cost me several thousand dollars in interest payments.

Looking at the bright side, it made me become a more conservative buyer. Only if the deal is truly a once in a lifetime deal would I put my house on the line again.

This type of financing should only be used if A, the equity is there to borrow from, and B, if all other borrowing will end up costing you more.

CONSIGNMENT

Over the years, you will establish relationships with others in the apparel trade, like your suppliers and other retailers.

Whenever possible, try to stock your store with their goods on a consignment basis. This means that you'll stock their inventory and pay (perhaps monthly) for only what you sell. This is easier said than done. There needs to be a trust factor, as well as a need for the supplier or other retailer to part with their merchandise.

The reasons why they'll sell on consignment is that they have an overstock, need to generate extra cash, and clear whatever is overflowing their warehouse. Another reason may be to make more than they normally would. The price will generally be higher than if you were to buy it outright.

However, if the merchandise sits on your shelves for months with no movement, the owner may decide to take it back. A supplier may be reluctant to provide you with prepacked items, as they will be broken once you begin selling. In my experience, suppliers don't want broken sizes returned to them. Such merchandise will be much harder to sell.

Consignment is the basis for how giant chains like *Home Depot* operate. Their shelves are stocked with merchandise provided by manufacturers and suppliers. When merchandise sells, they pay the supplier. The more the items sell, the more shelf space they will allocate for their product. The less it sells, the more likely the supplier will be tossed out like yesterdays newspaper.

It's interesting to note that the suppliers must offer a no-hassle return policy. If, for whatever the reason, a customer returns an item, the supplier or manufacturer must take it back, no questions asked.

That doesn't sound fair, but when you consider the amount of sales a giant chain can provide, it's worth the risk.

Consignment is viewed slightly differently than sale terms in the eyes of the law, in that the merchandise is always under the ownership of the consignor (the supplier). If you (the consignee), decide to close shop and make a run with the merchandise, you will more than likely have police officers show up at your door charging you with theft. It's the same as stealing.

I would love to open a store with nothing but consignment goods. What risk do I have? How can I lose? I can have nothing but fresh and current goods all year long!

I have heard of some European franchises offering fully consigned inventory to their partners. I have no doubt that if the formula works, it will spread like wild fire.

PERSONAL CREDIT CARDS

I realize that most of you are thinking that credit cards charge the highest interest fees. While this may be true with most cards, there are a number of financial institutions offering credit cards at very competitive rates (under 10%). There are a number of reasons for this. First, the market has become very competitive, so the banks will do practically anything to get you to use their card. The other reason is that the credit card companies make a percentage from the retailer where the card is used for purchases.

Make sure that the rate of the card is a permenant one. Often times credit card companies offer an introductory rate that is only valid for six months. After that time elapases the rate jacks up to regualr rates of over 15%.

The important thing to remember is to pay back the amount used as soon as possible and never make only the minimum payment! Paying the minimum, if you buy nothing else, will take years to pay off the balance! This is by no means the best solution for financing!

I learned, first hand, the devastating effects of misuse of credit cards. But, if used responsibly, they can provide your business with a great source of available funds.

Don't stop here; get creative! These are only a few examples of how to raise funds for your business. Hopefully, your business will flourish and you won't have a need for financial assistance. Until that day comes, it will be wise to invest some time and thought in determining the best way to handle your company's finances.

AT THE END OF THE DAY

We have now reached the end of the book. I hope you had as much fun reading it as I had writing it. You are now armed with enough information to set up your new apparel venture.

CONGRATULATIONS!!!!

The next important step to your success is actually getting up off your ass and doing it.

You don't need to watch another one of those Anthony Robbins commercials to remind you. Start small and confident, and I assure you that your business will grow.

Take the time to do it right!

The most important advice I will leave you with is to apply common sense whenever possible.

Read my book several times. You'll always pick up on something new, or something that makes more sense to you when you read it a second or third time, or maybe just something that you missed the first time around. Use this book as a reference guide. Refer back to it as often as needed. Make notes.

My goal in writing this book is that each and every person who reads it walks away with a clearer understanding of the business and makes use of any or all of the many techniques I've used in my career.

My thanks to all and a sincere GOOD LUCK!

GLOSSARY OF TERMS

The following are terms you will hear from time to time, so you need to learn the lingo.

CPP Canada Pension Plan. Obviously, this will only apply if you live in Canada. This is another piece of the employee's wage that is submitted to the government. When the employee turns old and grey (65 years old), it will be returned in a very low monthly check.

Customs Broker is the person or company in charge of clearing your shipment through customs. They'll prepare and obtain all the necessary documents in order for the shipment to cross the border. You can do this yourself, but I don't recommend it. For the customs broker's very nominal fee, it isn't worth the hold-up at customs.

Freight Forwarder is the person or company in charge of getting your shipment from point A to point B. Their offices are usually located near an airport. Their job is to book your shipment on a boat, plane, or truck, or all of the above. Sometimes your suppliers will use their own freight forwarders and you'll only be responsible to clear shipments through customs.

Jobber is someone or a company who purchases job lots, usually large quantities of factory overruns and overstock. Job lots are sometimes sold by weight or by the container. A jobber will pay next to nothing but will usually purchase large quantities.

Leasehold improvement is another term for renovations on the property for which you have signed a lease agreement. Usually, all improvements will require approval in writing from the landlord prior to commencing the work.

Letter of Credit, or LC, is a method of payment through the bank, which is somewhat of an insurance policy when dealing with suppliers from overseas. Essentially, you both enter into a contract outlining all the specifics of the merchandise. If you order blue jeans and red skirts arrive, you have the option of not releasing the funds. This can be avoided, to a degree, by hiring a third party inspector to check the goods before they depart from the supplier for their destination.

Line of Credit. A banking term. It works the same as a credit card, and only operates through the account. Interest is charged as funds are used. There may also be a monthly fee to keep it operational.

NSF (non sufficient funds) To put it simply, this is when a check bounces. The funds are not in the account. This will happen to you at least once in your career. Most of the time, it happens when a company mismanages their books. A business may have issued too many post-dated checks, or have automatic payments being withdrawn on the account.

Offer to Lease is a legally binding contract, which outlines all the necessary information about the property and the lease terms, which will tie you and the landlord into the lease agreement. The offer is as important as the actual lease agreement.

PO, or Purchase Order, is usually a form provided by the supplier which is filled out with items chosen for the store. When referring to the PO, always use the PO number (usually found in the top right hand corner) to identify the exact order placed. This is especially important when making and ordering changes.

POS System stands for Point of Sale Terminal. This is a fancy term for your cash register or computer.

RA Number This is a Return Authorization Number provided by a wholesaler/distributor. Most returns will be rejected if they arrive without prior approval and the RA number which goes with it.

Selling at Keystone is a term meaning the item must be sold at the suggested retail price, usually double the cost. This may appear on an invoice from a designer brand.

Shrinkage. This is an industry term for loss of inventory, usually through theft, both internal (employee), and external (customer).

UI Unemployment Insurance, otherwise known as "pogee." This is a weekly contribution from the employee's wage. It is submitted to the government, and can be used when there is no work. The amount is based on the income earned. Unfortunately, as a small business owner you don't qualify to receive benefits in the event you have to close up shop. Otherwise everyone and their grandmother would open and close shop in order to collect UI.

Vacation Pay will come off the wage as well, usually 5% of the total amount. The employee has the right to request his/her vacation pay at the end of every year, or at the end of employment, whichever comes first. Believe it or not, most employees don't bother asking for it when exiting from their job! Oh well . . .

APPENDIX

Here are some websites offering top brand designer clothing at discounted prices to get you started. Always remember to do as much homework as possible prior to buying.

www.1dwi.com

www.aaacloseoutsnetwork.com

www.amazingwholesalescarves.com

www.atlanticsurplus.com

www.authenticstyles.com

www.awesomewear.com

www.baniantrading.com

www.baseline-clothing.com

www.benelias.com

www.bestdealwholesale.com

www.bluemoondirect.com

www.brandemporium.com

www.cawholesale.com

www.citymoda.com

www.closeoutheaven.com

www.clothesoutfactory.com

www.countryside-closeouts.com

www.dealerleather.com

www.designappeal.com

www.eagletrade.com

www.eclothingclub.com

www.extremedeal.com

www.fragrancewholesale.com

www.gazoz.com
www.gdcdistribution.com
www.gifts-for-less.com
www.globalsources.com
www.highendcloseouts.com
www.hotandy.com
www.hotfashions.ws
www.islandwholesaler.com
www.jdcloseouts.com
www.jetapparel.com
www.jilliandistributors.com
www.julie-ann.com/brandname.html
www.kellys-kloset.com
www.kidswholesalewearhouse.builderspot.com
www.liquidationmerchandise.com
www.liquidationoverstock.com
www.luxurybrandsllc.com
www.mbkwholesale.com
www.mdminternational.net
www.mybargainbin.com
www.quiknet.com/~kbo
www.redtagclothing.com
www.rlctrading.com
www.royalmerchandising.com
www.siswholesale.com
www.smartbargains.com
www.spclothing.com
www.thecloseoutclub.com
www.thewholesaledirect.com

www.transamwholesale.com
www.upscalew.com
www.urbanweardirect.com
www.usacloseouts.com
www.venturedesignsusa.com
www.viatrading.com
www.vistawholesale.com
www.wholesaleclothingmart.com
www.wholesale-handbags.com
www.wmsclothing.com
www.zazausatradeshoes.bcentralhost.com

SAMPLE ADVERTISEMENTS

HAPPY BIRTHDAY!

FROM ALL OF US AT

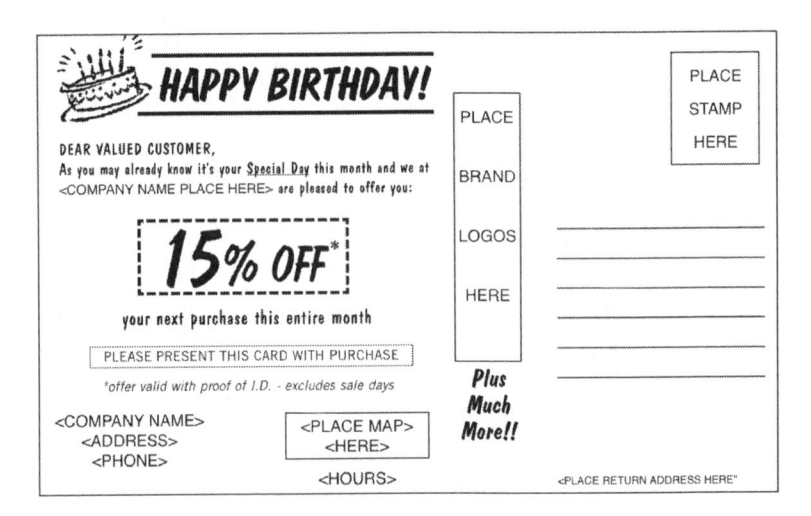

<COMPANY NAME>
<PLACE HERE>

<SEE BACK>

HAPPY BIRTHDAY!

DEAR VALUED CUSTOMER,
As you may already know it's your <u>Special Day</u> this month and we at <COMPANY NAME PLACE HERE> are pleased to offer you:

15% OFF*

your next purchase this entire month

PLEASE PRESENT THIS CARD WITH PURCHASE

*offer valid with proof of I.D. - excludes sale days

<COMPANY NAME>
<ADDRESS>
<PHONE>

<PLACE MAP>
<HERE>
<HOURS>

PLACE BRAND LOGOS HERE

Plus Much More!!

PLACE STAMP HERE

"<PLACE RETURN ADDRESS HERE>"

SAMPLE CLUB CARD

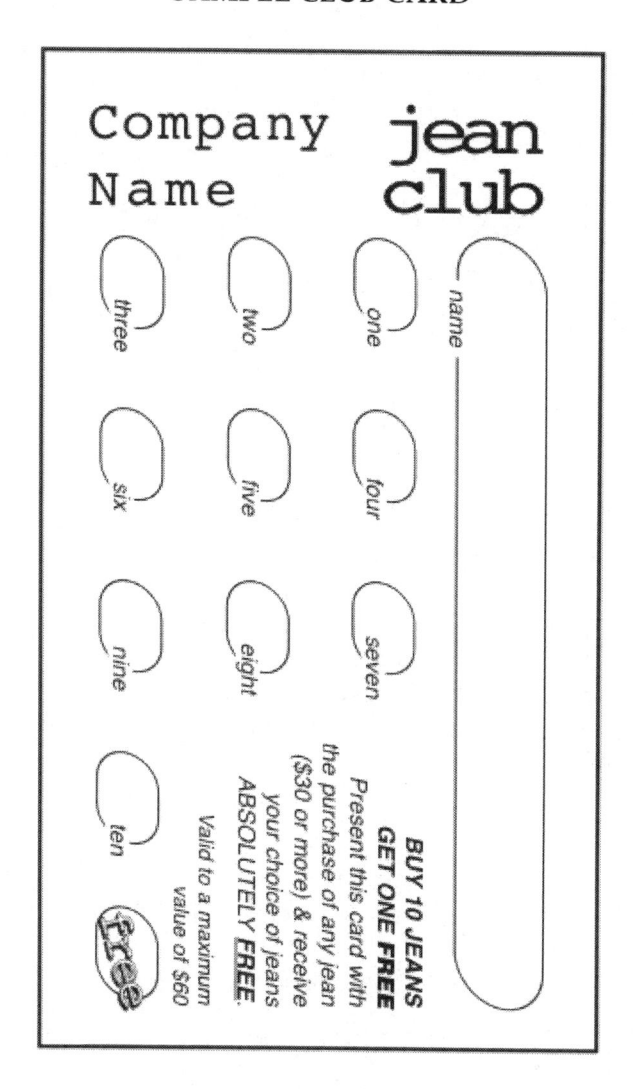

COMMERCIAL LEASE

This lease is made between _____, herein called Lessor, and _____, herein called Lessee.

Lessee hereby offers to lease from Lessor the premises situated in the City of _____, County of _____, State of _____, described as _____, upon the following TERMS and CONDITIONS:

TERM and RENT

Lessor demises the above premises for a term of _____ years, commencing on _____ and terminating on _____ or sooner as provided herein at the annual rental of _____ dollars ($) _____ payable in equal installments in advance on the first day of each month and no later than the tenth day of said month, for that months rental, during the term on this lease. All rental payments shall be made to Lessor at the address specified above.

USE

Lessee shall use and occupy the premises for the express purpose of_____. The premises shall be used for no other purpose. Lessor represents that the premises may lawfully be used for such purpose.

CARE and MAINTENANCE of PREMISES

Lessee acknowledges that the premises are in good order and repair, unless otherwise indicated herein. Lessee shall, at his own expense and at all times, maintain the premises in good and safe condition, including plate glass, electrical wiring, plumbing and heating installations and any other system or equipment upon he premises, and shall surrender the same at termination hereof, in as good condition as received, normal wear and tear excepted. Lessee shall be responsible for all repairs required, excepting the roof, exterior walls, structural foundations, and:

ALTERATIONS

Lessee shall not, without first obtaining the written consent of Lessor, make any alterations, additions, or improvements, in, to or about the premises.

ORDINANCES and STATUTES

Lessee shall comply with all statutes, ordinances and requirements of all municipal, state and federal authorities now in force, or which may hereafter be in force, pertaining to the premises, occasioned by or affecting the use thereof by Lessee.

ASSIGNMENT and SUBLETTING

Lessee shall not assign this lease or sublet any portion of the premises without prior written consent of the Lessor, which shall not be unreasonably withheld. Any such assignment or subletting without consent shall be void and, at the option of the Lessor, may terminate this lease.

UTILITIES

All applications and connections for necessary utility services on the demised premises shall be made in the name of Lessee only, and Lessee shall be solely liable for utility charges as they become due, including those for sewer, water, gas electricity, and telephone services.

ENTRY and INSPECTION

Lessee shall permit Lessor or Lessors agents to enter upon the premises at reasonable times and upon reasonable notice, for the purpose of inspecting the same, and will permit Lessor at any time within sixty (60) days prior to the expiration of this lease, to place upon the premises any usual To Let or For Lease signs, and permit persons desiring to lease the same to inspect the premises thereafter.

POSSESSION

Should Lessor be unable to deliver possession of the premises at the commencement hereof, Lessor shall not be liable for any damage causes thereby, nor shall this lease be void or voidable, but Lessee shall not be liable for any rent until possession is delivered. Lessee may terminate this lease if possession is not delivered within _____ days of the commencement of t he term hereof.

INDEMNIFICATION of LESSOR

Lessor Shall not be liable for any damage of injury to Lessee, or any other person, or of any property, occurring on the demised premises or any part thereof, and Lessee agrees to hold Lessor harmless form any claim for damages, no matter how caused.

INSURANCE

Lessee, at his expense, shall maintain plate glass and public liability insurance including bodily injury and property damage insuring Lessee and Lessor with Minimum coverage as follows:

Lessee shall provide Lessor with a Certificate of Insurance showing Lessor as additional insured The Certificate shall provide for a ten-day written notice to Lessor in the event of cancellation of material change of coverage. To the maximum extent permitted by insurance policies, which may be owned by Lessor or Lessee, Lessee and Lessor, for the benefit of each other, waive any and all rights of subrogation that might otherwise exist.

EMINENT DOMAIN

Should the premises or any part thereof or any estate therein, or any other part of the building materially affecting Lessees use of the premise, shall be taken by eminent domain, this lease shall terminate on the date when title vests pursuant to such taking. The rent, and any additional rent, shall be apportioned as of the termination date, and any rent paid foe any period beyond that date shall be repaid to Lessee. Lessee shall not be entitled to any part of the award for such taking or any payment in lieu thereof, but Lessee may file a claim for any taking of fixtures and improvements owned by Lessee, and for moving expenses.

DESTRUCTION of PREMISES

Should an occurrence of a partial destruction of the premises during the term hereof, from any cause, Lessor shall forthwith repair same, provided that such repairs can be made within sixty (60) days under existing governmental laws and regulations, but such partial destruction shall not terminate this lease, except that Lessee shall be entitled to a proportionate reduction of rent while such repairs are being made, based upon the extent to which the making of such repairs shall interfere with the business of Lessee on the premises. If such repairs cannot be made within said sixty (60) days, Lessor, at his option, may make the same within a reasonable time, this lease continuing in effect with the rent proportionately abated as aforesaid, and in the event that Lessor shall not elect to make such repairs which cannot be made within sixty (60) days, this lease may be terminated at the option of either party. In the event that the building in which the demised premises may be situated is destroyed to an extent of not less than one-third of the replacement costs thereof, Lessor may elect to terminate this lease whether the demised premises be injured or not. A total destruction of the building in which the premises may be situated shall terminate this lease.

LESSORS REMEDIES on DEFAULT

Should Lessee default in the payment of rent, or any additional rent, or defaults in the performance of any of the other covenants or conditions hereof, Lessor may give Lessee notice of such default and if Lessee does not cure any such default within _____ days, after the giving of such notice (or if such other default is of such nature that it cannot be completely cured within such period, of Lessee does not commence such during within said _____ days and thereafter proceed with reasonable diligence and in good faith to cure said default), then Lessor may terminate this lease on not less than _____ days notice to Lessee. On the date specified in such notice the term of this lease shall terminate, and Lessee shall then quit and surrender the premises to Lessor, but Lessee shall remain liable as hereinafter provided. If this lease shall have been so terminated by Lessor, Lessor may at any time thereafter resume possession of the premises by any lawful means and remove Lessee of other occupants and their effects. No failure to enforce any term shall be deemed a waiver.

SECURITY DEPOSIT

Lessee shall deposit with Lessor upon the signing of this lease the sum of _____ Dollars ($) _____ as security deposit for the performance of Lessees obligations under this lease, including without limitation, the surrender of possession of the premises to Lessor as herein provided. If Lessor applies any part of the deposit to cure any default of Lessee, Lessee shall on demand deposit with Lessor the amount so applied so that Lessor shall have the full deposit in hand at all times during the term of this lease.

TAX INCREASE

Should there be an increase in taxes during any year of the term of this lease in the City, County, or State real estate taxes over and above the amount of such taxes assessed for the tax year during which the term of this lease commences, whether because of increased rate of valuation, Lessee shall pay to Lessor upon presentation of paid tax bills an amount equal to _____% of the increase in taxes upon the land and building in which the leased premises are situated. In the event that such taxes are assessed for a tax year extending beyond the term of the lease, the obligation of Lessee shall be proportionate to the portion of the lease term included in such year.

COMMON AREA EXPENSES

Should the demised premises be situated in a shopping center or in a commercial building in which there are common areas, Lessee agrees to pay his pro-rata share of maintenance, taxes, and insurance for the common area.

ATTORNEY FEES

Should a lawsuit be necessary for the recovery of the premises, or for any sum due hereunder, or because of any act which might arise out of the possession of the premises, by either party, the prevailing party shall be entitled to all costs incurred in connection with such action, including a reasonable Attorneys fee.

NOTICES

Notices given, or that might be required to be given by either party shall be accomplished by mailing same postage prepaid, to Lessee at the premises, or Lessor at the address shown below, or at such other places as might be designated by the parties from time to time.

HEIRS, ASSIGNS, SUCCESSORS

This lease is binding upon and inures to the benefit of the heirs, assigns, and successors in interest to the parties.

OPTION to RENEW

Provided that Lessee is not in default in the performance of this lease, Lessee shall have the option to renew the lease for an additional term of _____ months commencing at the expiration of the initial lease term. All the terms and conditions of the lease shall apply during the renewal term except that the monthly rent shall be the sum of _____Dollars ($) _____. The option shall be exercises by written notice given to Lessor not less than _____ Days prior to the expiration of the initial lease term. Should Lessee fail to give notice in the manner provided herein within the time specified, this option shall expire.

SUBORDINATION

This lease is and shall be subordinated to all existing and future liens and encumbrances against the property.

ENTIRE AGREEMENT

The foregoing constitutes the entire agreement between the parties and may be modified only in writing, signed by both parties. The following Exhibits, if any, have been made a part of this lease before the parties execution hereof:

Signed on this _____ day of _____, _____.

By: _____ By: _____
       (Lessee)   (Lessor)

By: _____ By: _____
      (Witness)   (Witness)

PARTNERSHIP AGREEMENT

THIS AGREEMENT made this _____ day of _____, 20____, by and among _____ (hereinafter referred to as "Partner One") and _____ (hereinafter referred to as "Partner Two").

WHEREAS, partner one and partner two desire to form a partnership in the State of _____.

NOW, THEREFORE, in consideration of the mutual covenants and agreements contained herein, the parties hereto, intending to be legally bound hereby, agree as follows:

1. The parties hereby form a partnership that will engage in the business of _____ under the name of _____.

2. The partners ownership interest and capital account shall be as follows: _____.

3. The principal office of the partnership is to be located at _____, or in such other place as the parties agree.

4. The partnership shall exist for a period of _____, commencing on _____, 20____, and shall continue until _____, 20____, unless terminated earlier as hereinafter provided.

5. Either party to this partnership agreement may withdraw from the partnership upon six (6) months notice to the remaining party to this partnership agreement.

6. The partners shall share the profits and losses of the partnership in relationship to their ownership interest.

7. This partnership agreement shall immediately terminate upon the death of either partner.

8. All controversies arising under or in connection with, or relating to any alleged breach of, this partnership agreement shall be settled by arbitration in accordance with the rules then obtaining of the American Arbitration Association, and judgment upon any award rendered may be entered in any court having jurisdiction.

9. This partnership agreement shall be binding upon and inure to the benefit of the parties hereto and their respective heirs, executors, administrators, successors and assigns.

10. This partnership agreement constitutes the entire agreement between the parties hereto and supersedes all prior agreements, negotiations and understandings of any nature with respect to the subject matter hereto. No amendment, waiver or discharge of any of the provisions of this agreement shall be effective against any party unless that party shall have consented thereto in writing.

11. This partnership agreement shall be construed, interpreted and enforced in accordance with the laws of the state of _____.

IN WITNESS WHEREOF, Partner One and Partner Two have caused this partnership agreement to be duly executed the day and year set out above.

IN WITNESS WHEREOF, the parties have executed this agreement the day and year first above written.

_____   _____
Signature   Date

EMPLOYEE APPLICATION

DEMANDE D'EMPLOI / APPLICATION FOR EMPLOYMENT

EMPLOI DÉSIRÉ / POSITION APPLIED FOR	SALAIRE DEMANDÉ / WAGES EXPECTED
	DATE DISPONIBILITÉ / DATE AVAILABLE

| NOM / SURNAME | PRÉNOM / FIRST | INITIALES / MIDDLE | TELEPHONE | NO ASS. SOCIALE/SOCIAL INSURANCE NO |
| ADRESSE / ADDRESS | RUE / STREET | VILLE / TOWN | PROVINCE | CODE POSTAL / POSTAL CODE |

POUVEZ-VOUS TRAVAILLER LÉGALEMENT AU CANADA / ARE YOU LEGALLY ELIGIBLE TO WORK IN CANADA   OUI/YES ☐   NON/NO ☐

ÉDUCATION / EDUCATION RECORD

	NOM INSTITUTION - ADRESSE / SCHOOL NAME / ADDRESS	DATE DE / A DATE FROM / TO	SUJET / SUBJECT	DIPLÔME OBTENU / DIPLOMA / DEGREE AWARDED
SECONDAIRE / SECONDARY SCHOOL				OUI/YES ☐ NON/NO ☐ TYPE TITLE
PROFESSIONNEL OU TECHNIQUE / BUSINESS TRADE OR TECHNICAL SCHOOL				OUI/YES ☐ NON/NO ☐ TYPE TITLE
COLLÉGIAL / COMMUNITY COLLEGE				OUI/YES ☐ NON/NO ☐ TYPE TITLE
UNIVERSITAIRE / UNIVERSITY				OUI/YES ☐ NON/NO ☐ TYPE TITLE

AUTRES COURS, SÉMINAIRES, OU ATELIERS / ADDITIONAL COURSES, SEMINARS, WORKSHOPS

DÉCRIVEZ TOUTE EXPÉRIENCE, APTITUDE OU CONNAISSANCE PERTINENTES AU POSTE DÉSIRÉ / DESCRIBE ANY OF YOUR WORK RELATED SKILLS, EXPERIENCE, OR TRAINING THAT IS RELATED TO THE POSITION BEING APPLIED FOR

LANGUE / LANGUAGE

	PARLÉE / SPOKEN	ÉCRITE / WRITTEN
ANGLAIS / ENGLISH	☐	☐
FRANÇAIS / FRENCH	☐	☐
AUTRES / OTHER	☐	☐

EMPLOIS PRÉCÉDENTS: (COMMENÇANT PAR LE PLUS RÉCENT) / EMPLOYMENT RECORD (MOST RECENT EMPLOYER FIRST)

COMPAGNIE / COMPANY NAME	DU / FROM	SALAIRE AU DÉPART / LAST SALARY	EMPLOI OCCUPÉ / JOB TITLE
ADRESSE / ADDRESS	AU / TO	$	RESPONSABILITÉS, FONCTIONS / DUTIES, RESPONSIBILITIES
	TYPE D'ENTREPRISE / TYPE OF BUSINESS		
RAISON DU DÉPART / REASON FOR LEAVING	SUPERVISEUR / SUPERVISOR		

COMPAGNIE / COMPANY NAME	DU / FROM	SALAIRE AU DÉPART / LAST SALARY	EMPLOI OCCUPÉ / JOB TITLE
ADRESSE / ADDRESS	AU / TO	$	RESPONSABILITÉS, FONCTIONS / DUTIES, RESPONSIBILITIES
	TYPE D'ENTREPRISE / TYPE OF BUSINESS		
RAISON DU DÉPART / REASON FOR LEAVING	SUPERVISEUR / SUPERVISOR		

COMPAGNIE / COMPANY NAME	DU / FROM	SALAIRE AU DÉPART / LAST SALARY	EMPLOI OCCUPÉ / JOB TITLE
ADRESSE / ADDRESS	AU / TO	$	RESPONSABILITÉS, FONCTIONS / DUTIES, RESPONSIBILITIES
	TYPE D'ENTREPRISE / TYPE OF BUSINESS		
RAISON DU DÉPART / REASON FOR LEAVING	SUPERVISEUR / SUPERVISOR		

COMPAGNIE / COMPANY NAME	DU / FROM	SALAIRE AU DÉPART / LAST SALARY	EMPLOI OCCUPÉ / JOB TITLE
ADRESSE / ADDRESS	AU / TO	$	RESPONSABILITÉS, FONCTIONS / DUTIES, RESPONSIBILITIES
	TYPE D'ENTREPRISE / TYPE OF BUSINESS		
RAISON DU DÉPART / REASON FOR LEAVING	SUPERVISEUR / SUPERVISOR		

AVEZ-VOUS DÉJÀ TRAVAILLÉ POUR CETTE COMPAGNIE ? / HAVE YOU EVER BEEN EMPLOYED BY THIS COMPANY BEFORE?	AVEZ-VOUS ÉTÉ RÉFÉRÉ PAR QUELQU'UN ? / WHAT SOURCE REFERRED YOU TO THIS COMPANY?
OUI ☐ NON ☐ / YES NO SI OUI / IF YES DU / FROM ____ AU / TO ____	
QUEL POSTE OCCUPIEZ-VOUS À VOTRE DÉPART ? / WHAT WAS YOUR POSITION? (WHEN YOU LEFT)	ACCEPTERIEZ-VOUS DE TRAVAILLER SUR QUART DE TRAVAIL ? / WILL YOU WORK SHIFT WORK? OUI ☐ YES NON ☐ NO
POUVONS-NOUS CONTACTER VOTRE EMPLOYEUR ACTUEL ? / MAY WE CONTACT YOUR PRESENT EMPLOYER? YES ☐ NON ☐ OUI NO	ACCEPTERIEZ-VOUS UN TRANSFERT (RÉPONDRE QUE SI PERTINENT) / ARE YOU WILLING TO RELOCATE? ANSWER ONLY IF JOB RELATED OUI ☐ YES NON ☐ NO PRÉFÉRENCES / PREFERRED LOCATIONS

PASSE-TEMPS, INTÉRÊTS, ACTIVITÉS (AUTRES QUE RELIGIEUSES, ETHNIQUES, RACIALES, OU POLITIQUES.)
OUTSIDE HOBBIES AND INTERESTS, SERVICE CLUBS OR PROFESSIONAL ASSOCIATIONS: (DO NOT LIST CLUBS OR ORGANIZATIONS OF A RELIGIOUS, RACIAL, POLITICAL CHARACTER.)

RÉFÉRENCES / REFERENCES

INDIQUER 2 PERSONNES (AUTRES QUE FAMILLE OU ANCIENS EMPLOYEURS);
LIST TWO PERSONS TO WHOM WE MAY REFER (NOT RELATIVES OR PREVIOUS EMPLOYERS)

NOM / NAME	ADRESSE / ADDRESS	TELEPHONE	USAGE INTERNE SEUL. OFFICE USE ONLY
OCCUPATION			
NOM / NAME	ADRESSE / ADDRESS	TELEPHONE	
OCCUPATION			

JE DÉCLARE QUE LES INFORMATIONS DONNÉES CI-HAUT SONT COMPLÈTES ET VÉRIDIQUES. JE COMPRENDS QUE SI JE SUIS EMBAUCHÉ, TOUTE FAUSSE DÉCLARATION DANS CETTE DEMANDE D'EMPLOI POURRAIT ENTRAÎNER MON RENVOI.
I HEREBY DECLARE THAT THE FOREGOING INFORMATION IS TRUE AND COMPLETE TO MY KNOWLEDGE. I UNDERSTAND THAT A FALSE STATEMENT MAY DISQUALIFY ME FROM EMPLOYMENT, OR CAUSE MY DISMISSAL.

SIGNATURE _____ DATE _____

USAGE INTERNE SEULEMENT / FOR OFFICE USE ONLY

COMMENTAIRES / COMMENTS

RESPONSABLE / INTERVIEWER

COMPLÉTER CETTE SECTION SEULEMENT SI LE CANDIDAT A ÉTÉ EMBAUCHÉ
THIS SECTION IS TO BE COMPLETED ONLY IF APPLICANT HAS BEEN HIRED

STATUT MARITAL / MARITAL STATUS	EN CAS D'URGENCE CONTACTEZ / IN CASE OF EMERGENCY NOTIFY NOM / NAME		
CÉLIBATAIRE ☐ SINGLE MARIÉ ☐ MARRIED	ADRESSE / ADDRESS		TELEPHONE
DATE DE NAISSANCE / DATE OF BIRTH JOUR / DAY MOIS / MONTH AN / YEAR	MÉDECIN PERSONNEL / FAMILY DOCTOR		TELEPHONE

DATE D'EMBAUCHE / DATE HIRED	DÉPARTEMENT / DEPARTMENT	SALAIRE DÉPART / STARTING RATE	NBRE HEURES / HRS / WEEK	POSITION	DATE DU DÉBUT D'EMPLOI / DATE EMPLOYMENT COMMENCED

CANADIAN FASHION SCHOOLS

Want to become a designer? If you can't get an entry level position with one of the great fashion moguls, enroll in fashion school. The following is a list to get you started.

Academie de Dessin de Mode Richard Robinson Academy of Fashion Design www.richardrobinson.com 447 Sussex Drive Ottawa, ON, K1N 6Z4 T 613-241-5233 | F 613-241-7676 info@richardrobinson.com	Academy of Design (Formerly International Academy of Design) www.aodt.ca 1835 Yonge St Toronto, ON, M5S 1X8 T 866-838-6542 | T 416-929-0121
Academy of Fashion Design www.aofdesign.com 218B Avenue B South, Saskatoon, SK, S7M 1M4 T 306-978-9088 | F 306-933-9362 fashiondesign@sasktel.net	Algonquin College www.algonquincollege.com 1385 Woodroffe Avenue, Ottawa, ON, K2G 1V8 T 613-727-4723
Blanche Macdonald Centre www.blanchemacdonald.com 460 Robson St., Vancouver, BC, V6B 2B5 T 604-685-0337 | F 604-685-0317 info@blanchemacdonald.com	Campus Notre-Dame De Foy www.cndf.qc.ca 5000 rue Clement-Lockquell, Saint-Augustin-de-Desmaures, QC, G3A 1B3 T 418-872-8041 | F 418-872-3448
Cegep Marie-Victorin www.collegemv.qc.ca 7000, rue Marie-Victorin, Montreal, QC, H1G 2J6 T 514-325-0150 | F 514-328-3830 promotion@collegemv.qc.ca	Coco Fashion Design Institute www.cocofashion.ca 348 Ryding Ave, Toronto, ON, M6N 1H5 T 416-739-0875 | F 416-739-0063 info@cocofashion.ca
Dalhousie University – Theatre Department - Costume Studies www.dal.ca	Ecole de Joaillerie de Montreal www.ecoledejoaillerie.com 900 - 416 Maisonneuve Montreal, QC, H3A 1L2 T 514-281-9922

1685 Argyle Street, Halifax, NS, B3J 2B5 T 902-494-2211	F 514-281-9933 ecolejoail.mtl@qc.aira.com
Ecole Holt Couture School of Couture Sewing and Design www.ecoleholtcouture.com 2227 - 20 Ave. SW, Calgary, AB, T2T 0M4 T 403-244-5460 | F 403-228-1416 info@ecoleholtcouture.com	**Ecole superieure de mode de Montreal (ESMM)** www.esmm.uqam.ca C.P. 8888 Succ. Centre ville, Montreal, QC, H3C 3P8 T 514-933-6633 | T 514-933-1807 mode@uqam.ca
Fanshawe College - Art and Design www.fanshawec.ca/EN/ 1001 Fanshawe College Blvd., PO Box 7005, London, ON, N5Y 5R6 T 519-452-4430 | F 519-452-4420	**George Brown College Centre for Fashion Studies and Jewellery** www.gbrownc.on.ca/fashionstudies/index.html Casa Loma Campus - 160 Kendal Avenue, Toronto, ON, M5R 1M3 T 416-415-5000, ext. 4840 info@gbrownc.on.ca
Georgian College www.georgianc.on.ca 1 Georgian Drive, Barrie, ON, L4M 3X9 T 705-728-1968 | F 705-722-1531 wmoosang@georgianc.on.ca	**Granton Institute of Technology** www.grantoninstitute.com 263 Adelaide St. W., Toronto, ON, M5H 1Y3 T 416-977-3929 | F 416-977-5612
HP Academy of Applied Arts and Design www.hpacad.com 885 Don Mills Rd. Suite 404, Toronto, ON, M3C 1V9 T 416-652-1881 | F 416-652-3531 inquiries@hpacad.com	**Humber College - Fashion Arts Diploma** www.humber.ca 205 Humber College Boulevard, Toronto, ON, M9W 5L7 T 416-675-5000 | F 416-675-2427 enquiry@humber.ca
John Casablancas Institute of Applied Arts www.jcinstitute.com/fashion.html 220 Cambie Street, Suite 150, Vancouver, BC, V6B 2M9 T 604-688-0328 | F 604-688-9365	**Kwantlen University College** www.kwantlen.ca/fashion Surrey Campus Admission Office- 12666 - 72nd Avenue, Surrey, BC, V3W 2M8 T 604-599-2000 | T 604-599-2100 |

info@johncasablancas.ca	F 604-599-2086 admissions@kwantlen.ca
LaSalle College www.collegelasalle.com 2000 Sainte-Catherine Street West, Montreal, QC, H3H 2T2 T 514-939-2006	**LaSalle College International Vancouver** www.lasallecollegevancouver.com 200 - 889 West Pender St., Vancouver, BC, V6C 3B2 T 604-683-2006 | F 604-683-6505
Lethbridge Community College www.lethbridgecollege.ab.ca 3000 College Drive South, Lethbridge, AB, T1K 1L6 T 403-320-3200 | F 403-320-1461 - Information Desk info@lethbridgecollege.ab.ca	**Mithe de Fontenay Unique Fashion Centre** 17 Sandpiper Link N.W., Calgary, AB, T3K 4L7 T 403-275-7322 | F 403-275-7322
New Brunswick College of Craft and Design www.nbccd.ca 457 Queen St. , Fredericton, NB, E3B 5H1 T 506-453-2305 | F 506-457-7352 nbccd.email@gnb.ca	**Okanagan Fashion Institute Inc.** www.okanaganfashioninstitute.ca 414 Cedar Avenue, Kelowna, BC, T 250-712-1136
Olds College www.oldscollege.ab.ca 4500 - 50th St., Olds, AB, T4H 1R6 T 403-556-8342 | F 403-556-4724	**OnlineFashionCourses.com** www.onlinefashioncourses.com 65 Carl Hall Rd. Unit 225 c/o 226, Toronto, ON, M2K 2E1 T 866-210-9842 info@onlinefashioncourses.com
Patty Shapiro & Associates www.pattyshapiro.com 555 Chabanel St. W. #R17 - Main Floor, Montreal, QC, H2N 2H7 T 514-389-5627 | F 514-389-9969 patty@pattyshapiro.com	**Ryerson University, School of Fashion** www.ryerson.ca/fashion/ 350 Victoria Street, Toronto, ON, M5B 2K3 T 416-979-5333 fshninfo@ryerson.ca

Seneca College of Applied Arts & Technology Fashion Arts www.senecac.on.ca Newnham Campus - 1750 Finch Avenue East, Toronto, ON, M2J 2X5 T 416-491-5050	The Art Institute of Vancouver www.wherecreativitygoestoschool.ca 2665 Renfrew Street, Vancouver, BC, V5M 0A7 T 1-888-718-9073 | F 604-684-8839 vancouverinfo@wherecreativitygoestoschool.com
The Sewing Studio www.lovesewing.com 266 Avenue Road, Toronto, ON, M4V 2G7 T 416-901-0758 info@lovesewing.com	University College of the Fraser Valley www.ufv.ca 33844 King Road, Abbotsford, BC, V2S 7M9

US INDUSTRY CLOTHING ASSOCIATIONS AND ORGANIZATIONS

American Apparel and Footwear Association www.apparelandfootwear.org 1200 - 1601 North Kent Street, Arlington, VA, 22209 T 703-524-1864 | F 703-522-6741 **Description:** The American Apparel & Footwear Association (AAFA) is the national trade association representing apparel, footwear and other sewn products companies, and their suppliers. AAFA's mission is to promote and enhance its members' competitiveness, productivity and profitability in the global market.	**Association of Image Consultants International** www.aici.org PO Box 20483, Kalamazoo, MI, 49019 T 269-873-1598 | F 269-327-4590
Cashmere & Camel Hair Manufacturers Institute www.cashmere.org 6 Beacon Street, Suite 1125, Boston, MA, 02108-3812 T 617-542-7481 | F 617-542-2199 info@cashmere.org **Description:** To maintain the integrity of cashmere and camel hair products through education, information and industry cooperation.	**Clothing Manufacturers Association of the U.S.A** 730 Broadway, 10th Floor, New York, NY, 10003 T 212-529-0823 | F 212-529-1739 kaplancma730@hotmail.com **Description:** The Clothing, Manufacturers Association of the USA, which represents manufacturers of men's and boys' tailored clothing throughout the USA.
Council of Fashion Designers of America www.cfda.com 1412 Broadway, Suite 2006, New York, NY, 10018 T 212-302-1821 info@cfda.com **Description:** The Council of Fashion Designers of America, Inc.	**Fashion Group International New York** www.fgi.org 8 West 40th Street, 7th Floor, New York, NY, 10018 T 212-302-5511 | F 212-302-5533 info@fgi.org **Description:** The Fashion Group International is a global non-profit

(CFDA) is a not-for-profit trade association of over 250 of America's foremost fashion and accessory designers.

association with over 6,000 professionals of achievement and influence representing all areas of the fashion, apparel, accessories, beauty and home industries.

Fashion Outreach
292 West 137th Street, Suite 1,
New York, NY, 10030
T 212-252-3571
Description: Fashion Outreach, a non-profit organization designed to assist individuals of all ethic origins entering the fashion industry.

Headwear Information Bureau
www.hatsworldwide.com
302 West 12th Street, Penthouse C,
New York, NY, 10010
T 212-627-8333 | F 212-627-0067
Description: The Headwear Information Bureau represents the men's and women's headwear industries with a comprehensive national public relations campaign. Its national membership includes designers, manufactures, and suppliers.

International Formalwear Association
www.formalwear.org/index.html
401 N. Michigan Avenue,
Chicago, IL, 60611
T 312-321-5139 | F 312-321-5150
Description: Founded in 1973, the International Formalwear Association (formerly the American Formalwear Association) is the only alliance of all factors in the formalwear industry with formalwear specialists, wholesalers, and manufacturers.

International Swimwear/ Activewear Market
www.isamla.com
658 - 13351-D Riverside Dr.,
Sherman Oaks, CA, 91423
T 818-986-2152 | F 818-9862637
Description: Founded in 1978 as a non-profit association of swimwear manufacturers to strengthen and unify the swimwear industry, ISAM (International Swimwear and Activewear Market) has become one of the largest markets to serve the swimwear and resortwear industry.

National Fashion Accessories Association
www.accessoryweb.com
350 5th Ave. Suite 2030,
New York, NY, 10118
T 212-947-3424 | F 212-629-0361

National Textile Association
www.nationaltextile.org
6 Beacon Street, Suite 1125,
Boston, MA, 02108
T 617-542-8220 | F 617-542-2199
Description: The non-profit trade

Description: Formerly known as the National Handbag Association, the NFAA has been the principal trade association for the Handbag and Fashion Accessories industry since the early 1900's.

organization represents more than 200 textile manufacturers and industry suppliers with operations in the United States, Canada and Mexico. NTA members' process fibres, spin yarn, knit and weave fabric, dye, print and otherwise finish fabrics in North America

Neckwear Association of America
151 Lexington Avenue, Suite 2-F,
New York, NY, 10016
T 212-683-8454 | F 212-686-7382
Description: The Neckwear Association of America (NAA) is a 50-year-old association serving the manufacturers of men's and boys' neckwear and the suppliers to the field. 100 member strong, which representing about 75 percent of the tie production in the United States.

New York Fashion Council
153 East 87th Street,
New York, NY, 10018
T 212-289-0420 | F 212-289-5917
Description: Producer of New York Women's Apparel Market.

The Fragrance Foundation
www.fragrance.org
145 East 32th Street,
New York, NY, 10016-6002
T 212-725-2755 | F 212-779-9058
Description: The Fragrance Foundation is the non-profit educational arm of the international fragrance industry. It provides information and tips about the appreciation, use and sales of fragrance and perfume. This foundation is an international source for historic, cultural, scientific and industry-related reference materials.

CANADIAN CLOTHING INDUSTRY ORGANIZATIONS AND ASSOCIATIONS

Apparel & Textile Assoc. of Sask. 1102 8th Ave., Regina, SK, S4R 1C9 T 305-565-0065 | F 305-565-1962	**Apparel B.C.** www.apparel-bc.org 1859 Franklin St., Vancouver, BC, V5V 1P9 T 604-986-2003 | F 604-986-2097 **Description:** Apparel-BC is a self-sustaining organization of apparel industry members, whose mandate is to create awareness - through advocacy, communication and promotion - of the fashion, design and needle trade industry in British Columbia. ABC also provides an industry link with government and media.
Apparel Connexion www.apparelconnexion.ca 1114 - 9310 St. Laurent Blvd., Montreal, QC, H2N 1N4 T 514-388-7779 | F 514-388-6926 **Description:** Formed to assist management and labour in achieving their human resources objectives in the apparel industry.	**Apparel Industry Development Coucil (AIDC)** www.toronto.ca/invest-in-toronto/fashion.htm Metro Hall, 55 John St., 8th Floor, Toronto, Ontario, M5V 3C6 T 416-397-4832 | F 416-392-3374 **Description:** A not-for-profit group that works with Ontario apparel firms to identify skills training and business development needs. The Council offers technical training such as machine mechanics, stitch construction and quality control as well as management workshops in product costing and lean manufacturing.

Apparel Manufacturers Institute of Quebec www.apparelquebec.com 555 Chabanel St. West, Suite 801, Montreal, QC, H2N 2H8 T 514-382-3846 | F 514-383-1689 **Description:** Voice of the apparel industry in the province of Quebec.	**Apparel Ontario** www.ontarioapparel.com 124 O'Connor Street, Suite 504, Ottawa, ON, K1P 5M9 T 613-231-3220 | F 613-231-2305 **Description:** Represents the apparel industry in Ontario.
Assoc. Clothing Mfg. of the Prov. of Quebec 801 - 555 Chabanel W., Montreal, QC, H2N 2H8 T 514-382-3846 | F 514-383-1689	**Assoc. for Occupational Health & Safety for the Apparel Sector** 1011 - 9310 St. Laurent, Montreal, QC, H2N 1N4 T 514-383-8317 | F 514-383-7938
Association of Image Consultants www.aici.org 3 Rochester St., Carleton Place, Ottawa, ON, K7C 2P9 T 613-253-0081	**Canadian Apparel Federation** www.apparel.ca 124 O'Connor Street, Suite 504, Ottawa, ON, K1P 5M9 T 613-231-3220 | F 613-231-2305 **Description:** The national industry association for Canada's apparel industry. It represents the industry in consultations with the federal government on trade, legislative, and regulatory matters. Services to members include newsletters, trade and customs information, marketing services, reference materials and other information. CAF also publishes Canadian Apparel magazine.
Canadian Association of Importers & Exporters www.iecanada.com 438 University Avenue Suite 1618, P.O. Box 60, Toronto, ON, M5G 2K8 T 416-595-5333 | F 416-595-8226 **Description:** Represents members'	**Canadian Association of Wholesale Sales Representatives (CAWS)** www.caws.ca 1771 Avenue Road, P.O. Box 54546, Toronto, ON, M5M 4N5 T 416-782-8961 | F 416-782-5876

views and interests before government, provides members with guidance on trade and customs issues, promotes Canada's international trade.	caws@bellnet.ca **Description:** CAWS is a non-profit national association that represents commission sales agents and selected regional markets (Trade Shows).
Canadian Textiles Institute www.textiles.ca 222 Somerset St. West, Suite 500, Ottawa, ON, K2P 2G3 T 613-232-7195 | F 613-232-8722 **Description:** National trade association representing Canadian manufacturers of fibres, yarns, fabrics, and other textile articles.	**Chinese Canadian Textile & Garment Mfgs.** 20 Carthage Ave., Scarborough, ON, M1R 4Y2 T 416-727-9449 | F 416-510-8617
Design Exchange www.dx.org 234 Bay Street, P.O. Box 18, Toronto Dominion Centre, Toronto, ON, M5K 1B2 T 416-363-6121 | F 416-368-0684 **Description:** Non-profit design association that advocates the importance of design in fashion, architecture, interior design, landscape architecture, graphic design, industrial and product design and new media.	**Enterprise Toronto** www.enterprisetoronto.com City Hall Office, 100 Queen Street West, Toronto, ON, M5H 2N2 T 416-392-6646 | F 416-392-1794 **Description:** An innovative public and private sector alliance created to provide one-stop sourcing of services and programs tailored to meet the needs of the City's Entrepreneurs and small businesses.
Fashion Design Council of Canada (FDCC) www.lgfashionweek.ca Toronto, ON, T 416-922-3322 | F 416-922-4292 **Description:** Non-profit organization with a mandate to promote fashion in Canada.	**Fashion Group International (FGI), Toronto Regional Office** www.toronto.fgi.org T 416-696-5554 **Description:** The Fashion Group International is a global non-profit association with over 6,000 professionals of achievement and influence representing all areas of the fashion, apparel, accessories,

	beauty and home industries.
Fashion Industry Liaison Committee (FILC) www.toronto.ca/business Metro Hall, 55 John St., 8th Floor, Toronto, ON, M5V 3C6 T 416-392-1296 | F 416-392-3374 **Description:** Toronto 's fashion industry voice at City Hall; comprised of volunteers from all industry sectors.	**Fur Council of Canada** www.furcouncil.com 1435 St. Alexandre, Suite 1270, Montreal, Quebec, H3A 2G4 T 514-844-1945 | F 514-844-8593 **Description:** A national, non-profit federation representing people working in every sector of the Canadian fur trade. This includes fur producers, auction houses, processors, designers, craftspeople and retail furriers.
Furriers Guild of Canada www.furcouncil.com 211 - 4174 Dundas St. W., Toronto, Ontario, M8X 1X3 T 416-234-9494 | F 416-234-2244 furriersguildca@ica.net **Description:** A non-profit organization that promotes Canadian fur retailers and manufacturers	**Men's Clothing Mfg. Assoc.** 801 - 555 Chabanel W., Montreal, QC, H2N 2H8 T 514-382-3846 | F 514-383-1689
Ministere du Development Economique Innovation Exportation www.mdeie.gouv.qc.ca 380 St. Antoine W._5th Fl._, Montreal, QC, H2Y 3X7 T 514-499-2500 | F 514-873-9913 **Description:** Supports economic and regional development.	**National Apparel Bureau** www.nabq.com 294 St. Paul W._2nd Fl., Montreal, QC, H2Y 2A3 T 514-845-8135 | F 514-499-8468 **Description:** Cultivates a quality of credit reporting that will provide members with the next best thing to being a secured creditor. Providing a collection service tailored to the specific needs of the apparel industry since 1932.

Ontario Fashion Exhibitors
www.ontariofashionexhibitors.ca
160 Tycos Drive, Suite 2219, Box 218,
Toronto, ON, M6B 1W8
T 416-596-2401 | F 416-596-1808
Description: A provincial, non-profit association, OFE's mandate is to provide successful markets to wholesale sales representatives and professional buyers within the fashion industry.

Quebec Fashion Apparel Mfrs. Guild
2020 Veniard,
St-Laurent, QC, H4R 1S5
T 514-384-3800 | F 514-384-3801

Retail Council of Canada
www.retailcouncil.org/default.asp
1255 Bay Street, Suite 800,
Toronto, ON, M5R 2A9
T 416-922-6678 | F 416-922-8011 or 1-877-790-4271 (Toll-Free)
Description: Retail Council of Canada's mission is to be the Voice of Retail in Canada by providing advocacy, research, education and services that enhance opportunities for retail success, and increase awareness of retail's contribution to the communities and customers it serves.

Royal Ontario Museum Textile & Costume Committee (TEX-CO)
1166 Bay Street Apt. 1504,
Toronto, ON, M5S 2X8
T 416-923-5915
Description: TEX-CO aims to raise public awareness and funds for future exhibitions of textiles and costumes through a series of annual fundraising events.

Shoe Manufacturers Association of Canada
Baie d'Urfe Business Centre 90 Morgan Road, Suite 203,
Baie-d'Urfe, QC, H9X 3A8
T 514-457-3436 | F 514-457-8004

Toronto Business Development Centre
www.tbdc.com
900 - 1 Yonge Street
Toronto, ON, M5E 1E5_
T 416-345-9437 | F 416-345-9044
Description: Assists entrepreneurs in the formation and development of enterprises so that those endeavours grow into successful job-creating businesses.

Toronto Fashion Incubator
www.fashionincubator.com
285 Manitoba Drive,
Toronto, ON, M6K 3C3
T 416-971-7117 | F 416-971-6717
Description: An innovative, non-profit, small business centre designed to support, promote and nurture new fashion entrepreneurs.

Union of Needle Trades Industrial & Textile Employees
200 - 9275 Clark,
Montreal, QC, H2N 2K3
T 514-381-4692 | F 514-383-3407

Windfall
www.windfallbasics.com
3 - 29 Connell Court,
Toronto, ON, M8Z 5T7
T 416-703-8435 | F 416-703-8437
Description: An award-winning, registered charity that receives donations of new clothing and distributes them to over 80 partner social service agencies in Toronto.

SURFACE TREATMENTS

Accurate Pleating
445 Richmond Street W Lower Level,
Toronto, ON, M5V 1X9
T 416-703-2813 | F 416-703-3954
Sewing Specialty: Pleating and Buttons

Acme Pleating Company
545 King St. West - Unit 101,
Toronto, ON, M5V 1M1
T 416-971-6125
acmepleating@gmail.com
Sewing Specialty: Pleating

Anna Panosyan
Toronto, ON,
T 416-513-1976
annapanosyan@web.de
Sewing Specialty: Textile design - felt, leather, crochet, wovens, trim and more No minimums, can do samples

ArtofWhere
www.artofwhere.com
372 St. Catherine St. W., Suite 126,
Montreal, QC, H3B 1A2
T 514-842-8333
info@artofwhere.com
Sewing Specialty: Custom fabric printing on natural and synthetic fabrics. $5 for a swatch, $24 to $35 per meter. No minimums. Cut and sew services for pillows, home decor, hats and fashion accessories

Axis Gear Company Ltd.
www.axisgear.ca
1541 Dundas St. W.,
Toronto, ON, M6K 1T6
T 416-537-9229 x109
F 866-840-1730
Sewing Specialty: Screen Printing & Spot Sublimation_Specializing in Eco-Friendly apparel, inks and processes. Line of Fair Trade Apparel available for printing.

By Design Screen Print
5666 Roberts St.,
Halifax, NS, B3K 6B6
T 902.455.7100 | F 902.455.1802
garab@bydesign.ns.ca
Services: silk screen printing and embroidery

Calgary Silk Screen & Embroidery
www.calgarysilkscreen.com
33800 19 St. NE,
Calgary, AB, T2E 6V2
T 403.295.8940 | F 403.275.2098

Embroidery Specialists
80 Travail Rd.,
Markham, ON, L3S 3H9
T 905-201-7115 | F 905-201-7116

Services: Silk screen printing, embroidery, cresting, podprinting.

Entripy Custom Screen Printing and Embroidery
www.entripy.com
333 Wyecroft Road, Unit 6 & 7, Oakville, ON, L6K 2H2
T 905-844-1291 | T 1-866-ENTRIPY
F 905-844-2836
Sewing Specialty: Custom screen printing and embroidery on t-shirts, sweatshirts, hats, golf shirts and more. Brands include Gildan activewear, American Apparel, Fruit of the Loom, Weir Golf Services: 100 white t-shirts, 1 colour, 1 location, print and setup included all for only $3.49 per T (top quality Gildan Ultra Cotton 10.1 oz, 100% cotton t-shirt)

Eye 2 Eye Imagine
www.eye2eye.org
6471 Northam Drive, Mississauga, ON, L4V 1J2
T 905-672-1116 | F 905-673-3067
Sewing Specialty: We print on any man-made fabrics - high resolution, vivid colours, permanent, NO minimums. Free graphical designs and image search

Fine Line Silkscreening
www.finelinesilkscreening.com
PO Box 120, 15 Colford Dr., East Chezzetcook, NS, B0J 1N0
T 902.827.5292 | F 902.827.5353
Sewing Specialty: Decals, banners, screenprinting, dyers, digital printers.

GRY Enterprises
60 Nugget Ave, Scarborough, ON, M1S 3A9
T 416-335-3606
gryfashions@aol.com
Sewing Specialty: Bridal, eveningwear, free hand embroidery, original embroidery designs.

Lamoa Stitch
708 Queensway, Etobicoke, ON, M8Y 1L3
T 416-503-0096 | F 416-521-9649
lamoastitch@hotmail.com

Magpie Artworks
www.magpieartworks.com
Ajax, ON,
T 905-426-3451

Masterworks Screen Printing
www.masterworks1.com
121 Telson Road, Markham, ON, L3R 1E4
T 905-940-1744 | F 905-940-9859

Precieux Embroidery
5621 Finch Ave. E. Unit 2a, Scarborough, ON, M1B 2T9
T 416-754-8372 | F 416-754-1541

masterworks@rogers.com	
Scythes - Flying Colours www.flyingcoloursintl.com 128 Sterling Rd, Toronto, ON, M6R 2B7 T 416-535-1151 | F 416-535-0971 **Sewing Specialty:** Custom printing, dyeing for virtually any textile.	**Spoonflower Custom Fabrics** www.spoonflower.com 200 N. Fifth St., Mebane, NC, 27302 T 919-321-2949 **Services:** Design and print your own fabric, NO minimums, fast turnaround time.

CANADIAN YARN SUPPLIERS

A to Z Alpacas
www.atozalpacas.com
Box 337, Vauxhall, AB, T0K 2K0
T 403-654-2810
atozalpacas@gmail.com

Aberton Textiles Ltd.
3700 Rue Staint Patrick,
Montreal, QC, H4E 1A2
T 514-932-3711 | F 514-935-6653

Akko Canada Ltd.
93 Steelcase Road East,
Markham, ON, L3R 1E9
T 905-477-3348 | F 905-477-2068
akko@interlog.com

Alsew Canada Inc.
6626 - 20A Street S.E.,
Calgary, AB, T2C 0R3
T 403-543-8923 | F 403-543-8922

Americo Original
www.americo.ca
456 Queen St. West,
Toronto, ON, M5V 2A8
T 416-777-9747
info@americo.ca

Anzee Knits Inc.
7150 Torbram Road, Unit #5,
Mississauga, ON, L4T 3Z8
T 905-673-9698 | F 905-673-7662
anzknits@yahoo.com

B. Spratt Textile Sales
4573 55A Street,
Delta, BC, V4K 3T2
T 604-946-7999 | F 604-946-0263

Bains Textiles Mills
1625 Begin Ville,
St-Laurent, QC, H4R 1W9
T 514-745-3333 | F 514-745-5553

Briggs & LIttle Woolen Mills
www.briggsandlittle.com
3500 Route 635,
Harvey York County, NB, E6K 1J8
T 506-366-5438 | F 506-366-3034

Calko Canada-Inc.
7250 Marconi Street,
Montreal, QC, H2R 2Z5
T 514-495-1531 | F 514-495-1629

Cannon Knitting Mills Ltd.
www.cannonknitting.com
8 Milner Ave,
Scarborough, ON, M1S 3P8
T 905-525-7275 | F 866-527-1986
sales@cannonknitting.com

Cap City Clothing Inc. / Prince Textiles
36 Los Alamos Drive,
Richmond Hill, ON, L4C 0G7
T 905-770-9969 | F 905-770-4668
capcityinc@rogers.com

Cory Haynes Textile Sales Agency 259 Edgeley Blvd. - Unit 10, Concord, ON, L4K 3Y5 T 905-760-8180 | F 905-760-8050 coryhaynes@on.aibn.com	**Cross Country Fashion Fabrics Inc.** P.O. Box 5, 314 - 9th Street W., Cornwall, ON, K6H 5R9 T 613-938-0097 | F 613-938-1836 ccff@ccfashion.com
CVT Knitting Mills Inc. 193 Jardin Drive, Concord, ON, L4K 1X5 T 905-738-0703 | F 905-738-0895 cvtknitting@sprint.ca	**Danatex Textiles** 3083 West 38th ave, Vancouver, BC, V6N 2X4 T 604-733-2025 | F 604-733-8644
Du Re Textiles Ltee. 10 Route 108 ouest, St-Ephrem-De-Beauce, QC, G0M 1R0 T 418-484-2927 | F 418-484-5640	**Elite International/Lamotex** lamotextrading@lamotextrading.com 433 Chabanel West, Suite #266, Montreal, QC, H2N 2J3 T 514-382-4136 | F 514-382-4138
Ern-Tex Inc 4360 Cote de Liesse, Suite 217, Mount Royal, QC, H4N 2P7 T 514-343-5252 | F 514-343-9550	**Fab-Knit Textiles Inc.** info@fabknit.com 939 Warden Ave, Toronto, ON, T 416-297-7525 | F 416-297-1589
Finetex Knitting Mills Inc. 34 Haas Road, Etobicoke, ON, M6R 2T6 T 416-746-7821 | F 416-746-4366	**FunTex** fun_rex@hotmail.com 300 - 8800 St. Laurent, Montreal, QC, H2N 1M4 T 514-382-7662 | F 514-382-6186
G&H Textiles Trading Inc. sunnylin@shaw.ca 21 - 220 Tenth Street, New Westminster, BC, V3M 3X9 T 604-522-8166 | F 604-522-8160	**Gentry Knitting Mills Limited** 150 Dynamic Drive, Scarborough, ON, M1V 5A5 T 416-299-5252 | F 416-299-4007
Golden Gong Ltd. 48 Mandalay Drive, Winnipeg, MB, R2X 2Z2 T 204-694-0460 | F 204-694-0972	**Hillsdale Mohair** Port Hood, NS, B0E 2W0 T 902-787-2770

Industrial Textiles
185 Limestone Cres.,
North York, ON, M3J 2R1
T 416-736-4261 | F 416-736-1830
order desk@itiglobal.com

Interlock Knit Canada Inc./T.I.K. Canada
larrygr@interlockknit.com
8531 Delmeade,
Mont-Royal, QC, H4T 1M1
T 514-343-5511 | F 514-343-5532

International Sew-Right Company
www.safetyclothing.com
6190 Don Murie St.,
Niagara Falls, ON, L2E 6X8
T 905-374-3600 | F 905-374-6121
intsewright@safetyclothing.com

Ivodex Enterprises Inc.
203 - 18 Four Seasons Place,
Toronto, ON, M9B 6E7
T 416-695-3922 | F 416-695-3382
ivodex@idirect.com

J. P. Agencies
728 Montrose Street,
Winnipeg, MB, R3M 3N3
T 204-488-4911 | F 204-488-4911

J.N. Sales
jnsales@rogers.com
59 Jonathan Gate,
Thornhill, ON, L4J 5J8
T 905-771-032 | F 8

Janus Textiles Inc.
4990 Courval,
St. Laurent, QC, H4T 1L1
T 514-735-3555 | F 514-735-3350

Jo/Ri Incorporated
228 - 433 Chabanel St. W.,
Montreal, QC, H2N 2J3
T 514-382-1074 | F 514-382-7266

Joy Textiles
4808 St. Laurent Blvd.,
Montreal, QC, H2T 1R5
T 514-845-1469 | F 514-276-332

Kaztex Canada Inc.
www.kaztexcanada.com
6659 Park Ave.,
Montreal, QC, H2V 4J1
T 514-495-4124 | F 514-495-3392
info@kaztexcanada.com

Kliffer Agencies
www.cansew.ca
266 McDermot Ave.,
Winnipeg, MB, R3B 0S8
T 204-942-4264 | F 204-947-9280
orderdesk@mts.net

Koigu Wool Designs
www.koigu.com
RR 1, Williamsford, ON, N0H 2V0
T 519-794-3066 | F 519-794-3130
info@koigu.com

Laxmi Knitting Mill Ltd.
3565 Jarry Est. Suite 402,
Montreal, QC, H1Z 2G1
T 514-721-9401 | F 514-721-9401

Lemtex Fabrics
22 Eugene Street,
Toronto, ON, M6B 3Z4
T 416-781-4209 | F 416-781-1877

Les Tricots Devino 400, 6e rue , Daveluyville, QC, G0Z 1C0 T 819-367-2121 | F 819-367-4026	**MacDonald Faber Ltd.** 952 Queen St. W., Toronto, ON, M6J 1G8 T 416-534-3940 macfab@myna.com
Majestex / Majestic Laces Ltd. www.majestex.com 140 Tycos Drive, Toronto, ON, M6B 1W8 T 416-783-4296 | F 416-783-5712 sales@majestex.com	**Manoir Inc.** www.manoir-inc.com 4500 Cousens , St. Laurent, QC, H4S 1X6 T 514-339-1150 | F 514-339-1290
Meridan Knitting Ltd. 110 Robinson St. S., Granby, QC, J2G 7L4 T 450-378-0131 | F 450-378-4315	**Metro Textiles Inc.** 430 Flint Road, Downsview, ON, M3J 2J4 T 416-665-1800 | F 416-665-2549
North East Knitting Mills 304 - 3565 Jarry Street East, Montreal, QC, H1Z 2G1 T 514-729-8030 | F 514-729-8007	**Patons Yarns** www.patonsyarns.com 320 Livingstone Avenue South, Listowel, ON, N4W 3H3 T 519-291-3780 | F 519-291-3232
Pep - Thai Int'l Corp. 2912 Valleyvista Drive , Coquitlam, BC, V3E 2P3 T 604-464-2318 | F 604-464-6318	**Phoenix Textile Agencies** 5872 David Lewis Street, Montreal, QC, H3X 4A1 T 514-738-1860 | F 514-738-132
S-Tex Inc. 99 Chabanel St. W., #405, Montreal, QC, H2N 1C3 T 514-381-8021 | F 514-381-8022	**Sager Group Inc** 7000 Park Avenue, Montreal, QC, H3N 1X1 T 514-276-3570 | F 514-276-3452
Siltex/Silbert-Werner Knitting Mills www.siltex.com 10 Robinson Street, Winnipeg, MB, R2W 4C6 T 204-582-2371 | F 204-582-3071	**Spinrite Lp** www.spinriteyarns.com 320 Livingstone Ave. S., Listowel, ON, N4W 3H3 T 519-291-3780 | F 519-291-3232

Spring Knitwear Inc. kix@idirect.com 291 Progress Avenue, Scarborough, ON, M1P 2Z2 T 416-297-0292 | F 416-297-7740	**Standard Textile Sales** 96 Manuel Drive, Dollard-des-Ormeaux, QC, H9A 2M5 T 514-684-0116 | F 514-684-0141
Sunco Trading Inc. 9 Crawford St., Markham, ON, L6C 2L4 T 905-887-0641 | F 905-887-1301 suncoinc.@yahoo.ca	**Sunne Way Entreprises Inc.** 7261 Victoria Park Ave, Markham, ON, L3R 2M7 T 905-477-8008 | F 905-477-7008 sway@idirect.com
Time Develop Ltd. 43 - 151 Nashdene Road, Scarborough, ON, M1V 4C3 T 416-335-1103 | F 416-335-1102 timedevelop@sympatico.ca	**Transglobal Apparel Services Inc.** 30 Chichester Place, #28, Toronto, ON, M1T 3S5 T 416-499-4610 | F 416-494-5376
Tri-Star Textiles Ltd. 8490 Jeanne-Mance, Montreal, QC, H2P 2S3 T 514-384-1970 | F 514-384-0534 tristar@qc.aibn.com	**Tricot Carol Inc.** www.tricarol.com 560 Sauve West, Montreal, QC, H3L 2A3 T 514-389-5667 | F 514-389-1266 sales@tricarol.com
USM Canada 7700 de Lamartine, Anjou, QC, H1J 2A8 T 514-355-3690 | F 514-355-5953	**Wah Fung Textile Inc.** 2855 Matte, Brossard, QC, J4Y 2P4 T 450-619-2528 | F 450-619-2692
Westrade Inc. 8571 Bridgeport Road, Richmond, BC, V6X 1R7 T 604-270-8737 | F 604-244-7260	

CANADIAN TEXTILE LABEL MANUFACTURERS

Alyea Associates Ltd. 29 Cheshire Dr., Etobicoke, ON, M9B 2N7 T 416-410-5417 | F 416-410-5417 **Description:** Labels: woven; Labels: printed; Crests; Tags	**Fashion Tag and Label Inc.** www.fashiontaglabel.com 758 Gordon Baker Rd., Toronto, ON, M2H 3B4 T 416-977-5155 | F 416-977-8698 **Description:** Manufacturing in Toronto since 1969. Started doing "student specials" in 1971 and have been supplying labels and tags to some of Canada's brightest and most successful designers for over 30 years.
Kemik Labels Ltd. www.kemiklabels.com 1275 Morningside Avenue, Unit 14, Scarborough, ON, M1B 3W1 T 416-282-4425 | F 416-282-1669 **Description:** Printed labels, pressure sensitive with adhesive on the back	**LabelNet Inc.** www.labelnet.ca 250 Dundas St. S. Unit 6/ 232, Cambridge, ON, N1R 8A8 T 519-740-8900 | F 519-740-8919 **Description:** woven & printed labels of all types, adhesive backings, iron-on or pressure sensitive, embroidered & high definition woven patches, crests, emblems, PVC (rubber) labels, hang tags
Laidler Label www.laidlerlabel.com 300 Kennedy Rd, Scarborough, ON, M1N 3P7 T 416-265-4438 | F 416-265-8738 **Description:** Printed and woven garment labels	**Laven Industries Limited** www.laven.com 570 Hood Road, Unit 10, Markham, ON, L3R 4G7 T 905-477-4410 | T 416-497-1500 F 905-477-6107 **Description:** Woven labels, printed labels, hang tags, PVC / rubber, heat transfers, lanyards, ribbons, leather and suede, stickers, patches and crests

Monique Collections
3001 Markham Rd, Unit 14,
Scarborough, ON, M1X 1L6
T 416-291-8932 | F 416-283-3668
Description: Labels: garment makers; Tags: identification

Orchid Label and Printing Co. Ltd.
3293 Dufferin Street,
Toronto, ON, M6A 2T4
T 416-789-1103 | F 416-783-8754
Description: Printed and woven labels

Paxar Canada Inc.
www.paxar.com
1920 Clements Road,
Pickering, ON, L1W 3V6
T 905-839-8057 | F 905-839-8169
Description: Woven labels, printed labels, bar code, graphics, product labelers, apparel systems, security solutions

R-Pac Canada
www.r-pac.com
236 Rittenhouse Rd,
Kitchener, ON, N2E 2V5
T 519-579-5194 | F 519-579-8704
Description: Printed and woven labels

Source ID
www.sourceid.ca
690, rue Hodge,
Saint-Laurent, QC, H4N 2V2
T 514-747-0403 | F 514-747-2396
info@sourceid.ca
Description: Woven and printed labels, integrated tagging, hang tags, pocket flashers, pressure sensitive labels, jewellery tags and labels, match books, strip labels, waistbands, string tags, price tags, care labeling

Trimtag Trading Inc.
www.trimtag.com
805 - 15 Wertheim Court,
Richmond Hill, ON, L4B 3H7
T 905-763-7300 | F 905-889-6409
Product Mix: Branding on zippers and zipper pulls, hangtags, notions, trims, woven & printed labels. Microweave Satin/Taffeta, Microweave Damask, Overprinting on Woven Labels, Die Cut/Button Hole Zipper Pull Labels, Printed Labels

Weber Marking Systems Canada Ltd.
www.webermarking.com/html/canada1.html
6180 Danville Road,
Mississauga, ON, L5T 2H7
T 905-564-6881 | F 905-564-6886
Description: Provides high-quality labels and labelling and coding products

CANADIAN FABRIC SUPPLIERS

Andrew Koenig International www.andrewkoenig.com 555 Chabanel West, Montreal, QC, H2N 2L1 T 514-388-1106 | F 514-388-5811 **Description:** Imported fabric from Europe and Asia	**Apparatex** 12122-68 Street , Edmonton, AB, T5B 1R1 T 780-477-2811 | F 780-477-2807 **Description:** Interfacings, linings; for catalogue, please ask reception.
Bon-Mar Textiles Inc. www.bon-mar.com 8448 St. Laurent, Montreal, QC, H2P 2M3 T 514-382-2275 | F 514-382-4661 **Description:** Lycra, polar fleece, supplex, swimsuit lining, Swarovski crystals, sequins, fringe, knits, nylons, notions, thread, elasics, snaps, microfibre, lining, interlining, chiffon, velour, velvet, stretch denim, taffeta, 3M Scotchbrite reflective materials, Thinsulate, Hi-Vis materials, rubber patches, custom heat transfers and other novelties	**Bourne Mills of Canada** www.bournemills.ca 17 - 200 Connie Cres., Concord, ON, L4K 1M1 T 1-800-268-1297 F 1-800-268-1264 **Description:** Full range of drapery linings, sheeting, bedding
Cador Textile Import Ltd. 91 Brandon Ave., Toronto, ON, M6H 2E2 T 416-531-9948 | F 416-531-9949 **Description:** 100% cotton, quilting	**Cancon Fashion Eco-Fabrics** www.canconfashion.com/eco-fabrics/ 555 Richmond St. W. #115, Toronto, ON, M5V 3B1 T 416-361-0469 | F 647-258-6992 **Description:** By Appointment Only_Cancon Fashion Eco-Fabrics are produced entirely in Montreal, QC, Canada. We aim to provide quality fabric alternatives to outfit the needs of eco-minded fashion, accessory and/or interior

designers.

Cannon Knitting Mills Ltd. www.cannonknitting.com 8 Milner Ave, Scarborough, ON, M1S 3P8 T 905-525-1275 | F 866-527-1986 **Description:** microfibre, nylon, pique, polyester & blends, polynostic, cotton, crepe, quilting, rayon, rib, fleece,spandex, terry, jacquard, jersey, knits, wool	**Cansew Inc. - Head Office** www.cansew.com 111 Chabanel West, Suite 101, Montreal, QC, H2N 1C9 T 514-382-2801 | F 514-385-5530 **Description:** Bindings and biases, braid/cord, elastic, fasteners, tapes, thread Brands: 3M, Bonfil Cansew, Dennison, Filtex, Kai, Madeira, Mundial, Poly Plus, Seweze, Velcro, Wiss
PCansew Inc. - Toronto Branch Office www.cansew.com 28 Apex Rd., Toronto, ON, M6A 2V2 T 416-782-1122 | F 416-782-8358 **Description:** Bindings and biases, braid/cord, elastic, fasteners, tapes, thread Brands: 3M, Bonfil Cansew, Dennison, Filtex, Kai, Madeira, Mundial, Poly Plus, Seweze, Velcro, Wiss	**Consoltex Inc.** www.consoltex.com 4981 Rue Levy, St-Laurent, QC, H49 2N9 T 514-333-8800 | F 514-335-8805 **Description:** For use in fashion, outerwear, home furnishing and industrial trades. Woven nylon, polyester & blends of manmade fibres.
Darlington Textiles 5800 St. Denis #209, Montreal, QC, H2S 3L5 T 514-271-0897 | F 514-271-1697	**Davey Fabrics & FabricMate Sewing Supplies** www.daveyfabrics.com 10505 169th Street, Edmonton, AB, T5P 4Y7 T 780-484-4422 | F 780-485-4442 **Description:** Denim, fleece, knits, cottons, poly/cottons, nylons, lycra, quilting, fiberfill,linings, notions, thread, zippers, snaps, elastic and trims. Sewing machine parts & accessories.

Delight Textiles 2 Midvale Rd, North York, ON, M6A 1Y7 T 416-781-0059 | F 416-781-2309 **Description:** Linings: acetate, polyester & blends Other: cotton, taffeta, interlining, lining, home textiles	**Designer Fabric Outlet** www.designerfabrics.to 1360 Queen St. W., Toronto, ON, M6K 1L7 T 416-531-2810 | T if busy call: 416-531-3796 | F 416-531-4114 **Description:** Upholstery, fashion fabrics, imports, notions, fabrics for drapes, silks, costume fabrics.
Dome Fabrics Ltd. 533 College St.Side Entrance, Toronto, ON, M6G 1A8 T 416-924-1178 | F 416-924-2272 **Description:** All types of fabrics, including polyesters, crepes, cottons.	**Dominion Textiles** 1950 Sherbrooke W., Montreal, QC, H3H 1E7 T 514-989-6050 | F 514-989-6214 **Description:** Woven cotton blends for ladies sportswear, outerwear, career apparel & rainwear.
E&R Global Inc. www.erglobal.ca 117 White Lotus Circle, Markham, ON, L6C 1V8 T 647-238-0222 **Description:** Organic and eco-fabrics such as organic cotton, silk, viscose rayon, bamboo, moda, hemp, recycled polyester and more. Also carries blends with lycra.	**Equus Fabrics** www.equusfabrics.com 190 Millway Ave. #2, Toronto, ON, L4K 3W4 T 905-761-9153 | F 905-761-9164 **Description:** Wolesale distributor of window hardware and drapery. Serving interior decorators, contractors and retail stores for fabric needs. Silk Fabrics, sheers, linings.
Fab Knit Inc. www.fab-knit.com 939 Warden Ave, Toronto, ON, M1L 4C5 T 416-297-7525 | F 416-297-1589 **Description:** Fleece, jersey, rib, interlock, performance fabrics, pique, jacquards.	**Fauck Canada** www.fauckleather.com 250 West Beaver Creek Rd. Unit 7, Richmond Hill, ON, L4B 1C7 T 905-886-3300 | F 905-886-8301 **Description:** Specialty: Leather Suppliers - lamb, calf, buffalo, goat, pig, deer, shearling

George Courey Inc.
6620 Ernest Cormier,
Laval, QC, H4P 1M2
T 514-342-6315 | F 514-342-8027
Description: A bit of everything

Gordon Fabrics Ltd.
11891 Hammersmith Way,
Richmond, BC, V7A 5E5
T 604-275-2672 | F 604-275-4978
Description: Textile convertor/wholesaler, evening, special occassion, sportswear, and retailer

Hersh Rostex Inc.
www.hersh-rsd.com
6855 Thimens Blvd.,
St. Laurent, QC, H4S 2C7
T 514-335-3511 | F 514-335-0830
Description: 100% wool and polyester wool blends in plain and fancies in weights of 260 grams to 440 grams and metons in cashand wool in 400and 580 grams; stretch corduroy and fancy corduroy

J. L. de Ball Canada Inc.
433 Chabanel St.West, Suite 1015,
North Tower,
Montreal, QC, H2N 2J9
T 514-381-4216 | F 514-382-4709
Description: Sells only velvet

J. P. Doumak Textiles
855 McCaffrey ,
St. Laurent, QC, H4T 1N3
T 514-342-9397 | F 514-342-9475
Description: Converter of novelty fabrics, tartans, woolen & worsted fabrics.

J.B. Martin Ltee
445, rue St-Jacques,
St-Jean-sur-Richelieu, QC, J3B 2M1
T 450-346-6853 | F 450-347-4910
Description: Produces only velvet

JB Silks
www.jbsilks.com
PO Box 75368, WR RPO,
Surrey, BC, V4A 0B1
T 360-778-1621 | T 1-877-877-3069
F 360-778-3946
Description: Huge selection of all types of silk fabrics available in many patterns and colours including embroidered, novelty and solid colours. Over 2000 distinctive silk fabrics are in stock and ready for immediate shipping. In business for over 25 years.

Kaztex Canada Inc.
www.kaztexcanada.com
6659 Ave. du Parc,
Montreal, QC, H2V 4J1
T 514-495-4124 | F 514-495-3392
Description: Microfibre, nylon, chiffon, chintz, polar fleece, coatings, polyester & blends, corduroy, printed, denim, rayon, faille, rib, satin, fleece, gabardine, georgette, jacquard, terry, jersey, twill, knits, velour, velvet, viscose, linen, lining, 100% cotton, polyand cotton and linen blends; denims, corduroys, twills, sheetings,

	velvets, linen and shirtings.
KB International 43 Kempenfelt Dr, Barrie, ON, L4M 1B8 T 705-739-0607 | F 705-739-0321 **Description:** Sales agents for mills from Germany, Spain, France, Italy and Austria. Working from home - will bring the collection to you for viewing.	**Kendor Textiles Ltd.** www.kendortextiles.com 1260 Clivedon Ave., Delta, BC, V3M 6Y1 T 604-434-3233 **Description:** Cottons, poly, linen
Lida Baday Ltd. 70 Claremont Street, Toronto, ON, M6J 2M5 T 416-603-7661 | F 416-603-3245 **Description:** By Appointment Only. Lida Baday Ltd. produces a high end women's wear collection and has a surplus of fabric from previous seasons now being made available to designers at a discounted price. A wide range of fabrics are available, imported from the finest mills in Europe, including: jerseys, wools, cottons, silks, metals and blends.	**Marina Textiles Inc.** www.marinatextiles.com 11 - 3535 Laird Road, Mississauga, ON, L5L 5Y7 T 905-828-0777 | F 905-828-6200 **Description:** Home decor fabrics in cotton, polyester and cotton/poly_Sheeting, flannel, twills, duck, denim
Mega Fabrics www.megafabrics.ca 877 Alness St. Unit 9, Toronto, ON, M3J 2X4 T 416-829-4269 | F 647-342-9044 **Description:** Bridal, cotton, silk, linen, rayon, wool, French laces, novelty fabrics and many, many more.	**Micki's Fine Linens** www.mickis.biz 131 Citation Dr unit 21, Concord, ON, L4K 2R3 T 905-738-1161 | F 905-738-3665 **Description:** Imported Fabrics from Europe for the special event, hospitality and display industries. Polyester, satin, taffeta, sheer, poly-cotton, designer ribbons

Parapad Inc./ Paratex 90 Louvain St. W., Montreal, QC, H2N 1B4 T 514-389-3539 | F 514-389-1123 Description: Carries interlinings, shoulder pads, sleeve heads, padding	**Parkhurst Knitwear** 1 - 20 Research Rd., Toronto, ON, M4G 2G6 T 416-421-3773 | F 416-421-9084 Description: Wool, Angora, Acrylic/Wool Blend, Cotton, Cotton Blends
Perfect Leather Goods 555 King St W., Toronto, ON, M5V 1M1 T 416-205-9775 | F 416-205-9940 Description: Specialty: All types of leather	**Robyn Mills Textiles** 9333 Blvd. St-Laurent #404, Montreal, QC, Description: Knit & woven fabrics from various sources and countries of origin. Ability to locate and source as per customer request.
Sea Leather Wear www.sealeatherwear.com 210 86th Avenue S.E. #86, Calgary, AB, T2H 1N6 T 403-689-4701 Description: Suede and glazed tanned fish leather	**Shergroup Textiles Ltd.** 160 Tycos Dr, Toronto, ON, M6B 1W8 T 416-787-0002 | F 416-780-1602 Description: Microfibre, nylon, polar fleece, polyester & blends, satin, twill, lining, pocketings
Syd Textiles & Sales Inc. 2700 Dufferin St., Unit 23, Toronto, ON, M6B 4J3 T 416-783-7730 | F 416-783-8720 Description: Fabric for bridesmaid dresses and eveningwear, stretch knits, and lace	**T. Pearlman & Assoc. Ltd.** 330 Spadina Road, Suite 1703 , Toronto, ON, M5R 2V9 T 416-925-4278 | F 416-925-5327 Description: Sales Agency for european mills, textile converters
Telio & Company (Montreal) www.telio.com 625 rue Deslauriers, Montreal, QC, H4N 1W8 T 416-532-9444 Description: Acetate, microfibre, brocade, nylon, chiffon, pique, polyester & blends, corduroy, polynostic, cotton, printed, crepe, denim, rayon, faille, rib, fiberfil, satin, fleece, shirting, silk,	**Telio & Company (Toronto)** 219 Dufferin St._Suite 106A, Toronto, ON, M6K 1Y9 T 416-532-9444 | F 416-532-0683 Description: Acetate, microfibre, brocade, nylon, chiffon, pique, polyester & blends, corduroy, polynostic, cotton, printed, crepe, denim, rayon, faille, rib, fiberfil, satin, fleece, shirting, silk, gabardine, spandex, georgette,

gabardine, spandex, georgette, suede, hemp, taffeta, tencel & blends, jacquard, terry, jersey, twill, knits, velour, lace, velvet, viscose, leather, warp knits, linen, wool, lining Wovens, knits, novelty, import lines	suede, hemp, taffeta, tencel & blends, jacquard, terry, jersey, twill, knits, velour, lace, velvet, viscose, leather, warp knits, linen, wool, lining Wovens, knits, novelty, import lines
Tex Leader International Ltde 8490 Jeanne-Mance, Town of Mount Royal, QC, T 514-341-5648 | F 514-341-6487 **Description:** Jersey knits, spandex	**Textile Bazaar** 501 Danforth Ave., Toronto, ON, M4K 1P5 T 416-465-4492 **Description:** Wool crepes and polyesters
Title Textile Company 525 Adelaide St. W., 2nd Floor, Toronto, ON, M5V 1T6 T 416-703-1099 | F 416-703-8255 **Description:** Solids, special occasion, line, wool, poly viscose, new high tec fabrics, laces, satin back crepes.	**Tonic Living** www.tonicliving.com T 416-699-9879 **Description:** Supplier of contemporary, retro modern printed cottons in wide width. Ribbon trim and home decor products also offered. 100% cotton and cotton/linen blends.
Tonitex Inc. www.tonitex.com 9630 St. Laurent Blvd., Montreal, QC, H2N 1R1 T 514-389-2938 | F 514-389-1548 **Description:** Various fabrics, printed cotton, vinyl, plastics, mesh, faux fur and more	**Tricots Canada U.S. Inc** 955 rue Morison C.P. 130., St-Hyacinthe, QC, J2S 7B4 T 514-774-5385 | F 450-774-9272 **Description:** Cut-and-sew knitted material
Tricots Liesse (1983) Inc. www.tricots-liesse.com 2125 rue Lily-Simon, Montreal, QC, H4B 3A1 T 514-485-9900 | F 514-485-3225 **Description:** Cut-and-sew knitted material	**Veratex Lining Ltd. (Montreal)** www.veratex.ca 5425 Casgrain, #701, Montreal, QC, H2T 1X6 T 514-274-4495 | F 514-274-2951 **Description:** Carries interfacgins, padding, lining, woven and non-woven fusibles and sew-ins, embroidery backings, pocketings,

	industrial linings & backings.
Veratex Lining Ltd. (Toronto) www.veratex.ca 250 Wildcat Rd, Toronto, ON, M3J 2N5 T 416-246-9800 | F 416-246-0320 **Description:** Carries interfacgins, padding, lining, woven and non-woven fusibles and sew-ins, embroidery backings, pocketings, industrial linings & backings.	**Way Key International Inc.** www.waykey.com 440 Tapscott Road Unit 11 - 14, Scarborough, ON, M1B 1Y4 T 416-292-6008 | F 416-292-0129 **Description:** 100% polyester
Wool House 438 Queen St. W., Toronto, ON, M5V 2A9 T 416-703-8679 | F 416-703-8679 **Description:** Microfibre, corduroy, cotton, quilting, denim, shirting, silk, gabardine, hemp, interlining, twill, laminating, linen, wool, lining. Wool worsted suitings from Italy, France, Germany and England. Cotton, silk, linen; mostly novelty, just natural fabrics; Egyptian cotton shirting, 100% cashmere and microfibre.	**Zinman D. Textiles Ltd.** 5445 de Gaspe, Montreal, QC, H2T 3B2 T 514-276-2597 | F 514-276-0352 **Description:** Carries all kinds of linings

US FABRIC AND TRIM SUPPLIER

Alicia Lace - Liberty Tex USA
www.alicialace.com
141 West 36th Street, 2nd Floor,
New York, NY, USA, 10018
T 212-967-7888 | F 212-967-8899
Description: Embroidered Fabric, Embroidered Lace, Beaded Fabric, Re-embroidery & Cut-Out Work, Beaded Appliques, Motifs & Trims, Cluny Lace

American Fabrics Company
450 7th Avenue, Suite 963,
New York, NY, USA, 10123
T 212-868-0100 | F 212-714-9385
Description: One of the world's largest suppliers of laces, embroideries, novelty trims, fabrics and prints

Artistic Ribbon and Novelty
www.artisticribbon.com
22 West 21st Street,
New York, NY, USA, 10010
T 212-255-4224 | F 212-645-6589
Description: Ribbons, rosebuds and bows

B&J Inc.
www.bandjfabrics.com
525 Seventh Ave, 2nd Floor,
New York, NY, 100018
T 212.354.8150
Description: Fabrics

Beads World Inc.
www.beadsworldusa.com
1384 Broadway,
New York, NY, 10018
T 212.302.1199
Description: Beads & Findings

Buttonwood Corp.
www.woodbuttons.com
260 West 39th Street, 3rd Floor,
New York, NY, USA, 10018
T 212-354-7591 | F 212-354-8291
Description: "The world's largest manufacturer of fine wooden buttons and toggles"

Carlcraft Knit Sales Inc.
www.carlcraft.com
1000 Wilt Avenue,
Ridgefield, NJ, USA, 07657-1512
T 201-729-9300 | F 201-729-9311
Description: One of the largest manufacturers of knit trim in the United States; specialize in collars, cuffs, braids, elastic bands, armbands and waistbands

Cinderella Trimmings & Ribbons
60 West 38th Street,
New York, NY, USA, 10018
T 212-840-0644
Description: Notions, buttons, trims; specialize in bridal

Fountain Set www.fshl.com T 212-868-9134 **Description:** Circular Knits	**Ginsburg Trim LLC** www.ginstrim.com 242 West 38th ST., New York, NY, 10018 T 212.244.4539 **Description:** Brainds, decorative trims, frog closures
Great Button Inc. www.great-buttons.net 1030 Sixth Ave, New York, NY, 11223 T 212.869.6811 **Description:** Buttons, buckles, beads etc.	**Hyman Hendler and Sons** www.hymanhendler.com 67 West 38th St., New York, NY, USA, 10018 T 212-840-8393 | F 212-704-4237 **Description:** Basic, novelty and vintage ribbons and trims, of their own design
Jay Company Trimmings www.jaytrim.com 22 West 38th Street, New York, NY, USA, 10018 T 212-921-0440 | F 212-575-2620 **Description:** The largest and most diverse selection of trim inventory in the world"	**JB Silks** www.jbsilks.com 4001 Irongate Rd., Bellingham, WA, USA, 98226-8028 **Description:** Fashion, Birdal, QUilting & Home Decor Silk Fabrics. New Products: Beaded Trims, Alencon & Chantilly Laces.
Lida Baday Ltd. 70 Claremont Street, Toronto, ON, Canada, M6J 2M5 T 416-603-7661 | F 416-603-3245 **Product Mix:** By Appointment Only._Lida Baday Ltd. produces a high end women's wear collection and has a surplus of fabric from previous seasons now being made available to designers at a discounted price. A wide range of fabrics are available, imported from the finest mills in Europe, including: jerseys, wools, cottons, silks, metals and blends.	**Lin's Trimming Co.** 256 West 38th St., New York, NY, 10018 T 212.764.2166 | F 212.391.2979 **Description:** Ribbons, trims, closures, buttons

Lion Button Company
246 West 38th Street,
New York, NY, USA, 10018
T 212-768-7090 | F 212-768-7095
Description: Notions, buttons, trims

M&J Trimming
www.mjtrim.com
1008 Sixth Ave,
New York, NY, USA, 10018
T 212-391-6200 | F 212-764-5854
Product Mix: Appliques, beaded fringe, beaded trim, beads, braided trim, buckles, buttons, closures, cords, flowers, fringe, fur & feathers, handles, iron-on trim, jacquards, lace, nailheads, pendants, rhinestones, ribbons, tassels, tools and glue

Malibu Textiles
49 West 37th Street,
New York, NY, USA, 10018
T 212-354-6707 | F 212-921-0251
Description: Lace; Converter; Trim

Match Feather Inc.
224 West 38th Street,
New York, NY, 10018
T 212.704.0111
Description: Ribbons, trims

Miju Sewing USA Corp.
306 West 37th St,
New York, NY, 10018
T 212.695.7122
Description: Notions & supplies

N.Y. Elegant Fabrics
www.nyelegantfabrics.com
222 West 40th St.,
New York, NY, 10018
T 212.302.4980
Description: Fabrics, tulle

New York Binding Co.
www.newyorkbindingco.com
43-01 22nd Street,
Long Island City, NY, USA, 11101
T 718-729-2454 | F 718-392-7070
Description: Fabricate trim

Panda International Trading of New York, Inc.
www.zipppershop.com
247 West 38th St.,
New York, NY, 10018
T 212.302.9434 | F 212.302-9488
Description: Zippers, notions, sewing supplies, dress forms and more

Paron Fabrics West www.paronfabrics.com 206 West 40th St, New York, NY, 10018 T 212.768.3266 Description: Silk, Linen, Cotton, Woolens, Synthetics, Jersey/Knits, Velvets, Tulle, Felt etc.	**Promo Trim** 37 Spring Valley Avenue, Paramus, NJ, USA, 07652 T 201-568-6519 | F 201-712-5445 Description: Trim, notions, heat seals, silk screen printing
Roth International www.rothinternational.net 13 West 38th Street, New York, NY, USA, 10018 T 212-840-1945 | F 212-391-1033 Description: Wholesale manufacturer and distributor of laces, buttons and beaded and embroidered trimmings for the women's garment and home decorative industry	**Royal Craft Trimming Corp.** 307 West 36th Street, 5th Floor, New York, NY, 10018 T 212-563-6330 | F 212-465-1257 Description: Trims, notions, embroidery
Samuel Ehrman & Co. 1410 27th Street, North Bergen, NJ USA, 07047-2181 T 201-866-5223 Description: Embroidery Supplies, Fabric	**Steinlauf & Stoller Inc.** 239 West 39th St., New York, NY, 10018 T 212 869-0321 | F 212 302-4465 Description: Extensive selection of notions and sewing supplies
Tender Buttons 143 East 62nd Street, New York, NY, USA, 10021 T 212-758-7004 | F 212-319-8474 Description: New and antique buttons	**The Fabric Stock Exchange** www.fabricstockexchange.com T 215-579-2791 | F 215-579-2813 Description: Silks, Linens, Cottons, Rayons, Polyesters, Wools, Better Blends. Solids, Prints and Novelties in stretch and non-stretch. Imported and domestic.

Tinsel Trading Company
www.tinseltrading.com
47 West 38th Street,
New York, NY, USA, 10018
T 212-730-1030 | F 212-768-8823
Description:: Appliques & ornaments, buttons & beads, cords, fabrics & threads, flowers & leaves, fringes, metal & metallic trims, passementerie, ribbons, stampings and sequins, tassels.

Titan Trading Co.
www.titan-trading.com
60 Eisenhower Dr,
Paramus, NJ, USA, 07652
T 210-368-5201 | F 210-368-5207
Description: Natural corozo, Vegetable ivory & Tagua nut buttons

Toho Shoji (New York) Inc.
www.toho-shoji.com/ny.html_
990 6th Avenue,
New York, NY, 10018
T 212-868-7465 | F 212-868-7464
Description: Jewelry findings, beads, chains, etc.

Touch of Lace
www.touchoflace.com
333 Bergen,
Fairview, NJ, USA, 07022
T 201-943-1082 | F 201-943-7163
Description: Laces, Schiffil, Multis, Embroideries

Waterbury Button Co.
www.waterburybutton.com
1855 Peck Lane,
Cheshire, CT, USA, 06410
T 203-271-9055 x0309 | F 203-271-9852
Description: US made metal fashion buttons, brass & nickel, antique finishes, custom logo buttons, jeans tacks, lapel pins, cufflinks

CANADIAN NOTIONS AND TRIM SUPPLIERS

Allstar Plastic Industries
www.allstarco.com
5730 Donahue Street,
Montreal, QC, H4S 1C1
T 514-337-0524 | F 514-337-6895
Description: Rhinestones and Jewels, Metal Ornaments, Caviar Beads, Sequins, Fabrication Accessories

American and Efird Canada
www.amefirdca.com
8301 Ray Lawson Blvd.,
Ville d'Anjou, QC, H1J 1X9
T 514-385-0880 | F 514-352-4814
Description: Thread, Embroidery Supplies, Notions

Apex Trimmings Inc. (Papillon Ribbon & Bow Inc.)
www.papillonribbon.com
9494 St-Laurent Blvd., Suite 902,
Montreal, QC, Canada, H2N 1P4
T 514-385-3757 | F 514-385-3758
Description: Bows, crochet, trims, ribbon, packaging (custom printing available)

Arton Beads
artonbeads.net/
523/525 Queen St. West,
Toronto, ON, M5V 2B4
T 416-504-1168 | F 416-504-7392
Description: Beads from around the world. Metal finding and beads, pendants, and chains. Glass, wood, acrylic/plastic beads and pendants. Glass seed beads in #4, #6, #10, #11, #13, and bugle #2 and #3, etc.. Swarovski crystal beads and pendants. Semi-precious stone beads and pendants. Sterling silver finding, beads and pendants. Fresh water pearls, shell beads and pendants. Wire, cord and stringing material. Tools, design boards, jewelry bags and boxes, displays and more.

Bamiyan Silver
www.bamiyansilver.com
55 Queen St. E. #1100,
Toronto, ON, M5C 1R6
T 416-603-3983 | F 416-603-6550
Description: Beads, findings, semi-precious and non-semi

Bead and Save Enterprises Inc.
www.beadandsave.com
7020 Kildare Road,
Montreal, QC, H4W 1B9
T 514-481-2213
Description: Online store with a large variety of lampwork,

precious stones, finished and unfinished chains, necklaces, bracelets, anklets, toe rings, pendants, rings, earrings, studs, hoops and jewellery accessories.

Tibetan-style glass beads used for jewellery making and home decor

Capitol Buttons
www.capitolbuttons.com
2501 Steeles Avenue W.,
Toronto, ON, M3J 2P1
T 416-650-0323 | F 416-650-0326
Description: Buttons and buckles made of ABS-plate, nylon, polyester, acrylic, metal, tortoise, silver, real gold, electro-plating; toggles for duffel coats, novelty zipper pulls, buckles, large pins for school uniform kilts, frogs for closings, embroideries and snaps. Also supplies part and dies for making your own covered buttons.

Century Products
www.centurycanada.com
275 Stinson,
Ville Saint- Laurent, QC, H4N 2E1
T 514-744-9944 | F 514-744-9469

Chaton Beads
www.chatonbeads.com
7541 St. Hubert,
Montreal, QC, H2R 2N7
T 514-278-8989 | F 514-278-5224
Description: Beads

Cooper 1001 Articles Inc.
www.cooper1001.com
5550 Fullum St. Suite 301,
Montreal, QC, H2G 2H4
T 514-273-9128 | F 514-273-9266
Description: We convert your leather or fabrics into stripping, straps, binding, lacing, braid, piping, cut fringes & tassels, covered buttons & buckles to be used in your products. We can also do embosing, perforating, bows & assemblies, nailheads and novelties.

Crystal Bead Shop Inc.
www.crystalbeadshop.com
3240 Dufferin St Unit 5,
North York, ON, M5A 2T3
T 416-868-1338
Description: Swarovski Beads, Swarovski Pendants, Swarovski Pearls, Swarovski Findings, Findings, Sterling Silver Findings, Gold Filled Findings, Beads & Rondelles, Japanese Seed Beads, Chain & Beading Wire, Display, Seashell Beads, Freshwater Pearls, Gift Pouch/Box, Plier, Books, Beading Supplies

F and F Trading Stone Co.
www.fftrading.com
1451 Castlefield Avenue,
Toronto, ON, M6M 1Y3
T 416-504-1416 | F 416-504-1415
Description: Rhinestones, Imitation Pearls, Beads, Chains, Findings, Jump Rings, Split Rings, Key Rings and numerous other items.

Frabels
www.frabels.com
5580 rue Par,
Montreal, QC, H4P 2M1
T 514-842-8561 | F 514-842-6599
Description: Rhinestones, beads of all materials, buckles, buttons, trimmings, transfers, sequin products, findings and more

H.A. Kidd and Company Limited
5 Northline Road,
Toronto, ON, M4B 3P2
T 416-364-6451 | F 416-364-5733

Hubschercorp Inc
www.hubscherribbon.com/
2325 52nd Avenue,
Lachine, QC, H8T 3C3
T 514.636.6610 | F 514.636.9725
Description: Ribbons, bows, tapes, transfers, woven labels

Infiknit Canada
542 Mount Pleasant Rd. Unit 104,
Toronto, ON, M4S 2M7
T 416-487-9401 | F 416-487-3296
Description: Organic cotton yarn, hemp yarn, natural buttons

Interlux Trimmings
www.interluxtrimmings.com
10100 Boul. Parkway,
Anjou, QC, H1J 1P5
T 514-272-5078 | F 514-272-6014
Description: Fringes, Cords, Uniform Braids, Lanyards, Shoe

John Bead
www.johnbead.com
20 Bertrand Avenue,
Toronto, ON, M1L 2P4
T 416-757-3287 | F 416-757-1069
Description: Beads, Stones, Sequins, Appliques, Buttons,

Laces, Piping, Crochet Lace, Custom Fabrics, Sequins, Trimmings, Tassels, Frogs & Shoulders, Yarn, Elastics	Buckles, Trims, Threads, Cords, Lacing, Wire, Bridal, Floral, Ribbons, Seedbeads, Pendants, Findings - Open to the trade only
Leather & Sewing Supply Depot Ltd. 7 Vanauley St. BSMT, Toronto, ON, M5T 2V9 T 416-913-4868 | F 416-913-4868 **Description:** Leather, zippers, buckles, webbing, snaps, threads, trims, elastic, cords, boning, underwire, fabric, notions & findings	**MacDonald Faber Ltd.** 952 Queen St. W., Toronto, ON, M6J 1G8 T 416-534-3940 macfab@myna.com
Marathon Threads Canada www.marathonthreadscanada.com 21 Muir Rd., Winnipeg, MB, R2X 2X7 T 204-694-9116 | F 204-694-9118 **Description:** Embroidery, Sewing, Quilting and Sewing threads and supplies	**Masterstroke Canada** www.masterstrokecanada.com 575 Lombardy Ave., Oshawa, ON, L1J 8H5 T 866-249-7677 **Description:** ribbons, trims, laces - prices are low to high depending on items
Mibo Buttons 6829 de l'Epee , Montreal, QC, H3N 2C7 T 514-377-6426 | F 514-277-6422 **Description:** Buttons	**Mokuba Ribbons & Trim** 575 Queen St. W., Toronto, ON, M5V 2B6 T 416-504-5358 | F 416-504-7318 **Description:** RIbbons, trims, lace, tapes etc.
Serigraphie WSM Futur Inc. 9735 St. Urbain, Montreal, QC, H3L 2T1 T 514-382-6061 | F 514-382-6066 **Description:** Branding on narrow fabric.	**Sterling Button** www.sterlingbutton.com 300 Geary Avenue, Toronto, ON, M6H 2C5 T 416-534-8693 | F 416-534-6359 **Description:** Manufacturer and distributor of all types of buttons

and buckles. Materials used include: Polyester, Nylon, Casein, Metal and ABS plated plastic, Corozo (Vegetable Ivory), Leather, Horn, Sea Shell (Trocas, Agoya, Mother of Pearl), Wood, and Rhinestone Buttons._Additional Services: _-Assemble fabric covered buttons and snaps in a wide variety of styles using your fabric_-Dye-to-Match our buttons to your colours

Stones & Findings
www.stonesandfindings.com
705A - 55 Queen St. E. ,
Toronto, ON, M5C 1R6
T 416-628-8550
Description: Beads, Chains, FIndings, Pearls, Crystals and more.

Sundrop Textiles Inc.
www.sundroptextiles.com
#310 - 2071 Kingsway Ave.,
Port Coquitlam, BC, V3C 6N2
T 604-464-5236 | F 604-464-5237
Description: Fabrics, patterns, notions, videos, courses, and sewing machines, specialize in hard-to-find, unusual fabrics and patterns for outerwear and active wear

The Beadery
www.thebeadery.ca
446 Queen St. W.,
Toronto, ON, M5V 2A8
T 416-703-4668 | F 416-703-3586
Description: Extensive selection of beads and supplies from all over the world, including gemstones, wood, seeds, handmade glass, brass silver, gold findings, and tools.

YKK Zippers
www.ykk.ca
11 Cidermille Ave., Unit #6,
Concord, ON, L4K 4B6
T 905-738-7941 | F 905-738-7948
Description: Zippers, hook & loop, buckles, webbing and snap & buttons.

PROMOTION

CANADIAN WEB MEDIA CONTACTS

Canoe.ca www.canoe.com 333 King Street East 3rd Floor, Toronto, ON, M5A 3X5 T 416-350-6150 | F 416-350-6238	**CHEEKMagazine.com** www.cheekmagazine.com 847 Adelaide St. W., Toronto, ON, M6J 3X1 T 416-703-6888
ellecanada.com www.ellecanada.com Toronto, ON,	**FashionWatch.com** www.fashionwatch.com 642 King Street West, 2nd Floor, Toronto, Ontario, M5V 1M7 T 416-504-8044 | F 416-504-3033
FashionWindows.com www.fashionwindows.com P.O. Box 12184, Dallas, TX, 75225_ T 214-293-8651 | F 214-245-5919	**FashionWireDaily.com** www.fashionwiredaily.com 27 West 24th Street, Suite 1105, New York, NY, 10010 T 212-792-8282 | F 212-897-3700
FashWeekly.com www.fashweekly.com/flashversion.html 14 Widmer St., Toronto, ON, M5V2E7 T 416-722-2757 | F 416-340-0532	**Inside Fashion TV** www.insidefashion.com 372 Richmond Street West, Suite 119, Toronto, ON, M5V 1X6 T 416 508 7898
MiniMidiMaxi.com www.minimidimaxi.com 253 College St., Suite 170, Toronto, Ontario, M5T 1R5 T 416-599-9225 | F 416-599-5430	**She Does The City** www.shedoesthecity.com T 416-551-4116
Style.com www.style.com New York, NY,	**Toronto Daily News** www.torontodailynews.com/index.php/style 24 Southport St. Suite 844, Toronto, ON, M6S 4Z1 T 416-760-9698

Toronto Street Fashion www.torontostreetfashion.com	**Toronto.com** www.toronto.com 80 Peter Street, Toronto, Ontario, M5V 2G5
wnetwork.com www.wnetwork.com 64 Jefferson Ave., Unit 18, Toronto, ON, M6K 3H4 T 416-583-2864 | F 416-530-5199	**WorthGlobalStyleNetwork** **WGSN.com** www.wgsn.com/public/html/ca Worth House - 157 Edgware Road, London, UK, W2 2HR T +44 (0)20 7785 7700 | F +44 (0)20 7258 3666
XYYZ.CA www.xyyz.ca 317 Adelaide St. W., Suite 907, Toronto, ON, M5V 1P9 T 647-291-5567	

CANADIAN IMAGE AND BRANDING CONTACTS

These contacts are great for branding your line in the most professional manner

Artists By Timothy Priano 6 Clarence Sq, Toronto, ON, T 416-340-9000 | F 416-603-9891	**Artists by Timothy Priano** 4446 St. Laurent Blvd. SUite 605, Montreal, QC, H2W 1Z5 T 514-288-9216 | F 514-288-9043
Beauty On The Go www.beautyonthego.ca Burlington, ON, T 905-320-3130	**Brendan Turner Photography** www.brendanturner.ca 204 Spadina Rd. 3rd Floor, Toronto, ON, T 416-471-6226
Daniel Alvarado Photography www.danielalvaradophotography.com 660 Elginton Ave W. Ste. #207, Toronto, ON, M5N 1C3 T 416.785.9294	**Gardner Productions** www.gardnerproductions.ca 45 Charles St. East LL17, Toronto, ON, M4Y 1S2 T 416-921-4915 x 201

JC Photography & Co. www.wix.com/jcandco/pp 80 John St., Suite 2505, Toronto, ON, M5V 3X4 T 647-859-5121	**Judy Inc** www.judyink.com 21 Isabella St., Toronto, ON, M4Y 1M7 T 416-962-5839 | T 778-237-5839 F 416-962-5849
KM Image Consulting www.km-ic.com 48 Leopold St, Toronto, ON, M6K 1J9 T 647-283-3712	**Marois Photography** www.maroisphotography.com 5480 Glen Erin Dr., Unit 106, Mississauga, ON, L5M 5R3 T 905-339-7539
Mike Lewis Photography www.mikelewis.ca 104-363 Sorauren Ave., Toronto, ON, M6R 3C1 T 416-992-5154	**Palettes Makeup Art** www.palettesmakeupart.com T 416-899-8983
Photo By Willie www.photobywillie.com 54 Spanhouse Crescent, Markham, ON, L3R 4E3 T 647-290-9191	**Plutino Group** www.plutinogroup.com 525 Adelaide Street West, Suite 501, Toronto, ON, M5V 1T6 T 416-504-1605 | F 416-504-9277
Sabu Photography www.sabu.ca 29 Polson Street, Unit 301, Toronto, ON, M5A 1A4 T 416-879-6525	**Shalan & Paul** www.shalanandpaul.com 550 Front St. W. #410, Toronto, ON, M5V3N5 T 647-261-6720
Sherman Laws www.shermanlaws.com 210 - 65 Overlea Blvd. Toronto, ON, M4H 1P1 T 416.449.4477 | F 416.449.0643	**Solarfocus Photo and Video** www.richardemmanuel.com 238 Supertest Rd., North York, ON, M3J 2M2 T 416.650.7868 | F 416.650.0260
SURreal Productions www.surreal-productions.com T 416.642-6858	**The Little Black Dress Personal Shoppers & Image Consultants** www.thelbd.net PO Box 1435, Stn K, Toronto, ON, M4P 3J7 T 877-537-1410

Zoom Professional Photographers
www.zoomphotography.ca
12 Birch Ave,
Toronto, ON, M4V 1C8
T 416.921.8004 | F 416.921.0094

CANADIAN MODELLING AGENCIES

Don't use a good looking friend to model your clothing line. A professional model can set you apart from the competition.

2NV Models Inc www.2nvmodels.com 75 Berkeley St, Toronto, ON, M5A 2W5 T 416 595-7059 | F 416-595-9785	**Angie's Models and Talent** www.angiesmodels.com 25A York Street, Ottawa, ON, K1N 5S7 T 613-244-0544 | F 613-244-0481
B&M Model Management www.bnmmodels.com 645 King Street West, Suite 401, Toronto, ON, M5V 1M5 T 416-504-5584	**Belle Mundo Agency** www.bellemundo.com 11 - 3820 Cote Ste. Catherine, Montreal, QC, H3T 1E1 T 514-733-8442
Ben Barry Agency www.benbarry.com 76B Dupont Street, Toronto, ON, M5R 1V2 T 416-899-9646	**Bickerton Models** 208 - 499 Main St. S., Brampton, ON, L6Y 1N7 T 905.457.7571 | F 905.457.3048
Broadbelt & Fonte 703 Evans Ave. Mezz., Toronto, ON, M9C 5E9 T 416-588-8806 | F 416-588-4984	**Carolyns Model & Talent Agency** http://www.carolynsonline.com 1965 Britannia Rd., West, #210, Mississauga, Ontario, L5M 4Y4 T 905 542 8885 | F 905 542 8887
Casting Factory Inc. www.castingfactory.ca 86 Yorkville Ave. Suite 200, Toronto, ON, M5R 1B9 T 416-601-5419 | F 416-601-5418	**Century Models and Talent Agency** www.centurymodels.ca 920 Yonge Street, T 416-773-1010 | F 416-773-1011
CoverModels Management www.covermodelsmanagement.webs.com	**Dulcedo Model Management** www.dulcedo.ca 209 St-Paul W., 3rd Floor,

30 Marier Ave., Ottawa, ON, T 613-745-0527	Montreal, QC, H2Y 2A1 T 514-312-5272
Elite Model Management Toronto 32 Britain St. 3rd Fl., Toronto, ON, M5A 1R6 T 416-369-9995 | F 416-369-1929	**Elmer Olsen Model Management** www.elmerolsenmodels.com 477 Richmond Street West, Suite 708, Toronto, ON, M5V 3E7 T 416-366-6335 | F 416-366-6332
Folio Montreal Model Management www.foliomontreal.com 295 rue de la Commune Ouest, Montreal, QC, H3Y 2E1 T 514-288-8080 | F 514-843-5597	**Ford Models** www.fordmodels.com 385 Adelaide Street West, Toronto, ON, M5V 1S4 T 416-362-9208
Fulcher Agency Ltd. www.fulcheragency.com 6 Wellesley Place, Unit 29, Toronto, ON, M4Y 3E1 T 416-922-1222	**Gemini Models** www.geminimodels.com 127 Weber St. W., Kitchener, ON, N2H 4A1 T 519-578-2111 | F 519-578-2226
Geoffrey Chapman Model & Talent Agency www.geoffreychapman.com 1 Dundas St. W., Eaton Ctr Tower, Suite 2500 Toronto, ON, M5G 1Z3 T 416-365-5682| T 905-374-3821	**Giovanni Model Management** www.giovannimodels.com 517 Wellington St. W. Base 1, Toronto, ON, M5V 1G1 T 416.597.1993
Giovanni Model Management www.giovannimodels.com 291 Place D'Youville, Montreal, QC, H2Y 2B5 T 514.845.1278 | F 514.845.2547	**I Model Management** www.imodelmanagement.ca 2C, 1230A 17th Ave SW, Calgary, AB, T 403-697-8554
Ice Model Management 439 King Street West, 4th Floor, Toronto, ON, M5V 1K4 T 416-644-8577 | F 416-644-8369	**ICON Model Management** www.iconmodels.ca 130 Spadina Avenue, Suite 402, Toronto, ON, M5V 2L4 T 416-504-ICON | F 416-504-7034

Images International Model Management 578 Point McKay Grove NW, Calgary, AB, T3B 5C5 T 403-283-6517 | F 403-283-6596	**International Top Models** 185 Somerset Street West, Ottawa, ON, K2P OJ2 T 613-236-9575 | F 613-236-9607
Jett Models / Act Talent www.jettmodels.com Loft 510-1540 West 2nd Avenue, Vancouver, BC, V6J 1H2 T 604-742-0881 | F 604-875-0891	**Look Management** 1529 West 6th Avenue, Suite 412, Vancouver, BC, V6J 1R1 T 604-737-5225 | F 604-737-7612
Mako Models www.makomodels.com 151 Bloor St. W., Suite 612, Toronto, ON, M5S 1S4 T 416-238-1988 F 1-888-385-8314	**Marquee Model Management** www.marqueemodels.ca 38 Fontenay Court #1202, Toronto, ON, M9A 4H5 T 416-435-4780
Minx Models www.minxmodels.com 1311 Howe Street, Suite 200, Vancouver, BC, V6Z 2P3 T 604-221-4080	**Model Management Group of Canada Inc. (MMG)** www.nymmg.com 642 King St. W., #406, T 416-918-7175
Models International Management www.modelsinternational.on.ca 256 Elgin Street, Ottawa, ON, K2P 1L9 T 613-236-9575 | F 613-236-9607	**Montage Inc** 3451 Street Laurent, Suite 400, Montreal, QC, H2X 2T6 T 514-284-4901 | F 514-284-3656
Next Models 6 Clarence Square, Toronto, ON, M5V 1H1 T 416-603-4807	**Next Montreal** 3547 boul. St-Laurent, Suite 401, Montreal, QC, H2X 2T6 T 514-288-9216 | F 514-288-9043
Now International 94 Bayfield Street, Barrie, ON, L4M 3A8 T 705-735-3200 | F 705-329-0123 now_models@hotmail.com	**Orange Model Management Inc.** www.orangemodels.ca 555 Richmond St. W #215, PO Box 409, Toronto, ON, T 416-977-6664 | T 514-284-6664

Orlando Galletta, Agence de mannequins
www.orlandogalletta.com
6397 rue St. Denis,
Montreal, QC, H2S 2R8
T 514-270-8236 | F 514-278-8807

Panache Model & Talent Management
897 Corydon Avenue, Suite 106,
Winnipeg, MB, R3M 0W7
T 204-982-6150 | F 204-474-2687

Plus Figure Models/Little Women Modelling Agency
1263 Bay Street, Suite 203,
Toronto, ON, M5R 2C1
T 416-961-6709 | F 416-923-5673

Reign Model Management
www.reignmodelmanagement.com
324 Glebemount Ave.,
Toronto, ON, M4C 3V5
T 416-357-2110

Sherrida Personal Management
110 Scollard Street, Suite 200,
Toronto, ON, M5R 1G2
T 416-928-2323 | F 416-928-0767

Specs Model Management
www.specsmodels.com
710 - 3981 St. Laurent,
Montreal, QC, H2W 1Y5
T 514.844.1352 | F 514.844.8540

Styles Model Management Inc.
www.toronto-modeling-agency.com
174 Spadina Ave.,
Toronto, ON, M1N 4M1
T 416-895-3011

Subzero Model Management
www.subzeromodels.com
439 King Street West, 4th Floor,
Toronto, ON, M5V 1K4
T 416-644-8575 | F 416-644-8369

Sutherland Model
www.sutherlandmodels.com
174 Spadina Avenue, Suite 100,
Toronto, ON, M5T 2C2
T 416-703-7070 | F 416-703-9726

Velocci
www.velocci.ca
439 Wellington Street West, Suite 202, Toronto, ON, M5V 1E7
T 416-595-9855

VMH Models
www.vmhmodels.com
1311 Howe Street, Suite 200,
Vancouver, BC, V6Z 2P3
T 604-221-4080

Vogue Models & Talent (Burlington.Toronto)
www.vmtm.com
433 Brant Street,
Burlington, ON, L7R 2G3
T 905-633-8182 | T 416-283-3231

W M Models Inc.
www.wmmodelsinc.com
403 - 19 Charlotte St.,
Toronto, ON, M5V 2H5
T 416-593-0853 | F 416-593-9890

PUBLIC RELATIONS – PR

A PR expert can have access to media outlets and magazines that can get you coverage on your line. In addition to their service you are buying their relationships.

1milk2sugars PR www.1milk2sugarspr.com 715 - 1117 Ste. Catherine W., Montreal, QC, H3B 1H9 T 514-807-9578 | F 514-338-0472	**Agence ZOI** www.agence-zoi.com 430 Ste. Helene, Suite 305, Montreal, QC, H2Y 2K7 T 514-282-9888
April Jackson Public Relations www.apriljacksonpr.com 196 Brunswick Ave. Toronto, ON, M5S 2M5 T 416-997-5405	**ASC PR Inc.** www.asc-to.com 110 Yorkville Ave., Toronto, ON, M5R 1B9 T 647-447-5909
Ashworth Associates Inc. www.ashworthassociates.com 745 Danforth Ave., Suite 303, Toronto, ON, M4J 1L4 T 416-603-6005 | F 416-603-9272	**Best PR Boutique** 379 Adelaide Street West, First floor, Toronto, ON, M5V 1S5 T 416.366.2378
Blessington Love PR 139 Main Street, Suite 203, Unionville, ON, L3R 2G6 T 905-513-1889 ext. 300 | F 905-513-9997	**Bounce Publicity Inc.** www.bouncepublicity.com 1029 King St. W. Suite 1005, Toronto, ON, M6K 3M9 T 416.909.4328 | T 647-340-4328 F 647-340-4329
Brill Communications www.brillcommunications.ca 125 John St., Toronto, ON, M5V 2E2 T 416-533-6425	**Budman and Associates** www.budmanpr.com 55 Avenue Road, Suite 2710, Toronto, ON, M5R 3L2 T 416-515-7667 | F 416-515-7372
Charm Communications www.charmcommto.com 28 Stadium Rd., #163, Toronto, ON, M5V 3P4 T 416-312-2060	**Crave Public Relations** www.cravepr.com 111 Merton St., Suite 204, Toronto, ON, M4S 3A7 T 416-850-3519

Depict Public Relations www.depictpr.com 31 Columbine Ave., Toronto, ON, M4L 1P4 T 416-303-0947	**Endalayon Corp.** www.Endalyon.com 654 Rogers Side Road, Kingston, ON, K7L4V1 T 613-572-7953
Energi Public Relations energipr.com 49A Spadina Ave., Toronto, ON, M5V 2J1 T 416-425-9143 | T 1-866-337-3362 F 416-703-2495	**Fashion Communications and Public Relations** 365 Woodsworth Road, Willowdale, ON, M2L 2T8 T 416-444-5333
FashionForFreedom www.expressionisnow.com 2135 Rue Beaudry, Montreal, QC, H2L 3G4 T 646-761-3680	**Faulhaber PR & Marketing** www.faulhaber.ca 1-835 Dundas Street West, Toronto, ON, M6J 1V4 T 416-504-0768
Flex PR www.flexpr.com 283 Danforth Ave. Suite 500, Toronto, ON, M4K 1N2 T 416-696-5554	**Fruitman Communications Group** www.rfcg.ca 301-10271 Yonge St., Richmond Hill, ON, L4C 3B5 T 905-780-0880 | F 905-780-1763
GA & Assoc. www.ga-associates.com 1220 St. Mathieu, Montreal, QC, H3H 2H7 T 514.933.2736 | F 514.932.9823	**Instigator Communications** www.instigatorcommunications.com 9 The Kingsway, Toronto, ON, M8X 2S9 T 416-993-3985
knexxion PR www.knexxion.com 6 Chatterton Court, Brampton, ON, L6W 4H1 T 416-473-8678	**limelitePR** www.limelitepr.com Vancouver & Victoria, BC, T 778-786-1495 | T 250-483-5442
Lotus Leaf Communications www.lotusleaf.ca 675 King St. W., Suite 306-307, Toronto, ON, M5V 1M9 T 416-928-1978 | T 416-702-5414 F 416-928-9641	**Lucid Communications** www.lucidcommunications.ca 51 Wolseley St. Suite 302, Toronto, ON, M6G 2S4 T 416-640-5675

MacKay & Co. www.mackayandco.com 44 Jackes Ave., Suite 1116, Toronto, ON, M4T 1E5_ T 416-485-5400	**Magnet Creative Management** www.magnetcreative.ca 921 College Street, Suite 1A, Toronto, ON, M6H 1A1 T 647.283.1931
Manning Selvage & Lee Public Relations www.mslworldwide.com 175 Bloor St. Eastm Suite 801, North Tower, Toronto, ON, M4W 3R8 T 416.967.3702 | F 416.967.6414	**Mary Symons and Associates** 32 Walker Avenue, Toronto, ON, M4V 1G2 T 416.996.6764
Matteson McCrea PR 1200 Bay Street, Suite 404, Toronto, ON, M5R 2A5 T 416-960-1900 ext. 224 F 416-960-8602	**MD Media Inc.** www.mdmediainc.com 111 Old Surrey Lane, Richmond Hill, ON, L4C 6R8 T 416-573-3960 | F 905-881-0463
Nancy Goldstein 95 Invermay Avenue, Toronto, ON, M3H 1Z6 T 416-398-1145 | F 416-398-6063 goldie99@interlog.com	**Northcott Communications** 102-1055 Southdown Rd., Mississauga, ON, L5J 0A3 T 905-274-1620 | T 416-562-5900
OverCat Communications www.overcatcommunications.com 17 Madison Avenue, Suite 222, Toronto, ON, M5R 2S2 T 416-966-9970 | F 416-966-8775	**pdaPR** www.pdaPR.com 163 Sterling Road, Suite 2, Toronto, ON, M6R 2B2 T 647-802-6166 | F 416-286-2512
Pennant Media Group www.pennantmediagroup.com 480 Adelaide St. West, Lower Level, Toronto, ON, M5V 1T2 T 416-596-2978	**PinkRed Public Relations** www.pinkredpr.com 642 King St. West #308, Toronto, ON, M5V 1M7 T 647-476-3023
SC\PR www.sc-pr.net 1121 Bay St. #604, Toronto, ON, M5S 3L9 T 416-351-7323	**that PR thing inc.** www.thatPRthing.com 100 - 21 St. Clair Ave E., Toronto, ON, M4T 1L9 T 416-923-6566 | F 416-923-3552

The Canadian Public Relations Society www.cprs.ca 4195 Dundas St. W. #346, Toronto, ON, M8X 1Y4 T 416-239-7034 | F 416-239-1076	The Musmanno Group www.themusmannogroup.com 229 East 60th St., Third Flr, New York, NY, US, 10022 T 212-308-2100 | F 917-591-9339
Third Eye Media www.thirdeyemedia.ca 69 Coady Ave, Toronto, ON, M4M 2Y9 T 416-778-5934 | F 416-778-8589	Torchia Communications www.torchiacom.com 205 Richmond Street West, Suite 602, Toronto, ON, M5V 1V3 T 416-341-9929 | F 416-341-0129

POPULAR INDUSTRY LINKS

About.com www.fashion.about.com **Description:** Find everything you want to know about fashion on this excellent search engine.	Apparel and Textile Care Symbols www.consumer.ic.gc.ca/textile **Description:** Download the Guide to Apparel and Textile Care Symbols which provides important information for designers and consumers
Apparel Search www.apparelsearch.com **Description:** An apparel industry directory providing members of the fashion industry with links to virtually every aspect of apparel, fashion, textiles and clothing. Apparel Search is the largest and fastest growing online guide to the Apparel & Textile Industry.	Apparel Search - Buying Groups www.apparelsearch.com/buying_groups.htm **Description:** A list of buying offices in the U.S.
ApparelNews.Net www.apparelnews.net **Description:** Apparel manufacturers, designers, and industry-related services use apparelnews.net to reach retailers and consumers; suppliers of goods	Branding & Marketing Blog brandandmarket.blogspot.com/ **Description:** A branding and marketing blogger dishes out good advice on how to DIY.

and services use us to reach apparel manufacturers. Also: research upcoming tradeshows on their tradeshow calendar.	
Business of Fashion www.businessoffashion.com **Description:** The leading authority on fashion and digital media.	**Canadian Apparel Industry - Industry Canada** strategis.ic.gc.ca/apparel Manufacturing Industries Branch, 235 Queen St. 6th floor, Ottawa, ON, K1A 0H5 T 613-948-4065 | F 613-954-3107 **Description:** Industry Canada's official government site for the Canadian apparel industry. Find statistics and analysis, trade and export information, company directories, event listings, regulations and standards, and business tips for the apparel industry.
CanadianRetail.com www.canadianretail.com **Description:** Canada's first and only retail-specific career website to connect retail job seekers with retail employers	**City of Toronto - Toronto Film and Television Office** www.toronto.ca/tfto/currentlist.htm **Description:** Find out which stars and major productions are currently filming in Toronto.
Common Machine Troubles cahe.nmsu.edu/pubs/_c/c-202.html **Description:** This handy checklist of common sewing machine troubles will help you solve technical issues such as stitch looping, thread breaking, puckered seams, skipped stitches and more	**Cotton Incorporated** www.cottoninc.com/CWFL **Description:** Source in cotton wovens, knits, lace/trim here

Coutorture www.coutorture.com **Description:** Features, photos, editorials and the latest fashion galleries	**Daily Candy Inc.** www.dailycandy.com **Description:** A free daily e-mail from the front lines of fashion, food & fun. Need to know what's happening in New York and L.A.? Get your daily fix here.
Design Boom Web Log www.designboom.com/weblog/index.php?CATEGORY_PK=24 **Description:** A design-related weblog on what's chic and new	**Designer Salaries** www.coroflot.com/community/results.asp?t=&survey_id=7 **Description:** Coroflot's International designer salary survey results (2007)
Drapers Record Online www.drapersonline.com **Description:** The UK's fashion industry news, jobs and trends	**Entrepreneur's Assessment Tool** www.bdc.ca/ **Description:** Would you make a good entrepreneur? Take the Business Development Bank of Canada's test to find out.
Entrepreneur.com www.entrepreneur.com/ **Description:** Resources on how to start your business, sales & marketing tips, how to grow your business & more.	**Expo Database** www.expodatabase.com **Description:** Over 10,000 exhibitions and 24,000 trade show dates are listed. A weekly e-mail newsletter will keep you up-to-date on tradeshows, exhibition organizers & news.
Export Source www.canadabusiness.ca/eng/105/165/ **Description:** New to exporting? Start here to develop your export marketing plan.	**Fabric Connect** www.gofabricconnect.com **Description:** A unique database of fabrics from different CanadianS and US suppliers - all under one roof.

Fabric.com www.fabrics.com **Description:** Discount to Designer online fabric store.	**Fashion Apparel Law Blog** www.fashionapparellawblog.com T (310) 228-3740 **Description:** A lawyer blogs about legal issues facing the fashion, apparel and textile industries
Fashion Capital www.fashioncapital.co.uk **Description:** Look up key trends for the season, get industry news and find suppliers. A one stop online support resource for all areas of the clothing and fashion industry.	**Fashion Era** www.fashion-era.com/Costume_films/costume_museum_attop_new.htm **Description:** Fashion-era contains 270 content rich, illustrated pages of Fashion History, Costume History, Clothing, Fashions and Social History.
Fashion Era: Pattern Drafting www.fashion-era.com/Pattern_drafting/pattern_drafting_atop.htm **Description:** How to pattern draft a basic straight skirt block and how to adapt the skirt block into styles_	**Fashion For Profit** www.fashionforprofit.com **Description:** Want to start a fashion business? Read this free e-guide that covers the key steps from product development to selling your line.
Fashion Lines www.fashionlines.com **Description:** An e-magazine featuring the latest European runway collections.	**Fashion Net** www.fashion.net/ **Description:** Your guide to all things chic.
Fashion Office www.fashionoffice.org **Description:** Runway collections and fashion news. Fashion trends in Eurpoe, Americas and Asia.	**Fashion Syndicate Press** www.fashionshowroom.com/ **Description:** View runway photos from international apparel, jewellery, bridal and swimwear collections including Anna Sui, BCBG, Donna Karan, M Siamo, Vera Wang, Zac Posen and many

	others.
Fashion Templates www.fashion-templates.com/ **Description:** Get visual tips and advice on everything from creating a fashion storyboard to fashion illustration.	**Fashion Trendsetter** www.fashiontrendsetter.com/ **Description:** Get information on trade shows, competitions, trend forecasting and more
Fashion Tribes www.fashiontribes.com **Description:** Your very own fashion expert with all the dish and expert advice. The daily diary details New York Fashion Week. Up-to-the-minute advice on the latest in fashion, beauty, lifestyle and pop culture.	**Fashion Week Daily** www.fashionweekdaily.com **Description:** Daily dish on the world's fashion weeks, news, parties and product launches
Fashion-411 www.fashion-411.com 855 York Mills Road, Toronto, ON, M3B 1Z1 T 416-446-6500 **Description:** Fashion trends and shopping guides for London, New York, Paris and Milan.	**FashionChalkboard.com** www.FashionChalkboard.com La Quinta, CA, 92253 T 310-309-9523
Footwear News www.footwearnews.com **Description:** Footwear and apparel industry news classifieds.	**I Want I Got** iwantigot.geekigirl.com **Description:** Fashion blog by Anita Clarke: Fashion & Toronto. Sales, Reviews, Designers, Models.
Infoexport www.infoexport.gc.ca **Description:** Get export market reports and business leads from around the world by signing up with the Virtual Trade	**Infomat** www.infomat.com **Description:** Find showrooms, designers, suppliers and other fashion industry info on this

Commissioner	excellent search engine.
Insolvency Helpline www.insolvencyhelpline.co.uk **Description:** Great tips on getting paid, dealing with bad cheques and late payers.	**International Trade Canada** www.infoexport.gc.ca **Description:** Get export market reports, tips for success and keep on top of trade issues.
Jargol www.jargol.com/guide/ **Description:** Research boutiques in Canada, the U.S. and Europe for your accessory or apparel line.	**Kauffman Foundation Resources** www.entreworld.org **Description:** A huge range of info on marketing, PR, market demographics, sources of financing and more.
L'Oreal Fashion Week www.lorealfashionweek.ca **Description:** Check out designer collections from L'Oreal Fashion Week held in Toronto.	**Label Talk** www.textileaffairs.com **Description:** Get the U.S. guide to label requirements of apparel care symbols and instructions.
Lessons From The Sustainable Factory Floor www.fashion-incubator.com **Description:** Fashion diary of an apparel industry pattern maker offering tips, advice and related fashion links.	**Livedress.com** www.livedress.com **Description:** Find stores near you and get updated information on sales at your favourite stores.
Look 4 Textile www.look4textile.com **Description:** LOOK4 TEXTILE's manufacturers section is one of the Internet's most complete company directories for textile companies manufacturing, converting, importing or representing textiles.	**Makeup, Hair & Styling: Portfolio Dos & Dont's** www.coroflot.com/public/help_portfolio_tips.asp **Description:** Need to pull together a winning portfolio? Get tips and advice here.

MastheadOnline www.mastheadonline.com **Description:** The magazine industry's source for headline news and job postings.	**Media Bistro** www.mediabistro.com/articles/cache/a7558.asp **Description:** Here's a great article on breaking into fashion journalism.
Mentors, Ventures and Plans www.mvp.cfee.org/en/ **Description:** Access information about a wide range of entrepreneurial programs available in Canada. Learn how to become an entrepreneur and start your own business.	**Michigan Retailers Association** www.retailers.com/eduandevents/askmiretailers.html **Description:** Opening a store? Ask a retailer for tips and advice.
Model Resource www.modelresource.ca **Description:** Wanna be a model or need to hire one? Check out this portal into the modeling world.	**New England Apparel Club** www.neacshow.com/members.asp **Description:** Looking for an accessory or apparel sales rep for New England? Start your search here! Also has information on tradeshows & exhibitions.
OmniTrans www.omnitrans.com **Description:** A one-stop service solution for Canada-U.S. transborder deliveries. A fully integrated customs brokerage and logistics network.	**Paramita Academy of Makeup Inc.** www.paramita.ca **Description:** Toronto school of make-up
Pattern Alteration cahe.nmsu.edu/pubs/_c/c-228.html **Description:** Download free instructions on how to make pattern alterations	**PR Web - The Free Wire Service** www.prweb.com **Description:** A free wire service for journalists. Post your press release for free!

Premiere Vision www.premierevision.fr/ Description: Premier fabric show in Paris	**Reliable Corporation** www.reliablecorporation.com Description: Shop for production equipment and supplies online.
Shapely Shadow www.shapelyshadow.com Description: Creates customized dress forms from 3D scanned fit models. Clients include HBC, Macy's, Reitmans and more.	**She Does The City** shedoesthecity.com Description: A place to find inspiration, and of course a guide for planning your week full of fun nightlife, cool art happenings, great films or fashion to find.
SnapFashun www.snapfashun.com/reportwest.htm Description: L.A. and European retail reporting, merchandising and design. A close up look at hot selling items in the trendiest cities. A first hand view for manufacturers and retailers.	**Style Dispatch** www.styledispatch.com Description: Headline industry news.
Style Sight www.stylesight.com Description: Trend analysis, forecasting and reporting for fashion design, merchandising and apparel mfg	**Textile Mirror** textilemirror.com Description: Online newspaper covering textiles, apparel and fashion news worldwide
The Alexander Report www.thealexanderreport.com Description: The complete apparel industry guide to business resources and services. Design, merchandising, product development, production and sales.	**The Daily Fashion Report** www.lookonline.com/blogger.html Description: Get the Daily Fashion Report for up-to-the-minute industry news and trends.

The Iconic Fashion Blog www.theiconicfashionblog.com **Description:** Fashion blog by Lisa Chau: runway reviews, trend reports and coverage of exclusive fashion events.	**The Look On-Line** www.lookonline.com **Description:** Welcome to The Daily Fashion Report by lookonline.com. Get your daily fashion news, insider gossip and special offers.
The Sartorialist thesartorialist.blogspot.com **Description:** Blog selected as one of Time Magazine's Top 100 Design Influences.	**The School of Professional Makeup** www.promakeupart.com **Description:** Fashion, bridal and special effects makeup to stage, television and film.
The Western Business Law Clinic www.law.uwo.ca/info-centres-progs/BusinessClinicAbout.html **Description:** The Western Business Law Clinic provides small start-up and early-stage businesses with student legal assistance. By connecting new entrepreneurs with law students, WBLC works to motivate small businesses by providing them with high quality economic development strategies.	**Toronto Street Fashion** www.torontostreetfashion.com **Description:** An online community featuring news, event photos, blogs and more.
Trend Hunter www.trendhunter.com/cool-hunting/category/Style-and-Fashion-Trends/_ **Description:** Discover a style trend—good, bad, ugly or strange—at this eclectic site. Find the latest on trends, galleries, videos more.	**Trendzine** www.fashioninformation.com **Description:** fashioninformation.com is a new concept in fashion reporting published exclusively on the Internet. A great womenswear forecasting and trend reporting service offering a close and detailed insight into fashion trends from a unique perspective

WireImage www.wireimage.com **Description:** A digital photographic press agency and wire service. See detailed images from the leading designer collections.	**Worth Global Style Network** www.wgsn.com/public/wgsndaily/ **Description:** WGSN Daily is the world's leading online research, trend analysis and new service for the fashion & style industries.

ORDER MY BOOK

How to Start a Clothing Empire!

I know, you loved the book so much you want to order more copies, perhaps for yourself or for a loved one. Mabye just a friend wanting to succeed in the wonderful world of Clothing. Here's How.

Visit www.paypal.com and make a payment of $39.95usd (per book- includes shipping within North America) to my account clothingempirebook@yahoo.com Include:

1. First and Last Name
2. Street address (including apartment number)
3. City
4. State or Province
5. Zip Code or Postal Code
6. Email Address (optional)
7. Phone Number (optional)
8. Country

Paypal will also give you the option to include a message. If there are any special instructions insert

Made in the USA
Middletown, DE
06 February 2016